Foreign Exchange Constraint and Developing Economies

Foreign Exchange Constraint and Developing Economies

Edited by

Aleksandr V. Gevorkyan

Henry George Chair in Economics and Associate Professor, Department of Economics and Finance, The Peter J. Tobin College of Business, St. John's University, New York, USA

Edward Elgar
PUBLISHING

Cheltenham, UK · Northampton, MA, USA

Published by
Edward Elgar Publishing Limited
The Lypiatts
15 Lansdown Road
Cheltenham
Glos GL50 2JA
UK

Edward Elgar Publishing, Inc.
William Pratt House
9 Dewey Court
Northampton
Massachusetts 01060
USA

A catalogue record for this book is
available from the British Library

Library of Congress Control Number: 2022948515

This book is available electronically in the **Elgar**online
Economics subject collection
http://dx.doi.org/10.4337/9781800880504

ISBN 978 1 80088 049 8 (cased)
ISBN 978 1 80088 050 4 (eBook)

Typeset by Deanta Global Publishing Services, Chennai, India
Printed and bound by CPI Group (UK) Ltd, Croydon, CR0 4YY

Contents

v

Contributors

Douglas Alencar is an Associate Professor of Economics in the Department of Economics, Federal University of Pará, Brazil. He holds his PhD from the Federal University of Minas Gerais, Brazil. During the 2015–2016 academic year, he was a Visiting Researcher at the University of Leeds, UK. He has been working on post-Keynesian macroeconomics, post-Kelekian models and, more recently, the effects of central bank policy on the regional banking system, economic activity and liquidity preference. He has published in the *Journal of Post-Keynesian Economics, Review of Political Economy* and *PSL Quarterly Review*, among others.

Hayk Avetisyan is the head of the Monetary Policy Department at the Central Bank of Armenia. He has more than 13 years of professional experience and expertise in macroeconomic modelling and forecasting, macroeconomic scenario-building, monetary policy design and analysis. He holds a PhD from the Armenian State University of Economics and an MPA from Columbia University, New York.

Uthman M. Baqais is a Chief Economic Specialist at the Saudi Central Bank and holds a PhD in economics from Colorado State University. He works as an economist, while also providing international affairs consultations and representing at international meetings. After graduating with his BA in economics in 2009, he joined the Saudi Economists Program at the central bank. His fields of concentration are international economics and development macroeconomics. He also holds two master's degrees in economics from Colorado State University and the University of Illinois.

Eduardo F. Bastian is an Associate Professor at the Institute of Economics, Federal University of Rio de Janeiro (IE-UFRJ), Brazil. He holds a BA, MSc and PhD in Economics from IE-UFRJ and was a visiting PhD student at the Faculty of Economics, University of Cambridge, and a visiting scholar at the Institute of Latin American Studies, Columbia University..

Georgia Bush is a Financial Sector Specialist at Banco de México, the Central Bank of Mexico. Her interests include international capital flows, global banking and currency markets. She completed her PhD in Economics at Rutgers University and her bachelor's degree at Harvard University. Prior to the PhD, she worked at Citibank and the Economist Group in research and management roles. Her academic work has been published in peer-reviewed journals such as the *International Review of Economics and Finance* and the *Review of International Economics*.

Esteban Pérez Caldentey is Head of the Financing Unit at the Economic Commission for Latin America and the Caribbean (ECLAC). He holds a master's degree and PhD in economics from the New School for Social Research. He is co-editor of the *Review of Keynesian Economics*, Editor-in-Chief of the *Palgrave Dictionary of Economics* and member of the advisory committee of International Economics Development Associates (IDEAS). He is the author of the first intellectual biography of Roy Harrod and has published extensively on Latin America and the Caribbean.

Claudia de Camino has a master's degree in economics from the Pontificia Universidad Católica of Chile. She currently works as a statistician in the Economic Statistics Unit of the Statistics Division of the Economic Commission for Latin America and the Caribbean (ECLAC). She also worked in the Economic Development Division at ECLAC, where she was in charge of analysing macroeconomic indicators, monitoring global economic growth, international trade, commodity markets and financial markets in order to analyse their impacts on the external sector of Latin American and Caribbean countries.

Otaviano Canuto, based in Washington, DC, is a senior fellow at the Policy Center for the New South, a nonresident senior fellow at the Brookings Institution, a professorial lecturer of international affairs at the Elliott School of International Affairs – George Washington University, a professor affiliate at UM6P and a principal at the Center for Macroeconomics and Development. He is a former vice-president and a former executive director at the World Bank, a former executive director at the International Monetary Fund and a former vice-president at the Inter-American Development Bank. He is also a former deputy minister for international affairs in Brazil's Ministry of Finance and a former professor of economics at the University of São Paulo and University of Campinas, Brazil.

Barry Eichengreen is George C. Pardee and Helen N. Pardee Professor of Economics and Political Science at the University of California, Berkeley, Research Associate of the National Bureau of Economic Research and Research

Fellow of the Centre for Economic Policy Research. He is co-author (with Asmaa El-Ganainy, Rui Esteves and Kris James Mitchener) of *In Defense of Public Debt* (Oxford University Press).

Luis O. L. Escobar-Farfán is a financial researcher at the Financial Stability General Directorate at Banco de México. He is responsible for the contagion studies done at the Central Bank and contributes to the stress testing analysis conducted twice a year and published in the *Financial Stability Report*. He also contributes to the analysis presented to the Monetary Policy Committee and to the Mexican Financial Stability Board. His research interests include financial networks, complex systems, financial stability, machine learning and financial risks related to climate change.

Łukasz Faryj is a PhD student at the College of Economics, Finance and Law at the Cracow University of Economics, Poland. His research is focused on behavioural theories of decision-making, primarily in the corporate finance area.

Erwin Flores-Tamés has been a data research assistant at the Complexity Science Hub Vienna since 2019, currently researching complexity economics and the effects of incomplete data on systemic risk measures. He has more than seven years of experience in financial stability topics, specifically on credit and systemic risks, including network analysis and complex data analysis.

Aleksandr V. Gevorkyan is a macroeconomist working on open economy macroeconomics and development, diaspora economics and post-social-ist transition economics. He is the Henry George Chair in Economics and Associate Professor at the Department of Economics and Finance of the Peter J. Tobin College of Business at St. John's University. Dr Gevorkyan is a member of the editorial boards at the *Review of Political Economy* and *Review of Keynesian Economics*. Dr Gevorkyan is the author of *Transition Economies: Transformation, Development, and Society in Eastern Europe and the Former Soviet Union* (Routledge, 2018).

Hugo C. Iasco-Pereira has a PhD degree in Economics at Federal University of Minas Gerais (UFMG), Brazil. He was a student at the Summer School on Latin American Economies of the Economic Commission for Latin America and the Caribbean (ECLAC). He also was a visiting scholar at Universidade Autônoma do México. He is a professor at the Federal University of Paraná (UFPR), Brazil. His research areas include heterodox macroeconomics, economic growth and distribution models (Kaleckian models).

Viacheslav Ilin is an Econometric Modeller at the International Monetary Fund. Previously, he has spent more than ten years in investment banking as a quantitative analyst and market risk manager overseeing bond, equity and derivative portfolios.

Samar Issa is an Assistant Professor of Business Analytics at Saint Peter's University, New Jersey. Dr Issa possesses a PhD in Economics and an MBA in Finance. She is a macroeconomist and an econometric modeller who has developed statistical and econometric models to address economic problems, such as default risk and credit flow. Her research focuses on the effects of leveraging in the banking industry, the corporate world and the oil market. She speaks four languages and worked for over a decade at US corporations, the United Nations and overseas.

Frederico G. Jayme Jr is a Full Professor of Economics at the Department of Economics and Director of CEDEPLAR at the Federal University of Minas Gerais, Brazil. He holds his PhD in Economics from the New School for Social Research, United States. In 2014 he was a Research Fellow at the Department of Land Economy, University of Cambridge, UK. Between 2015 and 2018 he was Alternate Executive Director of Brazil and Suriname at the Inter-American Development Bank in Washington, DC. He has published in the *Journal of Post-Keynesian Economics*, *World Development*, *Review of Political Economy* and *Metroeconomica*, among others.

Elżbieta Kubińska is an economist in the Department of Risk Management and Insurance at Cracow University of Economics, Poland. Her background is in financial mathematics; now her interests are focused on behavioural finance and modelling of financial markets.

Anna Macko is an adjunct in the Department of Economic Psychology and a researcher at the Center for Economic Psychology and Decision Sciences at Kozminski University, Poland. Her research interests include risk, entrepreneurship, ethical decision-making and factors influencing decisions to trust.

Serafin Martínez-Jaramillo leads the Environmental and Social Risks Analysis and Policy unit at Banco de México. His interests include environmental risk analysis, financial networks and machine learning. Serafin has published in *IEEE Transactions on Evolutionary Computation*, *Journal of Financial Stability*, *Neurocomputing*, *Journal of Economic Dynamics and Control* and *Computational Management Science*, among others. He holds a PhD in Computational Finance from the University of Essex, UK, and is an editor at the *Journal of Financial Stability*, the *Latin American Journal of Central Banking*, the *Journal of Economic Interaction and Coordination* and *Complexity*.

Fabricio J. Missio is an Associate Professor of Economics in the Department of Economics, Federal University of Minas Gerais (UFMG), Brazil. He holds his PhD in Economics from UFMG and was a visiting researcher in 2011 at the Department of Land Economy, University of Cambridge, UK. His PhD thesis received the CAPES thesis award in 2013. His research areas include macroeconomics, growth and distribution and economic policy, especially in emerging economies. He has published several papers in the *Journal of Post-Keynesian Economics*, *Metroeconomica*, *Structural Change and Economic Dynamics* and *PSL Quarterly Review*, among others.

Dave Seerattan is an economist studying the financial sector issues in the Caribbean and emerging economies. He now teaches money and finance at the University of the West Indies, St. Augustine. He also headed the Caribbean Centre for Money and Finance over the period 2015–2017 and has been a member of the Caribbean Regional Financial Stability Coordination Council. He has also served as a member of a number of Trinidad and Tobago Government Cabinet-appointed and other Caribbean-wide committees on the financial sector.

Cecilia Vera is an Economic Affairs Officer within the Economic Development Division at the Economic Commission for Latin America and Caribe (ECLAC) in Santiago de Chile. She coordinates the economic projections team, the monitoring and analysis of the global macroeconomic situation and, also, the monitoring of the external sector for the Latin America and Caribbean region. She has a master's degree in Economics, with distinction, from the London School of Economics and Political Science (LSE) and has authored numerous publications, some of which can be consulted at: https://ideas.repec.org/f /pve280.html.

Joanna Wyrobek is an economist specializing in corporate finance, internationalization, fraud detection and modelling of financial processes. She holds the Corporate Finance Chair and is an Associate Professor at the College of Finance, Law and Economics at the Cracow University of Economics, Poland.

Dmitry Yakovlev is a Senior Research Officer at the International Monetary Fund. Prior to joining the Fund, he worked as an economist and analyst at various banks and asset management companies.

Foreword

The COVID-19 pandemic and economic crisis have been the ultimate stress test for the global economy and not least for capital-flow-dependent emerging markets. The news so far is a mix of good and bad. The situation continues to evolve with economic recovery in the US and Europe, slower growth in China, the emergence of new COVID variants and the slow pace of vaccination in the developing world. With the onset of the pandemic in March 2020, nonresident investors pulled roughly $100 billion of portfolio capital out of emerging markets. Impressively, however, nonresident flows then stabilized and reversed: for the remainder of 2020 and 2021, nonresident portfolio flows into emerging markets, including China, turned strongly positive. This was quite unlike earlier crises, when nonresident investors were quick to cut and run. The difference in behaviour presumably reflects a perception of the existence of stronger policy frameworks in emerging markets and developing countries.

There are still other indications of stronger policy frameworks in emerging markets and sounder debt management by governments. Central banks in Mexico, India, Russia and Brazil were able to cut policy rates sharply following the onset of the crisis. This is what 'normal' central banks enjoying policy credibility are able to do. But it is quite unlike the past, when the requisite credibility had been lacking, emerging markets suffered capital outflows and central banks were forced to perversely tighten in the teeth of an economic slowdown (or worse). In 2020–2021, in contrast, the situation was different.

In addition, a number of emerging markets were able to loosen fiscal policy, providing essential support to families on lockdown and applying a stabilizing fiscal impulse to the macroeconomy. That fiscal-policy response was modest compared to the actions of advanced-country governments but impressive, nonetheless, by emerging-market standards. Again, this reflects the progress emerging markets have made in strengthening their fiscal policies and frameworks, not in all cases perhaps, but in a substantial number.

Finally, governments in emerging markets have made progress in issuing domestic currency-denominated debt, beginning to address the problem of 'original sin' about which some of us have written over the years. I say 'beginning to address' because external borrowing by corporates is still very heavily denominated in dollars. In consequence, depreciation of the local currency can create very serious financial difficulties, in turn preventing the authorities from taking recourse to the exchange rate instrument. Public debt may be local currency-denominated to an increasing extent, but this is no panacea. That debt is still heavily sold to foreign investors. As Hyun Shin and his colleagues at the Bank for International Settlements have shown, if there is a negative shock to the economy causing the exchange rate to weaken, foreign investors may rush for the exits even faster than before, since they now suffer the 'double whammy' of capital losses from currency depreciation and capital losses from lower bond prices.

And then there are future challenges. Not for the first time, the external environment facing emerging markets may turn less favourable as a result of events in the world's two largest economies. As I write, there are signs that the US Federal Reserve System is contemplating the possibility of tapering its asset purchases and then, some quarters later, beginning to normalize the level of interest rates. Financial-market participants appear confident that emerging markets will avoid the kind of taper tantrum suffered in 2013, mainly because their external funding requirements are more modest. I'm not so sanguine.

In addition, not only has the Chinese economy slowed, but the heavily indebted property developer Evergrande is experiencing serious financial problems. A default could roil financial markets and weaken foreign financial institutions holding its dollar-denominated bonds, causing 'common-creditor contagion' to other emerging markets. Again, financial market participants appear to be confident that the Chinese government can contain the fallout, on the grounds that China's is still a heavily controlled economy. The authorities can step in to reorganize the company; it can order the big banks to provide debtor-in-possession finance. Again, I'm not as sanguine as many other observers.

The one thing of which we can be confident is that policymakers in emerging economies will have plenty of capital flow-, exchange rate- and financial market-related challenges going forward.

Barry Eichengreen
University of California, Berkeley
September 2021

Preface and acknowledgements

Work on this project began in early April 2020 as the COVID-19 pandemic unleashed its full rage. The collective shock and associated profound sense of uncertainty were compounded by immense macroeconomic stress on the global economy, disproportionately affecting developing nations. For emerging markets (EM), the sudden loss of foreign exchange due to the reversal of capital flows, breakdown in supply chains and effective lockdown of the global economy inflicted a particular pain. The sovereign debt crisis of massive proportions appeared to be inevitable at the time, leading to sharp currency depreciations and prompting (a still ongoing) conversation on new sustainable models of economic development. Nothing seemed to remain the same.

It was in such environment that the idea for this book first appeared. At a broad conceptual level, the book is about macroeconomic challenges to small open economies dependent on foreign exchange flows. Stated differently, the chapters in this collection frame their analysis in the context of developing economy's integration and participation in the larger international capital market in the face of persistent uncertainty. As such, the majority of the contributions attempt to assess both risks and opportunities as well as policy options across a range of emerging and frontier markets from a variety of methodological approaches.

More concretely, the book is organized around three major topics: 1) international capital markets; 2) currency valuations and exchange rate dynamics; and 3) pandemic-induced international economy trends in a complex mix of developing economies' realities. Such organization is intentional in the attempt to inform the growing academic and policy literature on foreign exchange constraint from a perspective of financial markets' operations and exchange rate (currency) management. Given the nature of the individual chapter discussions, this collection deviates, somewhat, from the traditional 'gap' models of foreign exchange in the post-Second World War development literature. However, transactions in foreign currency, availability of foreign exchange, ability to maintain monetary sovereignty and at the same time deploy effective balance of payments management policies have become instrumental in the macroeconomic frameworks of the past two decades.

Consider, for example, the problem of sovereign debt – now an essential element in the small economies' development and operational mode. Since the onset of the pandemic, two trends of immediate concern have evolved: 1) problems of advanced economies and 2) difficulties facing developing countries. In the case of the former, the concern is somewhat counterbalanced by the relatively strong macroeconomic structures in each case. The economies of North America, the EU, the UK, Japan and Australia are characterized by relatively resilient industrial sectors, deeper financial markets and an overall greater share of high-skilled labour. In addition, these countries usually conduct trade in their own currencies, also known as reserve currencies, which eliminates several layers of financial and currency crisis risk. Finally, early into the pandemic, the advanced economies have been able to deliver, at least partial, immediate economic stimulus (e.g. the $2 trillion package introduced in the US and continued public and economic policy transformations).

The situation is the opposite in emerging and developing countries. These economies, spread across the Global South, Eastern Europe and Central Asia, are structurally weaker. Many of them rely on commodity exports and are financially underdeveloped if one would assess their financial markets' depth, escalating debt obligations, lacking foreign exchange and limited banking systems. As the global economy is thrown into recession, demand for primary commodities has followed the already too familiar cycle of uncertainty, while geopolitical tensions lead to another round of trade squeeze, and eventual domestic macroeconomic pressures. Such trends significantly cut foreign capital flows (and availability of foreign exchange) into those regions. In an ever-globalizing economy, despite the recent challenges, where access to innovative technology matters to the overall socio-economic outcome, foreign exchange constraint becomes a key determinant of the direction of the general development process.

One of the strengths of this book is that it is bringing under one thematic umbrella scholars with a diverse range of institutional and conceptual views, yet all actively working on the problems of foreign exchange in policy and development. The studies arranged here revolve around a mix of conceptual, theoretical, empirical and applied policy investigations, equally ranging from general to enriching country-specific discussions.

The book opens with a brief foreword by Barry Eichengreen on the rising (and persistent) challenges to capital-flow-dependent EM almost two years since the onset of the pandemic. There is some optimism in his assessment, especially upon the reflection on some countermeasures adopted across advanced and emerging markets. Yet, as Eichengreen puts it, he is not so 'sanguine' about developing economies being able to avoid the next bout of external pressure, even despite their modest funding needs. The heavy accumulating burdens in the operations of the international economy and the EM structural dependence on trade and finance pose a significant risk of renewed macroeconomic deterioration. Time will show, of course, but this important introduction sets the stage for what follows in the rest of the book.

In what is the book's first chapter within Part I, I try to sketch some additional background on the problem of foreign exchange constraint in connection with development challenges. There is hardly a better country case for such an analysis than the small economies of the post-socialist Caucasus and Central Asia. There is of course an embedded bias in this analysis, given my main research focus, yet, I believe it is justified. The past 30 years have been transformational for these economies, going from an absolute lack of independent economic policymaking to generally complete autonomy, while still attempting to fully integrate into the global economy. In this chapter, I attempt to develop an analytical framework for an informed analysis of capital markets resilience in the region with attention to foreign exchange constraint–related factors and country nuance.

Chapter 2 by Hayk Avetisyan, Viacheslav Ilin and Dmitry Yakovlev connects with the earlier mentioned risks in the sovereign debt that became evident at the start of the pandemic. Specifically, the authors are looking into whether the yields on domestic long-term bonds across emerging markets were reflective of the fundamentals and if the fiscal stress from the pandemic was correctly priced in. This is an important conversation, as following the sudden deterioration of the capital markets conditions across almost all developing countries, by mid-2020 the majority of the emerging markets' yields stabilized. In this comparative study, relying on a series of interviews with portfolio managers, the authors find that despite investors' overall restored belief in the short-run credibility of countercyclical monetary policy, which helped anchor short-term forward rates at historically low levels in virtually all EMs, the lack of credibility of fiscal and monetary policies in the long run kept longer-term forward rates at significantly distressed levels in countries with pronounced political constraints that tended to undermine the feasibility of necessary fiscal adjustments.

In the third chapter, Uthman M. Baqais focuses on the role of wealth composition, particularly natural capital, to explain capital flows. This chapter is motivated by the recent literature on upstream capital flows – a negative association between net capital inflows and economic growth with explanations about human capital and institutional quality. The chapter relies on a recent database on wealth and empirically examines the role of initial wealth composition while revisiting the allocative efficiency hypothesis across 108 countries during 1995–2015. Baqais confirms the significance of wealth composition in explaining capital flows, but no evidence of the allocative efficiency. The relevant finding here is the implication that capital mobility could allow subsoil resource–abundant countries to better smooth the use of resource windfalls by reducing their foreign exchange constraints.

The concluding chapter in Part I, Chapter 4 by Claudia de Camino, Esteban Pérez Caldentey and Cecilia Vera, draws our attention to the role of non-financial corporations as financial intermediaries in Latin America (LAC). The chapter focuses on intercompany loans, which behave like portfolio flows despite being classified as foreign direct investments. Such trends, according to the authors, heighten LAC's vulnerability to short-term fluctuations and as such exert additional macroeconomic pressure by strengthening the foreign external constraint and raising financial stability and fragility concerns. The authors find a strong correlation between intercompany loans and the business cycles in several Latin American countries, especially during crisis periods. As such, they conclude, intercompany loans are key to explaining the extent to which LAC's business cycles are driven by domestic or external (i.e. foreign exchange) factors as well as the transmission mechanisms linking those conditions.

The heading of Part II of the book, 'Currency and exchange rate', speaks for itself. This group of chapters is dedicated to the analysis of currency dynamics and exchange rate management and risks in an open economy. Here questions of dominant currency, currency networks, international reserves management, exchange rate risk and role of the exchange rate in development all come together. This section starts with Chapter 5 by Georgia Bush, Serafin Martínez-Jaramillo, Luis O. L. Escobar-Farfán and Erwin Flores-Tamés on currency network analysis. The chapter also explores dynamic currency networks over time looking at exchange rate correlations for 66 currencies in the period 1995–2018 to study currency centrality. This chapter adds to the emerging literature on dominant currency and the role of currency associations in foreign exchange management and development. Applying a range of empirical and filtering techniques in the context of foreign exchange networks, the authors compare pre-, during and post-global financial crisis (GFC) currency relationships. Focusing on the Mexican peso, the chapter also analyses currency centrality with implications for developing economy currencies. With its methodological improvements on foreign exchange network construction, the chapter makes an important contribution to the analysis of the recent dynamics of EM currency centrality.

Chapter 6 then by Eduardo F. Bastian continues with developing what it calls a neo-Kaleckian open economy analysis framework for the short-term limits of real exchange rate targeting in a country facing foreign exchange constraint. The chapter connects with the traditional 'gap' literature on foreign exchange, mentioned earlier. The model developed in the chapter evaluates different policies and shocks, namely progressive wage policies, public consumption increases, terms-of-trade shocks and industrial policies. Bastian shows that real exchange rate targeting under foreign exchange constraint limits real wage increases in the short term. Deviations from this outcome depend on what the author refers to as 'good luck in the form of positive terms of trade shocks' and a sound industrial policy.

Keeping the policy objective in focus, Dave Seerattan in Chapter 7 studies optimal levels of foreign exchange reserves across small economies with application to the Caribbean. The chapter is explicit about the vulnerability of small open economies to a range of international shocks and structural weaknesses with consequent greater exposure to capital flight. Seerattan argues that such circumstances require a greater share of international reserves for developing economies relative to larger advanced economies (or even stronger EMs). The chapter finds that the optimal reserves amount for small open economies is ultimately a function of the probability of and the way in which they respond to domestic and external shocks, their access to and cost of alternative sources of international liquidity, the relative costs of international reserves, the risk preference of the local authorities and difficult-to-measure idiosyncratic factors. The Caribbean case is instructive here as only a handful of countries have consistently reached the estimated optimal reserves levels. As such, the author concludes that in these economies (and those fitting a similar profile) greater attention should be given to resolving structural weaknesses, for example, low international competitiveness, high exposure to natural disasters, dependence on international commodity cycles and high levels of indebtedness which drive their relative need for international liquidity and insurance that international reserves provide.

Chapter 8 by another group of authors, Elżbieta Kubińska, Joanna Wyrobek, Łukasz Faryj and Anna Macko, brings us back to Eastern Europe in a way reconnecting with the post-socialist economies discussed in Chapter 1. However, the contrast between the two country cases could not be much more evident. In this chapter, the authors focus on assessing the risks of currency derivatives as a probable cause of the financial crisis in EMs. The chapter focuses on the case of Poland since the GFC, exploring the behavioural and macroeconomic reasons behind Poland's exporters' preference for foreign exchange market options with positive short-term characteristics (zero cost and attractive exchange rate) yet with significant long-term risks (less attractive exchange rate, outweighed impact in case of negative payoffs). As the Polish currency, zloty, lost value in the GFC, exporters incurred significant losses. The authors rely on their unique survey of micro, small and medium-sized enterprises in Poland, examining the degree of knowledge about financial instruments and cognitive inclinations in behavioural finance. The overall conclusion is that part of the motivation to engage in riskier foreign exchange transactions was due to the entrepreneurs' conservatism heuristics, intuitive way of processing information and overconfidence. However, equally important (and in that somewhat echoing the findings in Chapter 4) were results about the individual companies' activity and significant exposure to international trade and finance.

In Chapter 9, concluding the conversation on currencies and exchange rates, Hugo C. Iasco-Pereira, Fabrício José Missio, Frederico G. Jayme Jr and Douglas Alencar develop what they refer to as a Kaldorian growth model of cumulative and circular causation to study the association between real exchange rate and long-run growth. The chapter connects with a larger literature and is in cross-reference with the work of Eduardo Bastian in Chapter 6 in our collection. In its innovation, this chapter sees the real exchange rate as an explanatory variable of labour productivity growth and proposes, in addition to the Kaldor-Verdoorn mechanism. The authors argue that a competitive real exchange rate can induce capital accumulation and technological progress, impacting labour productivity. The findings suggest that a competitive real exchange rate is associated with a greater (lower) long-run growth, in economies under a profit- (wage-) led regime of demand and capital accumulation. Relying on a set of OECD countries, the chapter develops an empirical analysis of the effect of a competitive real exchange rate on labour productivity, confirming a positive association. Such effect occurs via the cumulative and circular causation induced by the faster (slower) pace of demand growth, reinforced by the greater (lower) capital accumulation, and by technological progress, induced by a competitive real exchange rate. However, the overall question remains if the same association might hold in the environment of a small open economy that is both facing a foreign exchange constraint and structurally limited in terms of domestic economy and export orientation.

The final section, Part III of the book, 'COVID-19 and open economy', comprises two chapters that offer both a general overview of by-now more or less identifiable challenges to global capital flows in the pandemic and a specific case study of a small open economy under foreign exchange constraint and with a complex (and some ways alternative) banking system. The section opens with Otaviano Canuto's Chapter 10 discussing EM and capital flows in a historical perspective from the GFC of 2008–2009 up until the latest pandemic. Since 2009, portfolio investments and other non-bank financial intermediaries have been responsible for an increasing share of foreign capital flows, while banking flows have shrunk in relative terms. Parallel to some of the points raised earlier (e.g. in the Foreword as well as in Chapters 1 and 2), this chapter analyses the extent to which normalization of monetary policies in advanced economies may lead to shocks in foreign exchange flows across EM. In addition, Canuto discusses the implications for exchange rate fluctuations between the US dollar and other major currencies on EM capital flows. The chapter concludes with an assessment of the range of policy instruments that EM might opt for to manage risks derived from such potential capital-flow volatility.

In the concluding chapter, Samar Issa focuses on the most recent economic crisis in Lebanon. As an applied case, the chapter examines the riskiness of Islamic banks (IBs) and conventional banks during the 2008 global crisis and the 2019 Lebanese crisis, and the likelihood of withstanding the impact of COVID-19 by estimating overleveraging of eight banks in Lebanon for the period 2000–2018. Issa finds that excess debt rather than the mere holding of debt to be the reason for the severe financial meltdown in 2008 as well as the 2019 crisis. Her results show that IBs performed better during the 2008 financial crisis as well as the recent crisis but were subject to the second-round effect of the global crisis. The author suggests that IBs' capital and liquidity buffers built since the crisis may help them overcome their borrowing costs and survive the latest twist of macroeconomic pressures. In these circumstances, Issa concludes, Islamic banks seem to provide a viable alternative financial system to the impaired domestic banking system in Lebanon, especially because their product structure is essentially asset-backed financing, whereas conventional banks rely heavily on leveraging. Should other small open economies attempt to learn from the IBs' prudent foreign exchange management policies? The question is certainly relevant in the times of broad-range search for resilient alternative macroeconomic policies.

As a compilation of individual contributions, this book first and foremost is a testament to the contributing authors' professionalism and dedication to their research fields. Despite the challenges of the pandemic this team has persevered to produce and deliver this high-calibre study. And all my profound gratitude goes to each individual author in this volume. I would also like to express my appreciation to those colleagues who considered participating in the project but had to withdraw due to circumstances beyond their control.

Of course, no substantial work can be completed without dedicated editors. And this volume would not have been possible without the initial interest and support from our editor Alan Sturmer whose encouragement and interest to work with me on the topic of this volume helped shape the contours of the initial idea into a meaningful collection. Much thanks is also due to Caroline Kracunas, Stephanie Mills, Elizabeth Clack, Arun Rajakumar and the entire support team at Edward Elgar for guidance with my questions through the writing process and for their thoughtful assistance with the book's production that helped us complete the project.

Over the period of working on the book, many of my colleagues have stepped up in many ways, offering their support and encouragement, and I would like to extend my special thanks to Charles M. A. Clark, Collin Constantine, João Pedro Farinha, Rebecca Maria Mari, Gary Mongiovi, Steven Pressman, Louis-Philippe Rochon, Norean R. Sharpe, Bruno T. Tomio, Guillaume Vallet, Matias Vernengo and many others. I am thankful to my family for their everlasting support of my research with all its ups and downs. I am indebted to Arkady Gevorkyan and Tarron Khemraj for their constructive critical advice on some of the organizational aspects of this study and their comments on my writing. Many thanks to Valentina Méndez Silva for her assistance with the preparation of the index for the book. I would like to thank everyone who participated in the 'emerging markets sessions' I organized during the Eastern Economic Association 2020 meetings in Boston, MA – our last in-person meeting before the pandemic – and which in some ways motivated this project. And finally, many thanks to the reader of this book. My hope is that this collection may open up some new informative and meaningful paths in your research and policy work or serve as a guide in the broader context of economic development.

Sometimes, it feels like the long year 2020 has not, yet, ended. The tragic loss of life due to the pandemic with its added social, political and economic stress is too overwhelming. Some pressures will remain, but it is with much hope for a better sustainable future that we continue our journey. This book is an attempt to broaden our view about developing countries, their emerging macroeconomic patterns and related policy questions of international capital flows in this rapidly transforming interconnected global economy.

Aleksandr V. Gevorkyan
Queens, NY
February 2022

PART I

Capital markets

1. Foreign exchange constraint and select developing economies: insights from the Caucasus and Central Asia

Aleksandr V. Gevorkyan

1.1 INTRODUCTION

As the COVID-19 pandemic launched a search for sustainable public health policy response, similarly, the concurrent macroeconomic and geopolitical pressures have thrown the global community towards a search for new development paradigms. Small open developing economies seem to have been affected the most by a barrage of direct and indirect impacts. Volatility in access to and availability of foreign exchange, drying liquidity in the domestic capital markets and balance-of-payments management – a foreign exchange constraint – are now essential to the longer-term evolution of their development models.

Recovery and structural shifts in the advanced economies seem to have directly affected the trends across a broad group of emerging markets (EM). This view is carried through several chapters of this study and has recently been emphasized by the International Monetary Fund January 2022 World Economic Outlook report. The policy targets of the advanced economies are locked on prioritizing outcomes in the domestic labour markets and sector growth, supporting local production by way of automation, introducing curbs to technological transfers or curtailing risk investors' appetites for foreign direct and portfolio investments, as monetary tightening to combat rising inflation is being signalled. In contrast, developing nations, by and large, generally reliant on international trade in primary commodities, have limited (if any) capacity or policy space to effectively tackle both the combined health and macroeconomic challenges. In short, two years since the beginning of the pandemic, the prospects for developing economies of stable diversified growth remain fragile.

The IMF's views on the global economy have varied between 2020 and 2022: from a hopeful potential resurgence of global trade and robust pace of global investment and consumer spending in January of 2020, revised in a few months to a view of 'global lockdown' with expected global economy contraction of 3.0 per cent, to a reserved recovery in early January 2022, again with hope this time of the success of vaccination campaigns and rebalancing of the global supply chains.[1] However, recent evidence on capital and foreign direct investment (FDI) flows suggests that recovery is expected to be uneven. Much of the resumption in global foreign exchange trends has gone towards developed economies, with negligible recovery of flows to structural sectors in developing economies, despite the latter sustaining double-digit declines during the pandemic (UNCTAD, 2022).

Furthermore, small developing countries that rely on tourism or workers' remittances (regular monetary transfers from their expatriate communities) have seen that dependence worsen through the pandemic. This observation is in contrast with a more often-mentioned global trend that on average reflects a large EM impact, leaving smaller economies aside. In post-socialist Southern Europe, the Caucasus and Central Asia, labour migrants' remittances serve as a critical economic buffer for many impoverished regions (e.g. Gevorkyan, 2022). With uncertainty in the advanced economies due to rising protectionist measures and escalating geopolitical risks, small developing economies with high remittances to income shares risk of compounding losses of financial flows to developing nations are rising.

One of the most visible manifestations of the foreign exchange constraint in developing nations today is their operational dependence on the international reserve currency (e.g. Gevorkyan and Khemraj, 2022). In this situation, developing nations rely on the supply of foreign exchange from their export revenues, which in turn depend on the global demand for commodities and developing nations' ability to continue to import export-necessary equipment and technology. Such centre-to-periphery dynamic has led to significant swings in the local currencies' valuations (e.g. UNCTAD, 2020a). As the US dollar or the euro, the world's main reserve currencies, strengthen on news of the respective economies' recovery and taming of the health crisis, the loss of relative values of the EM currencies vis-à-vis their trading part leads to further decline in the developing nations' purchasing power with direct impact on poverty and economic depression.

Cline and Vernengo (2016) suggest that shocks to aggregate terms of trade are an external source of financial crises in the EM. Often the first line of adverse response to an externally induced shock is a rapid depreciation of the domestic currency vis-à-vis the hegemonic currency and a possible loss of international reserves. The extent of foreign reserves loss may vary depending on the currency regime, reserves composition and the central bank's balance between a monetary policy and exchange-rate target (Gevorkyan and Khemraj, 2019). Note that globally by the end of 2020 up to 60 per cent of the total currency international reserves were held in US dollars, 21.3 per cent in euros and the rest in other currencies, according to the IMF. At the same time, in purely flexible exchange-rate regimes, the international reserves may be minimal, though this is rarely the case across emerging markets (e.g. Flood and Marion, 2002). The rise in popularity and economic significance of a range of cryptocurrencies adds to the puzzle of small countries' abilities to circumvent foreign exchange constraints.

Incidentally, Eichengreen et al. (2017) in their economic history-based analysis develop a systemic view of the international reserve currency. A plurality of dominant currencies is possible conditioned on the state of the global economy and country-specific pull factors. Those pull factors, in turn, are shaped by the macroeconomic stability and relative economic scale of the reserve currency issuing economy, predictably of its political cycles, national security and, most critically, the existence of internationally competitive, efficient, deep, and broad liquid financial markets with a variety of financial instruments open to the global economy. It is the combination of those factors that explain the US dollar's privileged position and consequent relevance to the developing nations' macroeconomics (Fields and Vernengo, 2013).

The view on the aforementioned availability of foreign exchange in the developing economies connects with the foreign exchange gap (constraint) literature since the early forays into development economics (e.g. Chenery and Bruno, 1962; Thirlwall, 1979; Taylor, 1994; Erten and Ocampo, 2013). Writing in this book, Eduardo F. Bastian in Chapter 6 explores the related topic of real exchange-rate targeting in a neo-Kaleckian open economy.

The small open economies in the Caucasus and Central Asia (CCA) region – Armenia, Azerbaijan, Georgia, Kazakhstan, the Kyrgyz Republic, Tajikistan, Turkmenistan and Uzbekistan – commenced their determined ascent to international capital markets after the 2008 global financial crisis (GFC). Following the EM trend, rising domestic financial markets and access to foreign exchange play an important role in the region's economic models. But lacking organically diversified financial markets or a capable domestic investor pool, the CCAs have primarily been benefiting from the good graces of foreign multilateral investors with limited foreign private investment in the primary commodity sectors.

Volatility in foreign capital flows and country-specific risks in the financial markets with limited depth may reveal more profound vulnerabilities to EM sustainable development exacerbating domestic macroeconomic pressures (e.g. Calvo et al., 1993; García-Kilroy and Silva, 2016; Carney, 2019). UNCTAD (2020b) warns against a possible 'lost decade' of development, as problems with foreign exchange liquidity are compounded by the inadequacies of the domestic macroeconomy – also relevant in the CCA. The pandemic has further exacerbated the rising socio-economic pressures across the entire Central and Eastern European and Former Soviet Union (CEE/FSU) region.

This chapter continues as follows. The next section sketches some key macroeconomic factors of the CCA economies. Section 1.3 introduces the fiscal side of foreign exchange constraint, namely, the schematics of the sovereign debt in the CCA and the ability of these countries to attract a diversified foreign investor. Section 1.4 elaborates on some of the trends in the broader external debt in the region, while section 1.5 continues with additional details on capital market vulnerabilities in the development context of a small open economy. Reflecting on the general discussion, section 1.6 advances an analytical framework of domestic capital markets' resilience in the CCA in the context of the broader discussion on foreign exchange constraint and development. The chapter concludes with a summary of key conceptual points.

1.2 MACROECONOMIC FACTORS IN THE CAUCASUS AND CENTRAL ASIA

Historical centralization of economic activity of the socialist economy led to deeper economic disruptions in the 1990s, with a delayed return to pre-reform income levels (Gevorkyan, 2018). Within the legacy system, the eight CCA countries, distanced from the major industrial hubs, relied on centralized financial transfers and material supply chains. As market reforms kicked in, economic disorganization of a Blanchard and Kremer (1997) type, prevailed. Macroeconomic losses of the early 1990s averaged 20 per cent of the gross domestic product (GDP) in the Caucasus (Georgia losing up to 45 per cent and Armenia 42 per cent in 1992 alone, according to the Conference Board [2020]). In Central Asia, output losses were more reserved, yet structurally significant. Across all countries, unemployment, outward migration and poverty would remain persistently high into the post-2008 GFC period (Gevorkyan, 2018). The dominance of primary commodity exports and high net outward migration exacerbate the CCA's on-average high susceptibility to volatility in foreign exchange flows.

Azerbaijan, Kazakhstan and Turkmenistan (and to some extent, Uzbekistan) ended up specializing in commodity exports (with shares of crude oil or natural gas in total exports accounting for 91.3 per cent, 64.7 per cent and 91.8 per cent respectively). Armenia and Georgia have also attempted to diversify their domestic economies in the service sectors (information and communications technology in the former and tourism and agriculture in both), capturing during 2016–2018 on average a 70 per cent share of GDP in Georgia and 57 per cent in Armenia (FocusEconomics, 2022).

Still, in their analysis, Iradian and LaRussa (2020) note a high degree of uncertainty about the future of the CCA's macroeconomic stability (a sentiment repeated in a more recent February 2022 update). The concern stems from the structural macroeconomic characteristics stipulated earlier, slower recovery in the services sectors, unclear effect of remittances and regional trade, as well as geopolitical risks. With these clarifications, prospects for growth are positive in the early months of 2022 but much depends on external factors and the CCA's ability to attract new investment.

1.3   FISCAL CONSTRAINT: SOVEREIGN DEBT AND TAPPING GLOBAL INVESTORS

1.3.1   General Framework

In terms of fiscal balances, the recent available data, summarized in Table 1.1, suggest the extent of the constraint facing the CCA. The combined public health needs and economic support measures have visibly exerted outsized pressures on the smallest economies, pushing fiscal spending up. It is not clear to what extent any of this might be compensated with corresponded tax revenues and any feedback from stimulus due to an unlikely quick economic rebound. This may suggest persistent elevated fiscal deficits in some non-energy exporters (e.g. Armenia, Georgia, Uzbekistan) and the arising need to compensate by stimulating external cash flows.

A characteristic of the energy-exporting CCA economies is the high share of state-owned corporations, which has relevance to the direction of spending. For example, as of January 2020 in Kazakhstan (where up to 30 per cent of the total fiscal expense is allocated to pensions and low-income support), 89 per cent of the state-owned enterprises were with 100 per cent of government capital participation, according to the data from the country's Ministry of Finance (Min Kaz, 2022). Though the state does not necessarily

Table 1.1   Fiscal balance, percentage of GDP

Country	2019	2020	2021	2022f	2023f
Armenia	−0.8	−5.1	−4.5	−3.2	−2.2
Azerbaijan	9.1	−6.5	−1.3	0.0	−0.6
Georgia	−1.8	−9.2	−6.6	−4.0	−2.8
Kazakhstan	−1.9	−3.1	−3.2	−2.8	−2.3
Kyrgyz Republic	−0.1	−3.3	−2.8	−2.7	−2.2
Tajikistan	−2.1	−4.4	−2.4	−1.9	−1.9
Turkmenistan	−0.4	−0.2	−0.3	−0.1	−0.2
Uzbekistan	−1.1	−4.8	−5.2	−3.6	−3.1

Note: Figures for 2022 and 2023 are forecast estimates.
Source: FocusEconomics (2022).

bear responsibility for any debt issued by such a company, the fiscal presence may imply reaffirmation of the borrower's solvency to the capital markets and implies a contingent liability in crisis times. Azerbaijan and Kazakhstan manage large sovereign wealth funds with reserves replenished from surplus revenues from the energy exports, at 90 per cent of GDP and 46 per cent of GDP respectively in September 2020, providing a possible emergency cushion to support domestic financial sectors (FitchSolutions, 2020).

Overall, public debt is modest for CCA but does hide some important country specifics. For example, Armenia has seen its government-debt-to-GDP ratio rise from the 2018–2020 average of 57.5 per cent to 61.5 per cent for the 2021–2023 estimated period. Similarly, in Georgia the respective ratios have changed from 46.4 per cent to 52.2 per cent and in the Kyrgyz Republic from 58.2 per cent to 60.7 per cent over the same period, according to FocusEconomics (2022). Public debt has also gone up significantly in Uzbekistan (from 28.1 per cent to 39 per cent), while estimated to be around the same (49.5 per cent) in Tajikistan and declining in Turkmenistan (from 32 per cent to 20.9 per cent).

Since the GFC, EMs have leveraged on the rising global liquidity and decreasing costs of borrowing, as global investors sought competitive capital markets. The literature suggests that developing economies may often see their costs of borrowing rise with perceptions of risks and capital costs in advanced economies, as the 2013 taper tantrum clearly suggested (e.g. Gevorkyan and Kvangraven, 2016). In addition, there has been a rise in both foreign and local currency borrowing across EMs driven by a mix of domestic and external factors (Dafe et al., 2017; Senga et al., 2018).

In this context, the CCAs have largely benefited from the participation of a range of multilateral investors in the governments' external debt programmes and of local financial and non-financial sectors in the local currency debt profiles. At this point, such an arrangement has offered a relative sense of protection against highly speculative capital flows, as domestic markets lack the needed depth. Table 1.2 summarizes some of the trends as of 30 September 2020 in government debt dynamics for select CCA countries.

The Asian Development Bank's (ADB) position in Kazakhstan's multilateral portfolio changed from 14.7 per cent of the total state external debt in January 2019 to 10.9 per cent as of January 2020 declined during 2020, with the Eurobonds at close to USD 9 billion representing a significant share (58.8 per cent of the total government's external debt). For the smaller CCA, credits and loans procured through multilateral organizations, such as ADB and others, are essential in guaranteeing the near-term stability of and development of the domestic capital markets. These loans normally entail a low borrowing cost and are significant concessionally, though subject to macroeconomic and

Table 1.2 Select indicators of government debt composition, as of 30 September 2020

Category	Armenia	Georgia	Kazakhstan	Kyrgyz Rep
Government's domestic debt balance, USD bln	1.9	1.7	18.5	0.647
Change in government's domestic debt Jan–Sept 2020, %	20.0	26.6	17.7	–2.2
Government's external debt balance, USD bln	5.6	6.7	15.2	4.18
Change in government's external debt Jan–Sept 2020, %	5.9	17.8	3.7	7.9
Multilateral debt, % of total government's external debt	76.9%	68.3%	37.0%	44.8%
Largest multilateral lender and % share of the total state external debt	International Development Association (21.6%)	Asian Development Bank (30.6%)	International Bank for Reconstruction and Development (24%)	International Development Association (35.7%) and Asian Development Bank (31.8%)
Bilateral debt, % of total government's external debt	22.6%	20.6%	4.2%	54.0%
Largest bilateral debt lenders and % share of the total state external debt	Russia (7.9%) and Germany (5.9%)	France (39.9%) and Germany (35.6%)	N/A	China via Exim Bank of China (79%)
Eurobonds or other, % of government's external debt	0.5%	11.2%	58.8%	1.2%

Note: Data for Kazakhstan reflects changes between 1 January 2019 and 1 January 2020; Kyrgyz Republic domestic government debt data is as of June 2020; '–' indicates negative change.
Sources: MinArm (2022), MinGeo (2020), MinKaz (2022), MinKyrgz (2022).

policy conditionalities. In fact, earlier in 2020, the Kyrgyz Republic was one of the beneficiaries of the World Bank's Debt Service Suspension Initiative with at the time estimated 'moderate' risk of external debt distress. In Armenia, the government's gross debt increased by almost USD 630 million or 8.5 per cent between January and the end of August 2020, mainly driven by the issuance of government treasuries bought by residents (rising by 20.4 per cent or USD 298 million to USD 1.76 billion on top of a smaller share of bonds denominated in foreign currency), while government's external debt increased by 5.9 per cent or USD 309 million.

1.3.2 Foreign Investors and Ownership of Government's Debt

Arslanalp and Tsuda (2014) offer a rare opportunity to study both foreign currency- and local currency-denominated general government's debt ownership by investor type and residence. The data is available for some but not all CCA economies (in Figure A1.1 of the appendix). Three country narratives seem to be emerging from this analysis in the CCA: small economies, large energy exporters (e.g. Azerbaijan and Turkmenistan, possibly with the addition of Uzbekistan) and an outlier, Kazakhstan.

Evolving foreign investor shares in the government debt ownership may be telling a story of macroeconomic and domestic capital markets maturity. Consider, for example, panel (a) in Figure A1.1 with Armenia's starting point in 2000 at 87 per cent of the government's debt claimed by foreign official investors. According to the statistical data from Armenia's Ministry of Finance (also reported in Table 1.2), those are primarily multilateral development institutions with long-term investments. Starting around the mid-2010s as the country entered the sovereign bond market the investor diversification changed with an increase in domestic (and later foreign) banking and non-banking sectors, along with changing shares of other foreign investors. Significantly, in Armenia the role of the central bank in what might be termed monetizing the government's debt is negligible.

Equally negligible has been the share of foreign investors holding Armenia's local currency-denominated treasury bonds. In fact, local-currency debt is a smaller share of the portfolio at about 22 per cent of the total government debt as of September 2020. According to the official data, the average share of non-resident investors in Armenia's local-currency debt has varied from 0.2 per cent to 0.5 per cent between December 2013 and December 2019, peaking at 1.8 per cent as of end of 2017 and as of September 2020 oscillating around 0.4 per cent with the remaining share allocated across residents (with up to 57.5 per cent concentration within the domestic banking system and 20 per cent in the non-financial sector at the end of the third quarter 2020, according to the Ministry of Finance data).

Following Armenia, Georgia is in panel (b) of Figure A1.1 where the central bank has initially played a greater role with a visible overall earlier diversification of the investor pool in more recent years. At the end of 2019, official foreign investors held 70 per cent of Georgia's sovereign debt, consistent with the multilateral and bilateral investors' significance (but above Armenia's 63 per cent). Recall that close to 80 per cent of the government's debt is in the form of external debt, in turn with 68.3 per cent (Table 1.2) held by multilateral organizations in foreign currency denominated credits or loans. As such, the share of the foreign ownership of the local currency debt is small, with greater allocations across domestic financial and non-financial sectors, as is indirectly confirmed by the World Bank's Quarterly Public Sector Debt (QPSD, 2020) online portal. But the high share of foreign-currency debt exposes the government to exchange-rate risk, as state revenues accrue in local currency (as reviewed here).

Due to the limited financing options in the Kyrgyz Republic, Tajikistan and Uzbekistan, Arslanalp and Tsuda (2014) do not report any data on these countries. Extrapolating from the QPSD (2020), it is possible to see that as of the second quarter of 2020, Tajikistan's local currency-denominated debt accounted for 15.2 per cent of the general government's debt of USD 3.6 billion. External creditors took up the foreign-currency debt share of 84.8 per cent of the total. Within the composition of debt, 74 per cent share was accounted for by mainly multilateral loans of USD 2.7 billion, with the remainder in domestic securities. No data was reported for other countries in the QPSD (2020).

Back in Figure A1.1, panel (c), Azerbaijan reports limited data but with a vast majority of debt issued in foreign currency, primarily owed to official (multilateral) foreign investors (up to 63 per cent in 2019) and some non-bank foreign investors. According to FitchSolutions (2020), despite Azerbaijan's manageable debt and the presence of a strong sovereign wealth fund, investment in the country's capital markets is discouraged due to the illiquid and underdeveloped nature of the national financial system. The financial sector is dominated by the local banking sector (over 90 per cent) with virtually no foreign investor participation in the local-currency bonds market.

The situation is different for Kazakhstan in panel (d), the most diverse and developed market within the CCA group. While the role of foreign investors is important, as of 2019 about half (48 per cent) of the total government debt was held by domestic non-financial corporations with minimal participation from the central bank. Local banking sectors' ownership shares over the past two decades ranged between 10 per cent and 20 per cent of the total debt. FitchSolutions (2020) points to the sustainability risk to Kazakhstan's largely foreign currency-denominated debt holders due to the waves of currency devaluation (2014 and 2015) and more recent losses due to the pandemic crisis.

For Turkmenistan in panel (e) of Figure A1.1, the data is rather scant but indicates relatively strong foreign investor share early after the transition reforms (about 11 per cent during and post-GFC) but declining to approximately 1 per cent as of the latest estimates, with a modest addition of foreign banks as holders of government-issued debt. The overall trend across CEE/FSU, according to Arslanalp and Tsuda (2014), is the rise in the share of foreign ownership of total government debt, which between 2007 and the fourth quarter of 2019 went up by four percentage points (from 48 per cent to 52 per cent). However, a more nuanced consideration is needed.

Compared to the leading CEE/FSU economies, the CCA countries are facing significant limitations in their capital markets deepening and marketability of their debt, and as such constrained access to international capital markets (Table 1.3). In Kazakhstan, the foreign investors have access to a much more diverse financial portfolio, which is not the case in the other commodity exporters Azerbaijan or Turkmenistan. The smaller economies have constrained capital markets, explaining the limited interest of the non-resident investors in the local currency-denominated securities. While such a structure limits the exposure of the smaller CCA economies to potential sudden outflows from the public debt by foreign investors, it also inadvertently cements

Table 1.3   Market capitalization in CCA and select CEE/FSU economies

	Market cap 2019, USD bln	Number of stocks*	Stock exchange established*	Market cap as share of GDP, %
ARM	0.3	10	2001	2.19
AZE	2.0	9	2002	4.16
GEO	0.7	21	1999 (2015)	3.95
KAZ	40.7	122 (7)	1993 (2017)	22.59
KGZ	0.4	19	1994	4.73
TJK	NA	NA	2015	NA
TKM	NA	NA	2017	NA
UZB	2.2	108	1994	3.80
Hungary	32.9	44	1990	20.4
Poland	151.6	459	1991	25.6
Russia	681.0	281	2011	40.1

Note: * If there is more than one exchange, the number of stocks and years of establishment of any subsequent exchanges are in parentheses.
Source: EBRD (2020) and WDI (2020).

the already missing financial deepening leading to the problems of foreign exchange constraint.

One recurring theme in the smaller economies with large expatriate communities (diaspora) has been a proposal for the diaspora bond *à la* Israel or India as a means of tapping the global financial resources and bringing large institutional investors into domestic capital markets (e.g. Gevorkyan, 2021, 2008). Diaspora investors are seen as 'first movers' and investors of last resort in little-known small economies. An altruistic diaspora investor agrees to a below-market rate of return (patriotic discount) and commits to a longer maturity. The instrument can be denominated in either local or foreign currencies. The bond would then be regulated by a State–Diaspora Supervisory Board (SDSB), with representatives from international banking, home country central bankers, policymakers, representatives from the diaspora and maybe observers. This remains a purely hypothetical, yet popular, proposal for boosting the domestic capital markets. Advancement of new local currency bond alternatives such as, perhaps, a diaspora bond may help smaller governments overcome their inability to tap the global markets and to borrow in their own currency, the 'original sin' (Eichengreen et al., 2005), diminishing financial dollarization. The shares of local currency debt in the CCA remain modest and of local significance.

1.4   FITTING INTO THE GLOBAL BOND MARKETS: GROSS EXTERNAL DEBT

The CCA sovereign bond spreads trail those of the MSCI Frontiers Markets index (Figure 1.1). At the same time, the degree of the CCA's intra-group variation over a five-year period between 2015 and mid-October 2020 is quite broad. After a tumultuous spring of 2020, the CCA spreads have converged to the late 2015 levels. A possible decoupling from the index is visible in Armenia and Azerbaijan, likely due to the October 2020 war. Assuming this risk perception is maintained, it is likely the sovereign spreads and future borrowing costs may continue to rise for the two economies. It is unclear if this would mean a reduced future borrowing by either of the two nations or a reduced demand for their debt from foreign creditors. Preliminary data seem to suggest borrowing to continue.

The CCA external debt patterns seem to have largely followed the countries' post-socialist macroeconomic transformations (see Figure 1.2). As tentative macroeconomic stabilization was achieved in the early 2000s, external debt shares started to modestly decline. The lowest shares for the group were reached right before the global financial crisis in 2008 after which the upward trajectory was resumed, as illustrated in Figure 1.2 by the

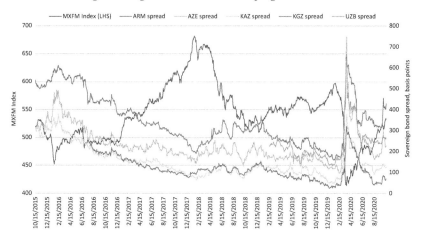

Note: MXFM – MSCI FM Frontier Markets Index.
Source: Bloomberg terminal.

Figure 1.1   Sovereign bond spreads and the MXFM index

Average transition economies (TE) and Average CCA changes. The forecast ratios for external debt to GDP are trending higher, with both Armenia and Georgia above others. Explaining these trends may be increased government borrowing and extension of multilateral credits with the expected emergent needs in the pandemic- (and war)-hit economies.

The oil- and natural gas-rich Azerbaijan and Turkmenistan and the more diversely endowed in resources Uzbekistan are all below the average trends (Figure 1.2). Kazakhstan, with its comparatively robust economy, tracks elevated shares of external debt to GDP, with Armenia and Georgia breaking into the highest thresholds.

The short-term debt component of the total external debt reveals some risk sensitivity for the CCA in the near term (Table 1.4). For the majority of countries, with some variations, most of the external debt has been long-term consistently since the late 1990s. A notable exception is Tajikistan with an elevated 20.5 per cent share of its external debt short-term and above the CCA and CEE/FSU averages.

As of 2019, Armenia and Georgia were trailing around the transition economies average of 13.4 per cent but above the 7.9 per cent for the CCA group. Relying on the directional guidance from publicly available sources, short-term debt has declined significantly over the past two decades for the energy-rich Turkmenistan (from 16.9 per cent to 0.14 per cent), Kazakhstan (from 10.2 per cent to 5.7 per cent) and Azerbaijan (from 9.6 per cent to 3.9 per cent).

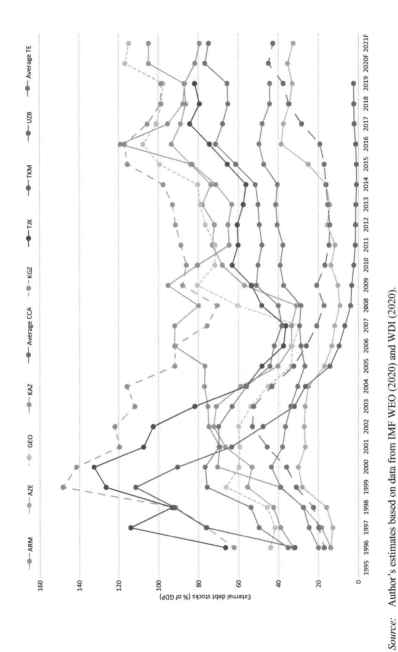

Source: Author's estimates based on data from IMF WEO (2020) and WDI (2020).

Figure 1.2 External debt stock as percentage of GDP

Table 1.4   Short-term debt, % of total external debt

Country	1996–2009	2010–2019	2019
Armenia	10.34	10.85	13.41
Azerbaijan	9.59	9.49	3.89
Georgia	6.30	14.40	13.15
Kazakhstan	10.21	5.78	5.75
Kyrgyz Rep	5.62	4.58	6.22
Tajikistan	5.51	18.50	20.49
Turkmenistan	16.97	16.98	0.14
Uzbekistan	5.70	4.36	5.57
Average TE	15.38	14.88	13.44
Average CCA	9.13	10.08	7.93

Source: Author's estimates based on data from IMF WEO (2020) and WDI (2020).

The trends in the short-term debt hint at the smaller economies being potentially prone to greater external pressure by way of the combined public and private foreign currency-denominated debt. For all of the CCA, most of the debt that might be carrying any potential destabilization risk to the domestic capital markets would be foreign currency denominated in form of state borrowing. That is shaped by the loans from multilateral organizations and bilateral agreements. As such, from an external investor's view, the risks remain relatively moderate. But what is the significance of these observations from the point of view of economic development?

1.5   CAPITAL MARKETS' VULNERABILITY IN A DEVELOPMENT CONTEXT

Financial openness (and deepening) characterizes a country's make-it-or-break-it moment in the global economy. In developing economies, the burden is often placed on the government to lead into international capital markets, overcoming the foreign exchange constraint. Once the market entry is made, the state strives to maintain market discipline, which in turn requires transparency in fiscal activities. Inability to accomplish this on a consistent basis dampens the foreign investors' enthusiasm for either local currency- or foreign currency-denominated bonds due to uncertainty.

Roos (2019) advances three enforcement mechanisms keeping the borrowing government in check with the international capital markets. The first is the 'market discipline', by which private creditors (a syndicate) may withdraw from the defaulted country and as such damage the economic development process. The second pertains to the conditionality of lending, which emanates from the frameworks of official or multilateral organizations' lending. The third mechanism comes from internal local businesses and political elites. A sovereign default or a government that might pursue independent policies disagreeing with the core creditor group might inflict unintended damages on the domestic corporations' terms of borrowing and future access to the global credit lines. Naturally, these factors compound the competitively weaker CCA economies compared to the larger EM country groups, connecting with foreign exchange complexity across developing nations.

Related to the factor of local business elites, Alfaro et al. (2019) find that across emerging markets, large domestic corporations are more financially vulnerable, while systemically important as the key players in the domestic bond markets and retaining significant market shares – a warning to Kazakhstan's model? Another vulnerability emanates, as Cerutti et al. (2019) suggest, from lacking diversity of creditors or significant reliance on global mutual funds. In such situations emerging markets grow more sensitive to sudden capital flow bouts, especially if the degree of financial openness is greater relative to the peers, for example, limited or absent capital controls.

A similar viewpoint is raised by Carney (2019), arguing that financial openness can be a 'double-edged sword'. Figure 1.3 contextualizes this in the CCA context. Higher volatility in capital flows can shave off a significant share of

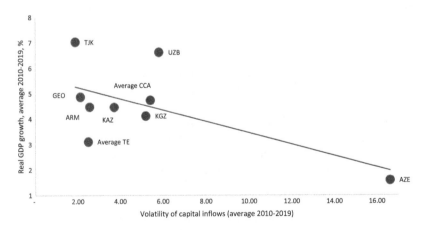

Note: Volatility is based on net inflows scaled by external debt liabilities.
Source: Author's estimates based on data from IMF WEO (2020) and WDI (2020).

Figure 1.3   Financial deepening: opportunity or vulnerability?

economic growth (the trendline in Figure 1.3 suggests higher volatility causes the economy to grow 0.2 percentage points slower over the reported period).

This is not a proposal for restricting capital accounts as a hypothetical solution to minimizing the foreign exchange market volatility. There are obvious macroeconomic and reputational downsides to such a policy that may be cutting off a country's access to foreign financial markets. Instead, and applied to CCA, here is an attempt to assess and illustrate the current capital market volatility, given, as argued earlier, the limited role of broad groups of institutional investors in the CCA markets.

Another conclusion from Figure 1.3 is that what amplifies the uncertainty in the little diversified CCA is the greater sensitivity to the external as opposed to domestic risk factors. For example, Li et al. (2020) find that while Kazakhstan is more resistant to the general emerging markets' volatility, the economy is sensitive to the global volatility index and changes in the crude oil price – the main export commodity. Gevorkyan (2019) arrives to a similar conclusion in the analysis of exchange market pressure for EM groups. There, crude oil exporters maintaining fixed (or pegged) exchange rates relied on the international reserves balances to sustain significant currency pressures to capital outflows. Here, FDI volatility has varied across the CCA over the past three decades, with energy-exporting nations benefiting from substantially larger inflows in absolute terms in proportion to their economies. Elsewhere, focusing on foreign exchange market pressure, Direye and Khemraj (2022) find that the central bank's one-sided Central Bank Bills sales can ease foreign exchange constraint and help to manage the exchange rate.

Reflecting on the 1997 Asian and 1998 Russian crises, Taylor (1998) makes a case against domestic and foreign private investors' speculative capital flow – 'hot money' – in a deregulated environment due to triggering potential currency and debt crisis. Effectively reconfirming that point, Carney (2019) warns that open EMs are more likely (he estimates three times more likely) to go through a financial crisis following sudden surges in capital flows. As a possible example, consider Uzbekistan's total external debt stock which rose 179 per cent between 2013 and June 2020, with 73.5 per cent of the total being long-term debt (CBU, 2020). Private sector external debt in Uzbekistan doubled reaching USD 10.1 billion and the government's external debt jumped 300 per cent for the same period!

1.5.1   A Developing Economy Context, Not Just the Financial Market

Aside from capital flows' volatility, in terms of external debt or FDI, the CCA region is facing currency pressures, consistent with the dominant currency argument discussed earlier (for the latest view see Gevorkyan and Khemraj,

2022). Corsetti and Marin (2020) argue that USD appreciation in times of crisis, for example, the pandemic recession, leads to sudden foreign exchange losses due to abrupt capital outflows from the EM. This then weakens the relative positions across CCA currencies in relation to either regional or global benchmarks, largely negating previous sovereign bond market gains, for example, pushing borrowing costs up. Reviewing exchange-rate trends for Armenia, Gevorkyan (2017) points to the importance of the external pressures, domestic banking sector competitiveness and the central bank's role in the country's foreign exchange market.

The recorded 2020 depreciation pressures on the CCA currencies run a risk of exacerbating access to credit in the region. Such burdens on the local consumer markets are important due to high shares of deposits and loans denominated in foreign currency, while income is earned and payments are made in the local currency. For the domestic consumer, dollarization also helps maintain a certain standard of living in macroeconomic uncertainty (Figure 1.4).

Dollarization has been quite stubborn in Georgia, only recently declining to 60 per cent of foreign currency deposits as a share of all deposits. In Armenia and the Kyrgyz Republic, with proactive central bank measures and the rise of the domestic investor, the dollarization rates are somewhat subdued (though still high in Armenia, despite the 2014–2015 steep decline). Feeding into the CCA dollarization, aside from the macroeconomic structure, is the high reliance on labour migrant remittances, averaging up to 35 per cent of GDP in the Kyrgyz Republic and Tajikistan. The transfers are an important supplement to the consumer markets in Armenia, Georgia, the Kyrgyz Republic and Uzbekistan.

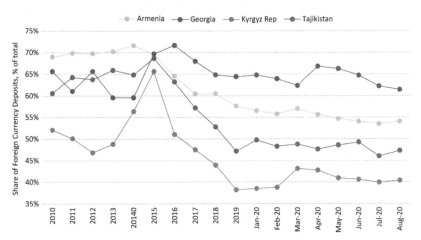

Source: Author's estimates based on data from countries' central banks (CBA, 2020; NBG, 2020; NBK, 2020; NBT, 2020).

Figure 1.4   Deposit dollarization in the CCA

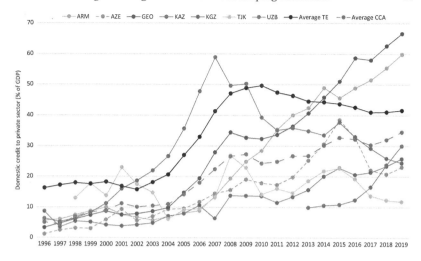

Source: Author's estimates based on data from IMF WEO (2020) and WDI (2020).

Figure 1.5   *Growth in domestic credit to private sector, percentage of GDP 1996–2019*

The aforementioned dynamics have gone parallel to rising trends in domestic credit growth (Figure 1.5) across CCA. A general testament to growing domestic financial markets, a cursory look at the recent trajectories raises a warning about rapid financial deepening and associated risks, consistent with the preceding discussion on fragile macroeconomic structures and accumulating debt in the near term.

The emphasis is on the speed of the rise in domestic credit (rather than the opening of the market) that is clearly visible in the post-GFC period. Compounding the factors of dollarization, reliance on remittances, limited international capital markets presence and lacking foreign exchange, such private credit growth may add to the state's contingent liabilities in the medium-term in the event of large-scale consumer or housing credit defaults with systemic risks to the economy.

1.6   A FRAMEWORK OF FOREIGN EXCHANGE CONSTRAINT AND CAPITAL MARKETS IN CCA

In the CCA, where the state is the major debt issuer, domestic capital markets' resilience may be gauged by the economy's capacity to maintain solvency, and attract and channel domestic and foreign capital flows effectively at upward or downward trends of the cycle. The CCA's generally stable capital market outlook is partly due to the existing fiscal capacity and partly due to the relative underdevelopment with limited exposure to the volatility of the global capital flows. As a summary of the preceding discussion, Figure 1.6 attempts to develop a conceptual framework of the CCA's capital markets and development mosaic.

Moving clockwise from the top, point 1, the first component in the framework is the macroeconomic structure and geography. The key energy exporters may continue to be able to attract substantial diversified foreign capital if primary commodities remain in global demand and much of the incoming loans and debt directly or indirectly targets the sector. That disproportionately sidelines the smaller economies where the scale of monetary balances is significantly lower. Geography plays a role in this as well, as the landlocked economies are left on the outskirts of the international trade routes and away from key business hubs and global value chain operations.

The second factor is the question of fiscal needs. At the time of writing, there is anticipation of widening fiscal deficits and a significant increase in general government debt. The strength of fiscal pressure and time demand on any extraordinary measures may be detrimental to a country's international capital markets position if the economy is also trying to attract FDI and

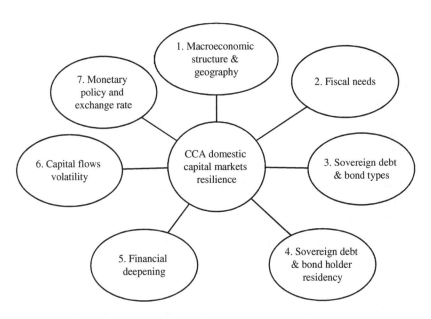

Figure 1.6   Analytical framework of domestic capital markets resilience in CCA

foreign portfolio investors or scale up any large infrastructure development projects.

The third factor is the question of sovereign debt (including the type of debt), for example, government-issued securities (e.g. Kazakhstan) or external loans and credits (e.g. smaller economies). Should the diaspora bond be seriously considered as an alternative to conventional ways of attracting foreign exchange into the economy? Could there be any other technologically more advanced financial schemes? These are the questions that each country will tackle individually.

The type of debt ownership is the fourth factor in Figure 1.6. Much of the foreign investors' ownership across the CCA consists of either multilateral lenders or other foreign governments as holders of the CCA's foreign currency-denominated debt. While this may be reducing the risk of 'hot money' volatility, the eight countries remain exposed to the currency risk, since revenues are generated in local currency terms and there are limited foreign exchange inflows to scale up development projects.

The fifth factor touches on financial deepening. Without financial infrastructure, the economy is unlikely to successfully attract long-term foreign investors. This is where a large-scale jump-start push by way of government action or a large (likely, state-owned) corporation's entry into the capital markets, could draw smaller economic agents into the market. It would be important to monitor ongoing innovation with the introduction of new debt instruments and reaching new domestic and foreign creditors (e.g. green bonds or diaspora bonds). A changing composition of creditors by residency may eventually come, signalling the economy's recognition in the global markets.

The sixth factor, capital flows volatility, relates to both the debt markets and FDI flows (with remittances added in some countries). This is about monitoring identifiable vulnerabilities overlapping the domestic bond market within the larger financial system. Volatility in foreign equity and portfolio capital flows may be evasive and not immediately identifiable in the available data and as such the destabilizing risk of too much financial opening (deepening) remains.

The final, seventh, factor, pertains to the monetary policy and, more narrowly in the CCA case, the exchange-rate management. From an economic development perspective, exchange-rate management, reliance on remittances and the significance of dollarization reveal some structural weaknesses in economies with pegged exchange rates. Either a sudden reversal of capital flows or a drop in currency valuation may have severe short-term economic effects on the weaker economies with limited international reserves cushion. As such, for the CCA, local currency-denominated bonds may indeed possibly help mitigate the instability in foreign capital flows, while also contributing to the domestic capital markets evolution. However, rolling out large-scale local-currency bonds to foreign investors, as local market participants are still lacking needed capacity, puts pressure on fiscal transparency and public policy realignments, which may not be seen as popular measures, especially during and coming out of crisis.

In the post-socialist CCA with underdeveloped financial infrastructure, there may not be sufficient demand for local bonds from either financial or non-financial domestic investors for a host of macroeconomic and other reasons. At the same time, foreign investors might prefer to stay out of a particular market either during the crisis or if there is no clarity about the country's prospects, in turn influenced by a larger EM portfolio view, instead of a country-specific approach. Macroeconomic idiosyncrasies and a host of external factors of capital flow volatility and currency pressures dominate the post-socialist CCA region. It is because of all of the aforementioned circumstances that the economies of the Caucasus and Central Asia are meaningful representations of typical development economies facing the foreign exchange constraint today.

1.7   CONCLUSION

The analysis of this chapter suggests that beyond the veil of emerging or frontier markets classification, the Caucasus and Central Asian economies retain unique idiosyncrasies. Domestic capital markets vary in the extent to which foreign investors are active in the CCA and structural dominance of the macroeconomic fundamentals determines external funding needs and developmental outcomes. Canvassing a vast CCA region, this chapter has constructed an analytical framework aiding in the assessment of the small open economy's resilience in facing challenges of foreign exchange constraint, access to global capital markets, exchange-rate management, mismatching macroeconomic diversification and development priorities. The attempt here is to provide a holistic foundation for any subsequent critical examination of the pertinent policy and research problems around foreign exchange constraint and developing economies.

NOTE

1.   According to FocusEconomics (2022), in 2020 the global economy contracted by 3.2 per cent.

REFERENCES

Alfaro, L., Asis, G., Chari, A., and U. Panizza. 2019. Corporate debt, firm size and financial fragility in emerging markets. *Journal of International Economics*, 118: 1–19.

Arslanalp, S., and Tsuda, T. 2014. *Tracking Global Demand for Emerging Market Sovereign Debt*. IMF Working Paper WP/14/39, Washington, DC.

Asian Development Bank (ADB). 2020. ADB to invest $40 mln in green bonds to upgrade water, sanitation in Georgia. https://agenda.ge/en/news/2020/2391.

Blanchard, O., and Kremer, M. R. 1997. Disorganization. *Quarterly Journal of Economics*, 112(4): 1091–1126.

Calvo, G., Leiderman, L., and Reinhart, C. 1993. Capital inflows and real exchange rate appreciation in Latin America: The role of external factors, staff papers. *International Monetary Fund*, 40(1): 108–151.

Carney, M. 2019. Pull, push, pipes: Sustainable capital flows for a new world order. Speech by Mark Carney, Governor of the Bank of England, Institute of International Finance Spring Membership Meeting, Tokyo.

Central Bank of Armenia (CBA). 2020. Databank. https://www.cba.am.

Central Bank of Uzbekistan (CBU). 2020. Statistics portal. Available online: https://cbu.uz/en/statistics/.

Cerutti, E., Claessens, S., and Puy, D. 2019. Push factors and capital flows to emerging markets: Why knowing your lender matters more than fundamentals. *Journal of International Economics*, 119: 133–149.

Chenery, H., and Bruno, M. 1962. Development alternatives in an open economy: The case of Israel. *The Economic Journal*, 72(285): 79–103.

Cline, N., and Vernengo, M. 2016. Interest rates, terms of trade, and currency crises: Are we on the verge of a new crisis in the periphery? In Gevorkyan, A. V., and Canuto, O. (eds.) *Financial Deepening and Post-Crisis Development in Emerging Markets: Current Perils and Dawns*. New York: Palgrave Macmillan.

Conference Board (TCB). 2020. Total economy database (adjusted version), May 2017. www.conference-board.org/data/economydatabase/.

Corsetti, G., and Marin, E. 2020. The dollar and international capital flows in the COVID-19 crisis. *VoxEU*. https://voxeu.org/article/covid-19-crisis-dollar-and-capital-flows.

Dafe, F., Essers, D., and Volz, U. 2017. *Localising Sovereign Debt: The Rise of Local Currency Bond Markets in Sub-Saharan Africa*. SOAS Department of Economics Working Paper 202.

Direye, E., and Khemraj, T. 2022. Central bank securities and foreign exchange market intervention in a developing economy. *Review of Development Economics*, 26: 280–297.

EBRD. 2020. *The Investor Base of Securities Markets in the EBRD Regions – March 2020*. 2nd ed. London: European Bank for Reconstruction and Development.

Eichengreen, B., Hausmann, R., and Panizza, U. 2005. The pain of original sin. In Eichengreen, B., and Hausmann, R. (eds.) *Other People's Money*. Chicago, IL: Chicago University Press.

Eichengreen, B., Mehl, A., and Chiṭu, L. 2017. *How Global Currencies Work Past, Present, and Future*. Princeton, NJ: Princeton University Press.

Erten, B., and Ocampo, J. A. 2013. Super cycles of commodity prices since the mid-nineteenth century. *World Development*, 44: 14–30.

Fields, D., and Vernengo, M. 2013. Hegemonic currencies during the crisis: The dollar versus the euro in a cartalist perspective. *Review of International Political Economy*, 20(4): 740–759.

FitchSolutions. 2020. *Country Risk Report (Armenia, Azerbaijan, Georgia, Kazakhstan, Kyrgyz Republic – Q4 2020)*. Fitch Solutions Group Ltd.

Flood, R., and Marion, P. 2002. *Holding International Reserves in an Era of High Capital Mobility.* IMF Working Paper No. 02/62.

FocusEconomics. 2022. FocusEconomics consensus forecast – CIS countries – February 2022. *FocusEconomics.* www.focus-economics.com.

García-Kilroy C., and Silva A. C. 2016. Post-crisis lessons for EME capital markets. In Gevorkyan, A., and Canuto, O. (eds.) *Financial Deepening and Post-Crisis Development in Emerging Markets.* New York: Palgrave Macmillan.

Gevorkyan, A. V. 2008. Fiscal policy and alternative sources of public capital in transition economies: The diaspora bond. *Journal of International Business and Economy*, 9(2): 33–61. https://doi.org/10.51240/jibe.2008.2.4.

Gevorkyan, A. V. 2017. The foreign exchange regime in a small open economy: Armenia and beyond. *Journal of Economic Studies*, 44(5): 781–800.

Gevorkyan, A. V. 2018. *Transition Economies: Transformation, Development, and Society in Eastern Europe and the Former Soviet Union.* Oxford: Routledge.

Gevorkyan, A. V. 2019. Exchange market pressure and primary commodity exporting emerging markets. *Applied Economics*, 51(22): 2390–2412.

Gevorkyan, A. V. and Khemraj, T. 2019. Exchange rate targeting and gold demand by central banks: modeling international reserves composition. *Emerging Markets Finance and Trade*, 55(1): 168–180.

Gevorkyan, A. V. 2021. *Diaspora Bonds: Can Success Be Replicated?* SSRN Working Paper (January 5). http://ssrn.com/abstract=3760281.

Gevorkyan, A. V. 2022. Diaspora and economic development: A systemic view. *The European Journal of Development Research,* Vol. 34: 1522–1541.

Gevorkyan, A. V., and Khemraj, T. 2022. *Dominant Currency Shocks and Foreign Exchange Pressure in the Periphery.* SCEPA Working Paper. https://www.economicpolicyresearch.org/.

Gevorkyan, A. V., and Kvangraven, I. H. 2016. Assessing recent determinants of borrowing costs in sub-saharan Africa. *Review of Development Economics*, 20(4): 721–738.

International Monetary Fund (IMF WEO). 2020. *World Economic Outlook database.* Available online: https://www.imf.org/en/Publications/WEO.

Iradian, G., and LaRussa, S. 2020 (July 31 and February 2022 update). *Caucasus and Central Asia Regional Report Navigating Through the COVID-19 Storm.* Institute of International Finance.

Li, H., Semeyutin, A., Lau, C., and Gozgor, G. 2020. The relationship between oil and financial markets in emerging economies: The significant role of Kazakhstan as the oil exporting country. *Finance Research Letters*, 32: 101–171.

Ministry of Finance of the Republic of Armenia (MinArm). 2022. Statistics and Reports. Online data resource. Available online: https://www.minfin.am/en/.

Ministry of Finance of Georgia (MinGeo). 2020. *Public Debt of Georgia: Statistical Bulletin #14 June.*

Ministry of Finance of the Republic of Kazakhstan (MinKaz). 2022. Online resources. Available online: https://www.gov.kz/memleket/entities/minfin/activities/directions?lang=en.

Ministry of Finance of the Kyrgyz Republic (MinKyrgz). 2022. Structure of public debt. Available online: https://minfin.kg/pages/182.

National Bank of Georgia (NBG). 2020. Statistics. Available online: https://nbg.gov.ge/en/page/statistics.

National Bank of the Kyrgyz Republic (NBK). 2020. Statistics. Available online: https://nbg.gov.ge/en/page/statistics.

National Bank of Tajikistan (NBT). 2020. Statistics. Available online: https://www. nbt.tj/en/.

Quarterly Public Sector Debt (QPSD). 2020. *Online Database*. Washington, DC: World Bank. http://datatopics.worldbank.org/debt/qpsd.

Roos, J. 2019. *Why Not Default?: The Political Economy of Sovereign Debt*. Princeton, NJ: Princeton University Press.

Senga, C., Cassimon, D., and Essers, D. 2018. Sub-Saharan African eurobond yields: What really matters beyond global factors? *Review of Development Finance*, 8: 49–62.

Taylor, L. 1994. Gap models. *Journal of Development Economics*, 45(1): 17–34.

Taylor, L. 1998. Capital market crises: Liberalisation, fixed exchange rates and market-driven destabilisation. *Cambridge Journal of Economics*, 22: 663–676.

Thirlwall, A. P. 1979. The balance of payments constraint as an explanation of international growth rate differences. *BNL Quarterly Review, Banca Nazionale del Lavoro*, 32(128): 45–53.

UNCTAD. 2020a. From the great lockdown to the great meltdown: Developing country debt in the time of Covid-19.

UNCTAD. 2020b. Trade and development report 2020. https://unctad.org/en/ PublicationsLibrary/tdr2020_en.pdf.

UNCTAD. 2022. Global foreign direct investment rebounded strongly in 2021, but the recovery is highly uneven. January 19. https://unctad.org/news/global-foreign-direct-investment-rebounded-strongly-2021-recovery-highly-uneven.

WDI. 2020. *Word Development Indicators*. Washington, DC: World Bank. http:// databank.worldbank.org/.

APPENDIX

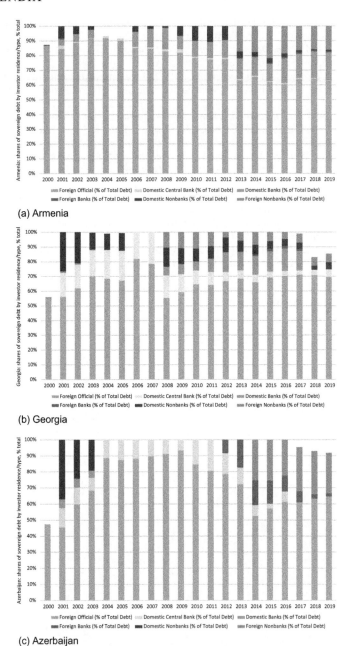

(a) Armenia

(b) Georgia

(c) Azerbaijan

Source: Extrapolated from the latest dataset based on Arslanalp and Tsuda (2014).

Figure A1.1 Share of sovereign debt held by investor residence/type, percentage of total

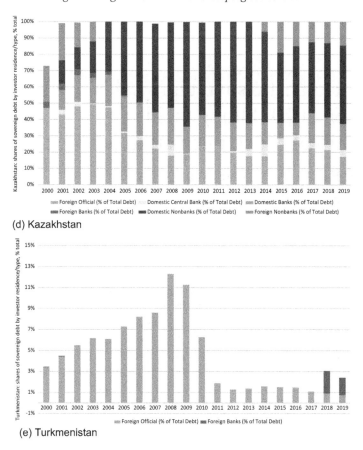

(d) Kazakhstan

(e) Turkmenistan

Figure A1.1 (Continued)

2. Domestic sovereign yields puzzle in 2020: falling yields amid a large fiscal shock in emerging markets

Hayk Avetisyan, Viacheslav Ilin and Dmitry Yakovlev

2.1 INTRODUCTION AND MOTIVATION

The first half of 2020 was a period of unprecedented uncertainty and extraordinary fiscal shocks in various countries across the globe. Yet, ten-year (10Y) yields in many emerging market economies (EMs) quickly stabilized at or below the pre-COVID levels simultaneously with rapidly widening expected budget deficits: Figure 2.1.1 demonstrates this counterintuitive dynamic for South Africa. However, at the same time, instantaneous forward rates at a ten-year time point (10Y FR) – indicators of investors' long-term outlook on sovereign and inflation risks along with various risk premia – remained elevated. Essentially, the stabilization of 10Y yields was a result of two opposing forces: 1) a massive drop in priced-in short-term forward rates in response to monetary policy easing; 2) an increase in long-term forward rates. Figure 2.1.2 provides an illustration of this for South Africa. Notably, while 10Y yields before the COVID shock and after the COVID shock were virtually the same, the underlying f-curves underwent a massive rotation (Figure 2.1.3 with f-curves as of two dates with equal 10Y yields = 9 per cent). As this chapter will explore further, EMs demonstrate significant cross-country heterogeneity with regard to the dynamics of instantaneous forward rates.

The COVID-19 shock was a perfect storm for studying the observed behaviour of macroeconomic and financial indicators versus the theoretical consensus in the literature and economic policy discussions about the dynamics of capital flows, country risk premium, interest rate term structure and the design of monetary policy reactions in emerging markets during global shocks. In this context, this chapter provides a series of stylized facts about the dynamics of domestic sovereign yield curves in emerging markets and the drivers of those fluctuations in the first stages of pandemic shock.

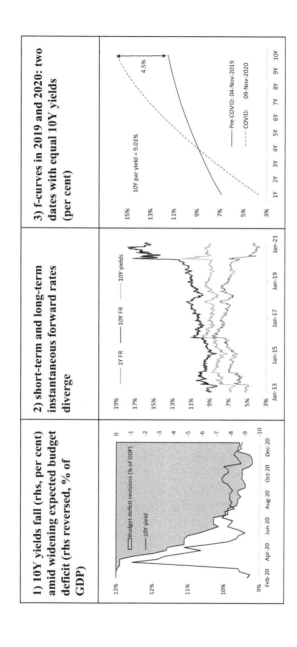

Source: Bloomberg, authors' calculations. Panel 1 shows the accumulated change in analyst forecasts of the expected budget deficit for 2020.

Figure 2.1   Components of 10Y yields in South Africa

A vast amount of existing literature has studied the determinants of the sovereign risk premia or bond spreads in emerging countries, and a few also researched the issues in the context of crises. While some analyses emphasize the role of such country-specific fundamentals as GDP growth, inflation or the external sector sustainability indicators (Bizuneh and Geremew, 2021; Taguchi and Bolortuya, 2021; Tebaldi et al., 2018; Martinez et al., 2013; Hilscher and Nosbusch, 2010; Eichengreen and Mody, 1998; Kamin and Von Kleist, 1999), clearly the debt and fiscal-related factors always stood at the table of researches that study the determinants of the sovereign debt spreads, and many found significant results (Palic et al., 2017; Baldacci and Kumar, 2010).

In addition to domestic fundamentals, in the era of globalized financial markets, bond spreads of emerging market countries are also affected by global financial and commodity market sentiments or cycles (Gevorkyan and Kvangraven, 2016; Bellas et al., 2010; Hilscher and Nosbusch, 2010; McGuire and Schrijvers, 2003; Kamin and Von Kleist, 1999). It is most pronounced especially in the short run when financial volatility is revealed to be a more important determinant of bond spreads than fundamental factors (Bellas et al., 2010). Moreover, Amsted et al. (2016) even found that country risk doesn't depend much on economic fundamentals but rather on the simple fact that a country is designated as an emerging market economy. In this context of risk-premium drivers, our discussion is closer to Remolona et al. (2008), who separated the default probability from the risk premium and revealed that country-specific fundamentals drive the former, while the latter is greatly affected by investors' sentiment (risk aversion).

Clearly, the role of different factors might intensify or change during global or domestic economic crises. For instance, Ebner (2009) and Aizenman et al. (2013) found significant differences in the government bond spread determinants in pre-crisis, during or after-crisis periods. In the context of Central and Eastern European countries, Ebner (2009) found that macroeconomic variables lose their importance, while the role of political, market volatility and global factors increases during crisis periods. In contrast, Aizenman et al. (2013), analysing CDS spreads in emerging markets, found that state fragility and external factors were important in the pre-crisis period, while elements describing the available fiscal and monetary space were key components of country risk determinants. A few studies have analysed the issue in the context of COVID-19 shock. Bizuneh and Geremew (2021), employing a panel estimation of 12 emerging countries, established that the magnitude of GDP decline during the COVID-19 pandemic defined the size of the risk-premium reappraisal by investors. In addition, Daehler et al. (2020) showed that the traditional macro-variables such as fiscal space, commodity revenues and mobility dynamics explained the variation of CDS spreads during the pandemic, while more specific COVID-19 mortality rates had little correlation with the risk premia in emerging countries.

Discussion in this chapter also relates to a strand of research that analyses the term premium dynamics in emerging countries in the face of spillovers from the international financial markets and how the macrofinancial fundamentals could define these effects. A small amount of literature that studied the issue in the context of emerging countries usually finds contradicting results unlike the literature on advanced economies. Some have revealed that similar to advanced countries, most of the yield curve volatility in emerging countries is associated with the term premium, rather than with expected short-term rate changes. Such results were obtained in the cases of Russia (Kryukovskaya, 2003) and Brazil (Caldeira and Smaniotto, 2019). Others found more support for the expectations hypothesis, which for example drives the yield spreads for India (Shareef and Shijin, 2016), Saudi Arabia (Harrathi and Alhoshan, 2020) and a sample of Asian countries (Guerello and Tronzano, 2016). In terms of the term-premium drivers, the studies show that market liquidity indicators, inflation, exchange rate, macroeconomic uncertainties as well as global market risk factor have positive contributions to the demanded premium (Ozbek and Talasli, 2020; Guerello and Tronzano, 2016). At the same time, some authors argue that given their fundamentals emerging countries have to pay high term premia to bondholders on long-term debt (Gevorkyan and Kvangraven, 2016), which consequently pushes them towards issuing at short-term maturities (Broner et al., 2013).

It is also widely accepted that monetary policy in advanced countries or their interest rates in general have significant spillover effects on emerging market yields. There is substantial amount of literature highlighting the US monetary policy and the US markets as influential global factors for credit and financial conditions in other advanced or emerging countries (Bruno and Shin, 2015; Rey, 2013). In addition, the correlation of emerging market bond yields with the prices of advanced country risk assets is also well documented (Obstfeld, 2015; Ammer et al., 2010). Different channels of transmission work here, including the risk-taking or search for yield, the synchronization of monetary or exchange rate policies across countries. The existing research shows that the US expectations component appears to be a more significant source of spillover than the US term-premium shocks (Mehrotra et al., 2019). On the other side, for receiving emerging countries, the effect is found to be concentrated in the term premium part of long-term yields (Ceballos and Romero, 2016; Albagli et al., 2018). Moreover, macrofinancial vulnerabilities in the receiving country matter for the magnitude of the transmission. In particular, Mehrotra et al. (2019) find that 'spillovers from US yields tend to be larger when a receiving emerging economy displays greater macrofinancial vulnerabilities' related to the current account, fiscal balances and the external debt.

From the policy perspective, our discussion in the chapter relates to the widely realized phenomenon of the 'procyclicality trap' in emerging countries. For example, in the context of monetary policy, it was documented in a paper by Vegh and Vuletin (2012). Facing an abrupt reappraisal of investors' risk perception that accompanies capital outflows, exchange rate depreciation and destabilization of inflation expectations, monetary authorities in emerging countries are usually forced to tighten policy conditions in the middle of a crisis. This raises the issue of monetary policy procyclicality in the face of economic shocks. As Vegh and Vuletin (2012) argue, the key solution is stronger institutions. However, during the COVID-19 shock, surprisingly to many researchers and policy practitioners, most emerging markets' central banks were able to decrease their policy rates and ease policy conditions (Cantu et al., 2021). Some authors argue that the level of initial inflation or the beneficial macroeconomic cyclical position clearly supported this (Aguilar and Cantu, 2020; Gelos et al., 2020). Others claim that the role of large-scale policy easing in advanced economies is undeniable (Aguilar and Cantu, 2020; Pordeli et al., 2021).

Most important however are the findings that attribute this escape from the procyclicality trap to a significant pre-crisis improvement of institutional factors related to monetary policy frameworks (Gelos et al., 2020). Interestingly, given the unprecedently active role of macroprudential policy during this crisis of COVID-19 (Yale CFRT, 2020), some authors demonstrate how it was important in creating space for monetary policy reaction and essentially boosting the effectiveness of policy responses (Paries et al., 2021). The literature however was not able to firmly establish whether the emerging monetary authorities took advantage of a combination of beneficial factors to act countercyclically during the COVID-19 crisis, or whether they have truly 'graduated' from the procyclicality trap by improving their institutional frameworks. Our findings in this chapter show that investors had mixed views on EM policies.

Finally, from the methodological point of view, our discussion in the chapter refrains from traditional econometric specifications widely used in the literature. Rather, we incorporate a series of interviews with market participants and portfolio managers. This, to our belief, provides a better understanding of investors' behaviour and state of mind during the very acute phase of the COVID-19 crisis, when most indicators of investors' expectations were either unreliable or lacked sufficient frequency.

The rest of the chapter is structured as follows. Section 2.2 provides a description of the quantitative concepts being used in the chapter as well as an overview of country buckets that are used for aggregation. Section 2.3 gives an overview of the dynamics of sovereign yields and forward rates at the very onset of the COVID crisis and highlights cross-country heterogeneity.

Section 2.4 discusses the factors leading to the elevated long-term forward rates and how they affected the issuance policies in EMs. Section 2.5 summarizes stylized facts presented in the chapter.

2.2 METHODOLOGY: COMPONENTS OF INSTANTANEOUS FORWARD RATES

Before discussing this chapter's methodology, we introduce the abbreviations used throughout the chapter.

z-curve – zero-coupon yield curve built based on domestic nominal fixed-rate sovereign bonds. It's a curve that allows equating the discounted cash flows from a bond with its current value:

$$P = \sum_t CF_t \cdot e^{-t \cdot z(t)} \qquad (2.1)$$

Here, P is the current value of a fixed-rate bond, CF_t is a stream of expected cash flows from the bond, $z(t)$ is the z-curve as a function of time to the future cash flow.

f-curve – instantaneous forward curve derived from the z-curve:

$$z(t) = \frac{\int_0^t f(\tau)\,d\tau}{t} \qquad (2.2)$$

Here, $f(\tau)$ is the f-curve as a function of time to the future cash flow. **1Y FR** – interest rate from the f-curve at the one-year time point: $1Y\,FR = f(1)$. **10Y FR** – interest rate from the f-curve at the ten-year time point: $10Y\,FR = f(10)$. **10Y yield** – interest rate from the sovereign par-curve at ten-year tenor (i.e. an equivalent of the yield-to-maturity of on-the-run bonds with ten years till maturity). The par-curve is derived from the z-curve.

While the relationship between 10Y yield and forward rates from the f-curve is very non-linear, conceptually a rough approximation may be perceived as a weighted average of points from the f-curve. Consequently, parallel shifts in the f-curve make the 10Y yield move in the corresponding direction, while the impact of rotations of the f-curve on the 10Y yield is rather muted. In this study, we focus on the dynamics of 1Y FR and 10Y FR as their variation captures a sufficient portion of oscillations of the f-curve.

Risk premium – a sum of all premia attributed to various risk factors relevant to forward rates at a given time point: term premium, premium for credit risk, premium for liquidity risk, etc. In the macrofinancial context, the front end (short end) and back end (long end) of the f-curve reflect two distinct sets of macroeconomic characteristics. The front end mostly reflects the expectations regarding the policy rate reaction to the *current domestic* economic cycle, while the back end generally reflects the *global secular* trends (secularly declining global potential GDP growth, declining term premium in advanced economies, impact of demographics on the real yields, etc.) and the long-term credit-risk premium of a given particular issuer. Consequently, the dynamics in 10Y FR is mostly synchronous across various countries (Figure 2.2.1), while 1Y FR shows considerable heterogeneity (Figure 2.2.2).

For emerging markets, the loading of the credit-risk premium in 10Y FR is very important and significantly affects both the dynamics on longer horizons as well as a reaction to a particular economic shock. For example, Figure 2.2.3 shows that a proxy combining US 10Y FR (i.e. global secular trend in long-term forward rates) and Hungarian CDS spread (i.e. country-specific credit-risk premium) explains a significant portion of the variation in Hungarian 10Y FR.

Two quantitative notes should be given when considering the usage of 5Y USD-denominated CDS as a component of local currency-denominated 10Y FR. First, while the precise value of the (unobservable) local currency-denominated credit spread differs from the (observable) USD-denominated CDS spread, still the USD-denominated spread is valuable enough as a regressor in the decomposition of the dynamics of domestic 10Y FR: complementing USD-denominated Eurobonds with cross-currency swaps may serve as a synthetic substitute for the domestic local currency bond and hence should be priced closely to avoid arbitrage. Correspondingly, the valuation of domestic sovereign bonds incorporates the variation in USD-denominated CDS spreads.

Second, as we are considering forward rates at 10Y tenor, it might at first seem appropriate to choose 10Y CDS hazard rates instead of 5Y CDS spreads as reference indices. However, 5Y tenor generally represents the most liquid tenor in the CDS market for EM sovereigns, while 10Y CDS is priced off 5Y CDS and may have less reliable quotes. Also, the hazard rate is computationally sensitive to inputs while we lack sufficient and reliable data for CDS spreads around 10Y tenor to build satisfactory estimates of the hazard rates.

The impact of the credit-risk premium in 10Y FR is much larger in EMs than in AEs, defines a starker heterogeneity with EMs and contributes to a more volatile historical dynamic. For example, Figure 2.2.4 demonstrates the difference between countries' 10Y FR and the 10Y FR of the US. For AEs, this spread is relatively close to zero with an insignificant intragroup variation between AEs and only moderate historical volatility. In contrast, for EMs the country differentiation with respect to the credit risk is much more pronounced, and historically the spread has been subject to a larger variation.

While the front end and back end of an f-curve are driven by conceptually different macrofinancial factors, there still may be a considerable degree of

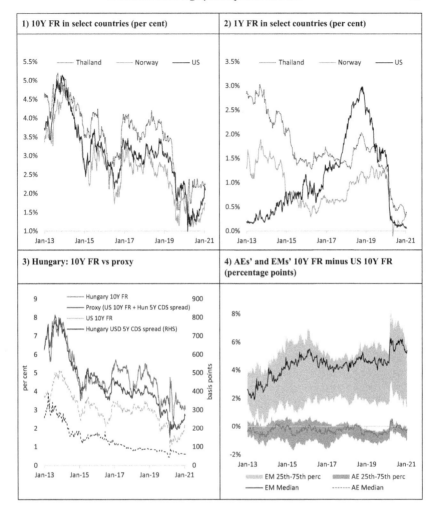

Source: Bloomberg, authors' calculations.

Figure 2.2 Dynamics of instantaneous forward rate curves

the arithmetic impact of one end on the other. For example, in some individual episodes, there may be a cross-impact of the long-term macroeconomic factors on the front end and short-term factors on the back end. For example, a spike in the long-term credit-risk premium (relevant mostly for the back end) may be a reflection of elevated general risk aversion, which impacts all the segments of the financial market, including the front end of the f-curve. An opposite example is an increase in the uncertainty regarding the short-term rates' path that arithmetically spills over into a slightly elevated term premium across all the tenors of the f-curve, including the back end. However, on the horizon of several years, it is safe to separate the factors affecting the front and back ends into different groups.

In this chapter, we consider 13 EMs, which we split into two groups: commodity exporters and others.[1] Some of the countries in the commodity exporters group are systematically placed at the bottom of the rankings based on income inequality (World Bank Gini index), political stability (World Bank's Political Stability and Absence of Violence/Terrorism index) and sovereign credit rating (Moody's rating). Consequently, the cumulative dynamics of the commodity exporters group are largely affected by those countries that are subject to the most pronounced fiscal risks and political rigidities to fiscal adjustments.

We analyse EM dynamics against that of advanced economies (AEs), also split into two groups: core AEs and smaller AEs.[2] The large depth and unique role of the financial systems of the core AEs limit their direct comparability to the dynamics in EMs. However, many smaller AEs have similar size, depth and degree of development as some of the most developed EMs. In other words, smaller AEs may serve as a reference point in assessing the degree of 'graduation' of macroeconomic policies and financial systems in the set of considered EMs. Comparing the timing and the size of COVID-related financial shocks in smaller AEs to those in EMs may help assess the EM-specific contribution to the dynamics of macrofinancial variables during the COVID crisis.

The econometric identification of the drivers of yield curves' rotation in EMs during the first months of the COVID crisis is severely limited due to the lack of reliable high-frequency series of market expectations regarding the expected paths of policy rates and other macrofinancial variables. The elevated uncertainty made analysts unable to form revisions to their previous expectations and/or unwilling to publish them in a timely manner. To overcome this problem of unrepresentative data, we conducted a series of interviews with market participants and portfolio managers from all EM countries in our sample to identify the drivers of the yield curves' variation during our period of interest. While we continue working on the quantification of this qualitative information and publishing it as separate indices, most conclusions in this chapter are based on the systematization of verbal accounts of market participants.

2.3   BASIC FACTS: THE DYNAMICS OF INSTANTANEOUS FORWARD RATE CURVES

The key difference in the market reaction in AEs and EMs to the onset of the COVID crisis lies in the market perception of the strength and credibility of the expected policy responses. The difference in dynamics between AEs and EMs is observed in 10Y yields, which represent an aggregate of the priced-in short-term and long-term forward rates. Figure 2.3.1 demonstrates that both groups of EMs experienced a temporary spike in 10Y yields at the onset of the COVID crisis.

In the very first weeks of the COVID crisis, markets were pricing in a pro-cyclical monetary policy response in EMs, based on the assumption that EM central banks will procyclically engage in defending their local currencies and will attempt to retain foreign investors. This priced-in expected policy response can be observed as a temporary spike in 1Y FR (Figure 2.3.2). However, the positive spillovers from the massive interventions of the Federal Reserve and ECB led to the stabilization of EM FX rates and allowed EM central banks to credibly conduct countercyclical monetary policy. The size of the consequent reduction in short-term forward rates was most pronounced among EM commodity exporters as they used to have inflation and policy rates higher than those in other EMs and, hence, had a larger space for policy rate cuts in the deflationary environment at the beginning of the pandemic. The massive drop in 1Y FR put strong downward pressure on 10Y yields and was responsible for the quick stabilization of 10Y yields as declining 1Y FR acted as a counterbalance to the elevated levels in 10Y FR (Figure 2.3.3). In other words, the quick stabilization of long-term domestic sovereign yields was achieved predominantly due to the credibility of the countercyclical monetary policy in the short-run horizon, while the long-run credibility of some EM commodity exporters remained questioned by the markets.

Another representation of this phenomenon is given in Figure 2.3.7 and 2.3.8: a massive change in 10Y FR for EM commodity exporters (x-axis on Figure 2.3.7) doesn't translate into any change in 10Y yields due to the equally impactful reduction in 1Y FR (x-axis on Figure 2.3.8). Figure 2.3.9 reiterates that countries with higher pre-COVID 1Y FR were able to experience a larger drop in 1Y FR.

The stress in 10Y FR was inevitable as there was a synchronized repricing of medium- and long-term credit-risk fixed-income securities across all the segments of the global financial market. Importantly, the unprecedently strong and timely response of the Fed and ECB allowed to stabilize the pricing of credit-risk instruments in all segments: for example, Figure 2.3.4 shows the dynamics of CDS spread indices for US Investment Grade and High Yield corporate issuers. Similarly, EM sovereign USD-denominated CDS spreads underwent synchronous moderation (Figure 2.3.5). However, for some EM commodity exporters, the repricing of the credit risk didn't explain the prolonged stress in 10Y FR for domestic local currency sovereign bonds: the long-term forward rates remained elevated even after the moderation in credit-risk indices (Figure 2.3.6). The interviewed market contacts pointed out two major

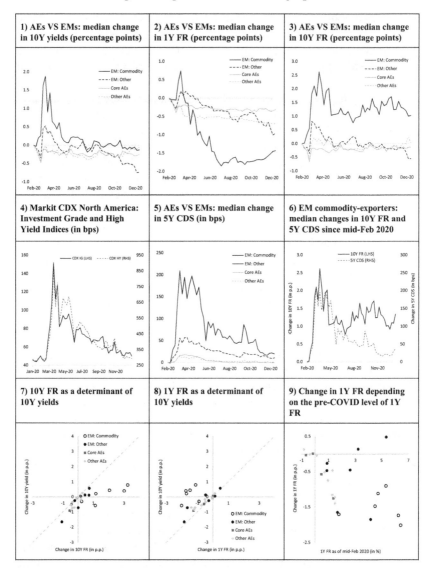

Note: The series in panels 1–6 are centred in mid-February 2020. The differences/changes in panels 7–9 are calculated between mid-February and end of June 2020.
Source: Bloomberg, authors' calculations.

Figure 2.3   Reaction to the onset of COVID-19 crisis: changes in forward rates since mid-February 2020

causes for the elevated risk premia in the long-term forward rates: uncertainty regarding the political feasibility of required post-COVID fiscal adjustments and the risk of neglecting the inflation targeting goal by the central banks.

2.4 FORWARD CURVES: THE STRESS IN LONG-TERM FORWARD RATES

Surprisingly, quantitative indicators do not show a clear picture of why the stress in 10Y FR had to be so long lasting for some commodity exporters. First, as Figure 2.4.1 shows, by mid-2020, the size of fiscal support in response to the COVID crisis had no particular impact on 10Y FR for AEs and non-commodity EMs. Also, the COVID-driven fiscal expenditure in EM commodity exporters wasn't considerably larger than that in other countries. The surveyed market participants commented that their trust in the fiscal prudence in AEs and most non-commodity EMs made them interpret the unexpected COVID-related expenditures as a transitory spike in sovereign debt to be faded out during the consequent sovereign deleveraging. In contrast, with regard to some EM commodity exporters, there was a pronounced concern that the lack of fiscal flexibility will make the new elevated levels of debt permanent despite the recovery in commodity prices, exacerbated by the fears of monetary financing.

Importantly, while the priced-in probability of this pessimistic fiscal scenario was responsible for most of the stress in 10Y FR in some EM commodity exporters, the published economists' projections and expectations do not make those countries differ meaningfully from their EM peers. Figure 2.4.2 demonstrates a set of long-term projections for the ratios of general government revenue and debt for 2025 (as they were perceived in mid-2020). Clearly, the lack of sufficient state capacity to tax made some commodity exporters have low revenue-to-GDP and high debt-to-revenue ratios. However, a similar situation was observed for some non-commodity EMs who didn't experience prolonged stress in 10Y FR. Similarly, the long-term expectations of GDP growth rates and inflation rates were virtually unchanged between pre-COVID and mid-2020 (e.g. Figure 2.4.3 for GDP growth rates). One of the reasons behind this lack of cross-country differentiation is that the projections are published for the baseline scenarios assuming optimal and prudent policy responses. Another reason is the inability and/or unwillingness of analysts to revise their long-term expectations amid the most turbulent and uncertain phase of the crisis. Consequently, it makes it nearly impossible to build a solid econometric framework explaining the dynamics of priced-in variables through the dynamics of the published analysts' expectations and projections.

To consider 10Y FR in the context of longer-term macroeconomic projections (serving as proxies for the steady-state levels of macroeconomic

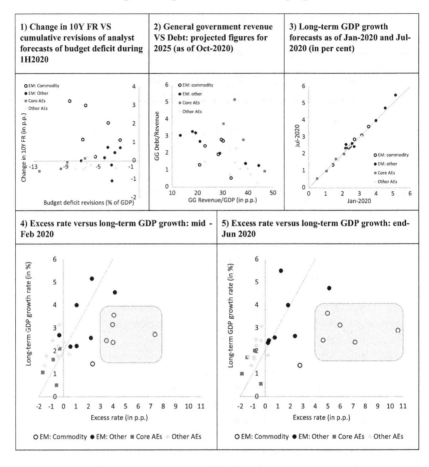

Source: Consensus Economics, IMF WEO Database, Bloomberg, authors' calculations.

Figure 2.4   Consensus expectations and projections

variables), we introduce the variable called excess rate (ER) as the difference between 10Y FR and steady-state inflation. Theoretically, the excess rate is the sum of the steady-state real interest rate (r^*) and the risk premium.[3] In most economic models, r^* is a linear transformation of GDP growth rate g: $r^* = \alpha + \beta \cdot g$. In the next step, we plot the excess rate versus the steady-state potential GDP growth rate. Correspondingly, abnormal deviations of the excess rate beyond levels justified by the GDP growth rate may be attributed to the elevated risk premium. Figures 2.4.4 and 2.4.5 show that while most AEs and EMs lie reasonably close to a straight line,[4] there are various outliers for which the large size of the excess rate can't be explained by the expected GDP growth; most of such outliers represent commodity-exporting countries. In other words, those EMs that experienced the largest increase in their 10Y FR in response to COVID-19 during 1H2020 were already facing elevated levels of risk premium even before the COVID-19 crisis. Further analysis shows that simple metrics like debt/GDP alone do not explain the cross-country variation in excess rates. It is in line with the economic intuition that would perceive the risk premium as a complex interplay of the degree of fiscal flexibility, the ability of a country to generate sustainable growth and the propensity of the sovereign to accumulate contingent liabilities and various off-balance-sheet tail risks.

As 10Y yields quickly declined to or below pre-COVID levels (Figure 2.3.1), various economists were puzzled why EMs did not finance their COVID-related expenditure through issuing long-term fixed-rate nominal bonds in the environment of presumably supportive yields. As it turns out, the answer lies in the increased slope of the forward curves (f-curves): in EMs, the stress in the longer-term forward rates was increasingly more pronounced with the increase in the distance to the time input for the f-curves. For illustrative analysis, we chose two time points for the f-curves: 7Y and 10Y. Most of the models that are used by market participants for the evolution of macrofinancial indicators assume the convergence of the modelled variables to their respective steady-states within at most five to six years. Thus, the 10Y–7Y term spread of the f-curves consists mostly of the marginal increase in the risk premia between those two time points.

Figure 2.5.1 shows an example of the rotation of f-curves during 1H2020: in Mexico the slope in the area 7Y–10Y is much larger as of end of June 2020 compared to pre-COVID levels, while the slope remains almost the same for the US. Figure 2.5.2 depicts the historical spread (10Y FR minus 7Y FR): for Mexico it stays close to record highs, while for the US the levels of the spread are rather moderate. Figure 2.5.3 shows the relative historical positioning of the spread for EMs and AEs in our sample: the slope of f-curves in AEs doesn't experience such a large increase as in EMs.

The 10Y–7Y FR term spread determines the relative attractiveness of issuing ten-year bonds versus issuing seven-year bonds and rolling them over for an additional three years. Essentially, the 10Y–7Y FR term spread is the risk premium that is paid for locking in the currently expected forward three-year rate – that is, the cost of hedging the variation in the future three-year rate. However, the historically high values of the 10Y–7Y FR term spread make such hedging prohibitively expensive. Thus, it is more beneficial for the issuer to issue seven-year bonds and be exposed to the risk of fluctuating three-year rates at the moment of rolling over the debt. In other words, the pronounced slope of the f-curves makes it optimal for an EM sovereign borrower to issue

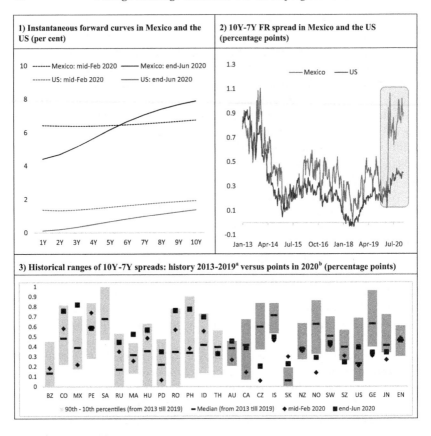

Notes:
a) Percentiles are calculated based on data with weekly frequency.
b) For South Africa and Brazil some of 2020 points are not depicted as they are larger than the size of the chart.
Source: Bloomberg, authors' calculations.

Figure 2.5   The slope of the back end of f-curves: spread 10Y FR minus 7Y FR

short- to medium-term bonds despite the presumably favourable levels of longer-term yields.

2.5   CONCLUSION

In the last two decades, most emerging markets were able to significantly reduce their foreign-currency sovereign debt and substitute it with domestic sovereign bonds. Many economists praised these developments as a final defeat of the Original Sin problem. However, it remained unclear how resilient and sustainable would be this new domestic financial architecture – in particular, whether emerging markets sufficiently graduated in their macroeconomic policymaking to make sure that this architecture may survive a major economic crisis. A particular concern was the degree of market participants' belief and trust in the credibility of a declared policymaking paradigm: should the investors lose trust in policymakers' commitment to orthodox policies during a major shock, it would become nearly impossible for the central banks to conduct countercyclical policy response.

In this chapter, based on the quantitative evidence and our interviews with market participants, we argue that investors had a mixed view of EM policies. At first, investors assigned a high probability of a procyclical monetary policy response. However, the spillovers from the massive interventions of the Fed and ECB allowed EM central banks to engage in credible countercyclical responses in the short run. While this helped to reduce the long-term yields, the uncertainty about the long-run dynamics in EM remained elevated for a prolonged period of time and was most pronounced in those countries that had the biggest political challenges to credible fiscal adjustments in the post-COVID recovery. Given that the long-term yields were at considerably low levels, it was puzzling why most EMs refrained from utilizing this opportunity by issuing longer-term bonds. As this chapter demonstrated, the elevated long-term forward rates made it prohibitively costly to issue long-term bonds versus the alternative of rolling over the short- and medium-term debt.

This chapter covers only the very onset of the COVID crisis, and further research is required to analyse the later periods of the COVID crisis, including the transmission of advanced economies' policy normalization into EMs' sovereign debt markets and unanchored inflation expectations in late 2021.

NOTES

1. Commodity exporters include Brazil, Mexico, Colombia, Peru, South Africa and Russia. The remaining EMs are Poland, Hungary, Romania, Malaysia, Indonesia, Thailand and the Philippines.
2. Core AEs are the US, UK, Germany and Japan. Other AEs include Norway, Sweden, Switzerland, the Czech Republic, Israel, Canada, Australia, New Zealand and South Korea.
3. The excess rate differs from the neutral real interest rate (used in macroeconomic literature) by a number of adjustments specific exclusively to the liquidity and structure of the sovereign bond market.
4. Many researchers choose $\beta \approx 1$ in the decomposition $r^* = \alpha + \beta \cdot g$. Those should refer to Panels 2.4.4 and 2.4.5 (Panels 4 and 5 in Figure 2.4) show a line with the slope coefficient equal to 1.

REFERENCES

Aguilar, A., and Cantu, C. 2020. Monetary policy response in emerging market economies: Why was it different this time? *BIS Bulletin No. 32.*
Aizenman, J., Jinjarak, Y., and Park, D. 2013. *Fundamentals and Sovereign Risk of Emerging Markets.* NBER Working Paper 18963.

Albagli, E., Ceballos, L., Claro, S., and Romero, D. 2018. Channels of US monetary policy spillovers to international bond markets. *Journal of Financial Economics*, 134: 447–473.

Ammer, J., Cai, F., and Scotti, Ch. 2010. *Has International Financial Co-Movement Changed? Emerging Markets in the 2007–2009 Financial Crisis.* Board of Governors of the Federal Reserve System, International Finance Discussion Papers, Number 1006.

Amsted, M., Remolona, E., and Shek, J. 2016. *How Do Global Investors Differentiate Between Sovereign Risks? The New Normal Versus the Old.* BIS Working Paper, No. 541.

Baldacci, E., and Kumar, M. 2010. *Fiscal Deficits, Public Debt and Sovereign Bond Yields.* IMF Working Paper, WP/10/184.

Bellas, D., Papaioannou, M., and Petrova, I. 2010. *Determinants of Emerging Market Sovereign Bond Spreads: Fundamentals vs. Financial Stress.* IMF Working Paper, WP/10/281.

Bizuneh, M., and Geremew, M. 2021. Assessing the impact of Covid-19 pandemic on emerging market economies' (EMEs) sovereign bond risk premium and fiscal solvency. *Eastern Economic Journal*, 47: 519–545.

Broner, F., Lorenzioni, G., and Schmukler, S. 2013. Why do emerging economies borrow short term? *Journal of European Economic Association*, 11: 67–100.

Bruno, V., and Shin, H. S. 2015. Capital flows and the risk-taking channel of monetary policy. *Journal of Monetary Economics*, 71: 119–132.

Caldeira, J., and Smaniotto, E. 2019. The expectations hypothesis of the term structure of interest rates: The Brazilian case revisited. *Applied Economics Letters*, 26(8): 633–637.

Cantú, C., Cavallino, P., De Fiore, F. and Yetman, J. 2021. *A Global Database on Central Banks' Monetary Responses to Covid-19.* BIS Working Papers, Vol. 934. https://www.bis.org/publ/work934.pdf.

Ceballos, L., and Romero, D. 2016. Decomposing long-term interest rates: An international comparison. *Journal of Fixed Income*, 26(1): 61.

Daehler, T., Aizenman, J., and Jinjarak, Y. 2020. *Emerging Markets Sovereign Spreads and Country-Specific Fundamentals During COVID-19.* NBER Working Paper No. 27903.

Ebner, A. 2009. An empirical analysis on the determinants of CEE government bond spreads. *Emerging Market Review*, 10: 97–121.

Eichengreen, B., and Mody, A. 1998. *What Explains Changing Spreads on Emerging-Market Debt: Fundamentals or Market Sentiment?* NBER Working Paper No. 6408.

Gelos, G., Rawat, U., and Ye, H. 2020. COVID-19 in emerging markets: Escaping the monetary policy procyclicality trap. *VoxEU.org*, 20 August.

Gevorkyan, A. V., and Kvangraven Harvold, I. 2016. Assessing recent determinants of borrowing costs in sub-saharan Africa. *Review of Development Economics*, 20(4): 721–738.

Guerello, Ch., and Tronzano, M. 2016. The expectations hypothesis of the term structure of interest rates and monetary policy: Some evidence from Asian countries. *Applied Economics*, 48(55): 5405–5420.

Harrathi, N., and Alhoshan, H. 2020. Validity of the expectations hypothesis of the term structure of interest rates: The case of Saudi Arabia. *Review of Middle East Economics and Finance*, 16: 1.

Hilscher, J., and Nosbusch, Y. 2010. Determinants of sovereign risk: Macroeconomic fundamentals and the pricing of sovereign debt. *Review of Finance*, 14(2): 235–262.

Kamin, S., and Von Kleist, K. 1999. The evolution and determinants of emerging markets credit spreads in the 1990s.

Kryukovskaya, O. 2003. Explaining the term structure of interest rates: The GKO market from 1996 to 1998. *EERC*, pp. 1–32.

Martinez, L., Terceno, A., and Terruel M. 2013. Sovereign bond spreads determinants in Latin American countries: Before and during the XXI financial crisis. *Emerging Markets Review*, 17: 60–75.

McGuire, P., and Schrijvers, M. 2003. Common factors in emerging market spreads. *BIS Quarterly Review*, December.

Mehrotra, A., Moessner, R., and Shu, Ch. 2019. *Interest Rate Spillovers From the United States: Expectations, Term Premia and Macro-Financial Vulnerabilities.* BIS Working Paper No. 814.

Obstfeld, M. 2015. *Trilemmas and Trade-Offs: Living With Financial Globalization.* BIS Working Paper No. 480.

Ozbek, I., and Talasli, I. 2020. Term premium in emerging market sovereign yields: Role of common and country specific factors. *Central Bank Review*, 20(4): 169–182.

Palic, P., Simovic, P., and Vizek, M. 2017. The determinants of country risk premium volatility: Evidence from a panel VAR model. *Croatian Economic Survey*, 19: 37–66.

Paries, M. D., Kok, Ch., and Rottner, M. 2021. *Reversal Interest Rate and Macroprudential Policy.* Deutsche Bundesbank, Discussion Paper, No. 24/2021.

Pordeli, S., Schofer, L., and Sutton, M. 2021. *The Response by Central Banks in Emerging Market Economies to COVID-19.* Reserve Bank of Australia, Bulletin, March.

Remolona, E., Scatigna, M., and Wu, E. 2008. The dynamic pricing of sovereign risk in emerging markets: Fundamentals and risk aversion. *Journal of Fixed Income*, 17: 57–71.

Rey, H. 2013. Dilemma not trilemma: The global financial cycle and monetary policy independence. *Jackson Hole Symposium Proceedings*.

Shareef, S., and Shijin, H. 2016. Expectations hypothesis and term structure of interest rates: An evidence from emerging market. *Asian-Pacific Financial Markets*, June.

Taguchi, H., and Bolortuya, M. 2021. *Determinants of Country Risk Premium Revisit: Evidence for Emerging Market and Developing Economies.* MPRA Paper No. 107078.

Tebaldi, E., Nguyen, H., and Zuluaga, J. 2018. Determinants of emerging markets' financial health: A panel data study of sovereign bond spreads. *Research in International Business and Finance*, 45: 82–93.

Vegh, C., and Vuletin, G. 2012. *Overcoming the Fear of Free Falling: Monetary Policy Graduation in Emerging Markets.* NBER Working Paper 18175.

Yale, Covid-19 Financial Response Tracker. 2020. *Yale Program on Financial Stability.*

3. Wealth composition, valuation effect and upstream capital flows

Uthman M. Baqais[1]

3.1 INTRODUCTION

A stable stream of foreign capital flows plays a critical role in the development process by augmenting capital stock accumulation and enhancing current account sustainability. On the one hand, standard neoclassical theory predicts that returns to capital should be higher in poor countries, in terms of capital–labour ratio, and hence global capital should flow in to exploit higher returns.[2] On the other hand, Lucas (1990) observes a puzzle that very little capital flows into poor countries, and Gourinchas and Jeanne (2013) find an allocation puzzle that fast-growing emerging markets and developing economies (EMDEs) have associated with net capital *outflows*. In a few words, the allocation puzzle is the Lucas paradox but in first differences.[3] Surprisingly, cross-country differences in natural resources have been neglected in the empirical literature on global capital allocation, although there is a wide literature on the natural resource–growth nexus. Primary goods exporting countries could be a major underlying source of the upstream capital flows due to their economic structure and the Dutch disease effects. Therefore, this chapter investigates the role of initial wealth composition on the medium- to long-term capital flows, while revisiting the neoclassical allocative efficiency hypothesis across 108 countries from 1995 to 2015. Wealth is defined more broadly as the sum of produced capital and urban land, net foreign assets, human capital, natural capital, social capital and domestic financial capital (Gylfason, 2004). Accordingly, I take advantage of a World Bank database on wealth accounting, supplemented by composite proxies. Moreover, I consider the role of valuation effects in studying capital movements, as emphasized by more recent literature (e.g. Lane and Milesi-Ferretti, 2007, 2017; Gourinchas and Rey, 2015).

Relevant literature on capital flows seems to adopt a view from growth accounting literature that cross-country differences in output growth mainly stem from total factor productivity (TFP) growth (e.g. Gourinchas and Jeanne,

2013). It implies that fast-growing economies would invest more and associate with higher returns to capital, so they should attract more capital inflows. Nevertheless, data on capital flows show the opposite pattern to the theoretical prediction. Previous studies, therefore, modify some assumptions of the neoclassical growth model (NGM) or incorporate other factors to provide some explanations. For instance, Lucas (1990) asserts that the answer to the puzzle is about cross-country differences in productivity growth stemming from a human capital spillover. Surprisingly, the recent few decades show that EMDEs have been associated with relatively higher growth rates but net capital *outflows* on average. Consequently, if the answer is not about human capital or even capital mobility, what could it be about? Alfaro et al. (2008) investigate empirically the Lucas paradox and conclude with institutional quality. Yet, the role of natural resources has been neglected in such empirical studies, so the current study aims to fill this gap among other considerations.

Although previous studies provide a set of possible explanations such as the Dutch disease effects (e.g. Prasad et al., 2007), natural resources do not appear in their empirical analyses of capital flows. Booms in commodity prices could lead to exchange rate appreciation and factor movement towards resource-intensive and non-tradable sectors; hence, the growth-inducing industrial sector shrinks over time. During busts, such countries may face economic and financial distress, especially through increasing foreign exchange constraints. Consequently, we should rethink that within an open-economy growth theory.

The permanent income hypothesis (PIH) is interpreted in the empirical literature of capital flows in contrast to that of natural resources. Gourinchas and Jeanne (2013) assert that the evidence of the allocation puzzle contradicts the implication of the PIH – faster-growing economies should invest and borrow more due to their expected higher growth rates. However, the role of natural resources is completely neglected in their analysis. With exhaustible natural resources, this chapter asserts that the PIH should be about smoothing consumption and the use of resource rents into human capital and productive physical capital. That is, resource-rich countries should save more during booms to better manage their economies during busts.

This chapter builds on economic growth theory to analyse capital flows based on two broad groups: 1) differences in initial factor supply abundance and 2) differences in productivity growth. Unfortunately, previous studies do not specifically control for cross-country differences in the abundance of natural resources that could drive the upstream capital flows. Interestingly, since the mid-1980s, there was concern that the GDP of resource-rich countries could be inflated due to the liquidation of natural capital rather than productive investments, and that motivates natural capital accounting efforts (Lange et al., 2018, p. 3). Lange et al., from the World Bank, construct a wealth accounting database and emphasize that cross-country comparison should focus on both income and wealth. Data show that human and natural capital assets account for a share of about 70 per cent of wealth across all county groups in 2014.[4] Thus, exploiting that database could help us better understand international capital flows.

This chapter, therefore, attempts to answer the following questions:

- Does the wealth composition matter in explaining the upstream capital flows?
- Does the allocative efficiency hypothesis hold true with the broad definition of wealth?
- Would decomposing natural capital into subsoil and non-subsoil types make a difference in explaining capital flows?
- Do valuation effects matter in the current international monetary and financial system?

To do so, it investigates the role of cross-country differences in initial wealth abundance measures and averaged real growth rates in explaining subsequent capital flows across 108 countries during 1995–2015. Besides the typical measure of net capital inflows, I consider other measures that adjust for official aid flows and valuation effects. A main hypothesis is that natural capital (especially, subsoil types: energy, minerals and metals) should play an important role in predicting net capital *outflows*.

An overview of the main findings indicates the importance of the measure choice of the net capital inflows and the initial composition of total wealth. Particularly, there is statistical evidence on the initial abundance of *decomposed* natural capital and net foreign assets positions. Thus, the introduction of natural capital highlights the role of economic management, unlike the standard neoclassical model. Policymakers in EMDEs could decide the pace of depleting natural resources and, hence, affect the GDP levels and growth rates (but through liquidation, not productive investment) along with the scale of capital movements when they mitigate the Dutch disease effects. A main policy implication suggests that countries with greater subsoil assets should improve their macroeconomic management through smoothing the use of resource rents, which helps reduce foreign exchange constraints, while developing a *dynamic* comparative advantage to achieve higher sustainable growth rates. Moreover, while the typical measure of capital flows shows evidence of persistent global imbalances, an alternative measure indicates a stabilization role of the valuation effects.

The remainder of the chapter is organized as follows. The next section discusses measurements and issues of wealth and capital flows, while section 3.3 develops a unified conceptual framework to establish a priori hypotheses. Section 3.4 covers data sources and summary statistics and develops an empirical approach. Section 3.5 reports main regression results, followed by a battery of robustness checks. The last section discusses major findings and policy implications and then concludes.

3.2 WEALTH AND CAPITAL FLOWS: MEASUREMENTS AND ISSUES

3.2.1 Importance of Wealth Composition

Lange et al. (2018) construct estimates of total wealth (W), defined as the sum of produced capital and urban land (K_P), net foreign assets (NFA or K_F), human capital (K_H) and natural capital (K_N).

$$W = K_P + K_F + K_H + K_N \tag{3.1}$$

Table 3.1 reports the share of each capital type in total wealth across country groups, based on per capita real income in 2014. Interestingly, the sum share of human capital and natural capital accounts for over 70 per cent of total wealth across all country groups, where the former is relatively higher in more developed economies.[5] Moreover, it is crucial to differentiate between OECD and high-income non-OECD countries, as the latter group has a noticeably different wealth composition. Hence, considering comprehensive data on wealth could reveal structural, economic explanations in predicting international capital flows.

Among many improvements, human capital and natural capital are calculated as *stock* units based on expected lifetime earnings. First, the human capital *wealth* is constructed based on over 1,500 global household earnings surveys to reflect expected lifetime earnings using Jorgenson and Fraumeni's (1989, 1992a, 1992b) approach, which asserts that higher lifetime earnings embody relatively higher skills. Second, natural capital reflects the present discounted value of expected lifetime net rents. Natural capital includes energy, minerals, metals, agricultural land, pastureland, forests and protected areas. It should also be noted that net foreign assets reflect the difference between a country's foreign assets and liabilities, the estimates of which are adopted from Lane and Milesi-Ferretti (2007, 2017).

Although this is the most accomplished effort yet for wealth accounting, there are some caveats. First, some components of natural capital are missing, including renewable energy, fish stocks and ecosystem services such as land and forest degradation. Second, the World Bank excludes *social capital* due to difficulties in obtaining robust estimates (see Lange et al., 2018). Besides, I argue that income distributional dynamics could vary across countries and adopting this human capital wealth measure could pose concerns.

Table 3.1 Wealth composition across country groups, 2014

Type of asset	Low-income countries (%)	Lower-middle-income countries (%)	Upper-middle-income countries (%)	High-income non-OECD countries (%)	High-income OECD countries (%)	World (%)
Produced capital	14	25	25	22	28	27
Natural capital	47	27	17	30	3	9
Human capital	41	51	58	42	70	64
Net foreign assets	–2	–3	0	5	–1	0
Total wealth, USD billion*	$7,161	$70,718	$2,47,793	$76,179	$7,41,398	$11,43,249
Total wealth per capita, USD*	$13,629	$25,948	$1,12,798	$2,64,998	$7,08,389	$1,68,580

(in constant 2014 USD)

Source: Lange, Wodon and Carey (2018, p. 8).

For a cross-country comparison, I believe that the calculation method is more about how relatively low-cost, rather than skilled, workers are. Moreover, Gylfason's (2004) definition of wealth is even broader, in which the sixth asset type is domestic financial capital. Although these limitations are beyond the focus of this study, I attempt to mitigate many of these issues, while exploiting the best available wealth estimates yet to predict international capital flows.

3.2.2   Alternative Measures of Net Capital Inflows

There is no direct, single and available measure of net (total) capital inflows in the data (Alfaro et al., 2014).[6] Although it could be possible to sum up many variables of capital flows per type, measurement issues and errors would arise, especially across a wide set of countries. Therefore, a typical measure used by previous studies is motivated by national income and balance of payments identities. Nevertheless, I observe some discrepancies when compared with alternative measures.

First, a country's net national (private and public) savings are equal to the current account balance:

$$(S-I)+(T-G)=(X-M)=CA \qquad (3.2)$$

Then, due to the double-entry accounting in the balance of payments (BOP), based on the fifth IMF manual edition, the sum of all components must always be zero:

BOP = Current Account + Capital Account + Financial Account

+Errors and Omissions = 0   (3.3)

BOP = $CA + KA + FA + EO = 0$

Alfaro et al. (2014) show that the KA constitutes a very negligible part, based on the data, because this account records capital transfers and the acquisition and disposal of non-produced, non-financial assets. Furthermore, they illustrate that the general practice is to consider negative (positive) values of EO as non-reported capital outflows (inflows). Therefore, the typical measure is the reverse sign of the current account (CA) balance, which could capture all reported and non-reported capital flows:[7]

$$\text{Net Capital Inflows} = -CA = FA + EO \qquad (3.4)$$

However, that measure neglects the fact that the *CA* comprises not only the trade balance but also aid flows and net investment income. Official aid flows are of particular importance to low-income countries, helping them even to finance trade deficits.[8] Net investment income could also play a critical role, especially when linking the recorded flow-unit *CA* balances to the stock-unit NFA positions in the current financial globalization era.

Alfaro et al. (2014) state that 'capital flows into low-productivity developing countries have largely taken the form of official aid/debt' (p. 3).[9] Hence, I should include net aid flows, reported in *CA*, to the other types of capital flow, reported in *FA*.[10] Consequently, the aid-adjusted measure of net capital inflows is as follows:

$$\text{Net}\,(\text{total})\,\text{capital inflows} = -CA + \text{Net Aid Receipts} \qquad (3.5)$$

The other alternative measure is emphasized by the recent literature on global imbalances (e.g. Gourinchas and Rey, 2015).[11] The *NFA* position of a country summarizes not only the cumulative *CA* balances but also reflects any valuation effects (*VE*) – capital gains/losses due to asset price changes and exchange rate movements, as in equation (3.6):

$$NFA_{(T)} = \text{Stock of Foreign}\,(\text{Assets} - \text{Liabilities})_{(T)}$$

$$= \sum_{t}^{T} CA_{(t)} + VE_{(T)} \qquad (3.6)$$

By the stock-flow accounting, a flow-unit measure can be computed to capture the *CA* balance plus any valuation changes in foreign assets and liabilities of a country in a specific year. Since the change in *NFA* reflects net capital *outflows*, reversing the sign allows us to capture net capital *inflows*. In other words, the negative change in *NFA* means a change in net foreign liabilities (*NFL*). Thus, the valuation-adjusted measure of net capital inflows is as follows:

$$\Delta NFL_t = -\Delta NFA_t = -\left(CA_t + \Delta VE_t\right) \qquad (3.7)$$

A country with a positive value of *ΔNFL* implies that it attracts net capital inflows, plus any capital losses (gains) if such value is greater (less) than that of the typical measure of equation (3.4) in a specific year.

Now the question comes of whether the three capital flow measures could be used as close substitutes for an empirical analysis. The correlations between those measures, normalized by nominal GDP[12] and averaged over 1996–2015, show that the typical (−*CA*) and aid-adjusted (−*CA*+Aid) measures are highly correlated at 0.93, so they could be used as close alternatives for a regression analysis. By contrast, there is a weaker correlation with the valuation-adjusted measure (*ΔNFL*) at 0.39, reflecting the importance of valuation effects in the global financial system. Consequently, more attention should be on the typical and valuation-adjusted measures.

3.3   CONCEPTUAL FRAMEWORK

This study mainly focuses on the supply side of the economy, as in the neo-classical growth model, to explain international capital flows during the convergence process. While the open-economy model illustrated by Gourinchas and Jeanne (2013) considers the accumulation of *financial wealth*, this study adapts the model by considering *total wealth*. Gourinchas and Jeanne present a growth model with initial abundance of both physical capital stock and net external debt stock. They argue that productivity growth in developing countries would catch up to some fraction of that in the US – the technological frontier. Thus, during the catching-up process, EMDEs would grow faster and attract more foreign capital inflows due to the law of diminishing returns. This is known as the allocative efficiency hypothesis – a positive association between productivity growth and net capital inflows.

Extending the standard open-economy growth model by considering a low of motion in terms of total wealth, as in Gylfason (2004), the model can be written in per capita units as follows:

$$y_{it} = A_{it} f_{it} \left(w_{it} \right) \tag{3.8}$$

Where: $w_{(it)} = k_{Physical_{(it)}} + k_{NFA_{(it)}} + k_{Human_{(it)}} + k_{Natural_{(it)}} + k_{social_{(it)}} + k_{Financial_{(it)}}$

The subscript (*it*) refers to a country and year, respectively.

Unlike the standard neoclassical growth model, by including natural capital we can also investigate the implication of natural resource management. For Gylfason (2004), natural capital has not only a direct negative effect on growth but also an indirect effect through *crowding out* other types of capital. By contrast, there are some successful, high-growth, resource-abundant countries such as Botswana, which was able to enhance human capital, and the United Arab Emirates, which diversified its economy into light manufacturing, telecommunications, finance and tourism (Van der Ploeg, 2011). These facts show the possibility of *crowding in* effects, too. Accordingly, in this chapter, I assert that the *indirect* effects of resource abundance are ambiguous.

Since some EMDEs have been associated with fast-growing economies, I could justify the use of the initial abundance of wealth composition for a better understanding of capital flows. I define the abundance measures similar to Gourinchas and Jeanne (2013) but for all types of capital stocks. Barbier (2007) also discusses a debate in the sustainable development literature about whether capital stock types could be substitutable. The *strong* sustainability argument states that *each type* of capital stock must be non-decreasing, while the *weak* sustainability only requires that the *total wealth* be non-decreasing. Accordingly, I must assume weak sustainability as a minimum requirement of sustainable growth. Figure 3.1 summarizes and visualizes the general conceptual framework.

In contrast to the crowding-out effects as illustrated by Gylfason (2004), I believe that, in the current financial globalization era, policymakers in resource-abundant countries have been accumulating NFA and allocating large shares of their annual budgets towards education, among other things. Thus, one could argue that financial globalization has allowed them to channel resource rents to a higher accumulation of NFA. That might help mitigate the Dutch disease effects by preventing the appreciation in real exchange rates, and by smoothing the use of natural resource windfalls. Thus, I emphasize that PIH is about smoothing consumption and the use of resource windfalls that could be channelled into human capital and physical capital. Accordingly, K_F management is crucial because that K_N could crowd in K_F during the development process.

Besides, I highlight the importance of natural capital in studying international capital flows. This is because per capita GDP is an erroneous measure of welfare, especially in the context of cross-country comparison. For instance, Stauffer and Lennox (1984), whose study was commissioned by OPEC, state, 'The GDP of oil-exporting states is exaggerated because some of their income is due to the consumption of depletable oil resources and hence is liquidation of capital, not income' (as cited in Neumayer, 2004, p. 1630). Consequently, the modified model illustrated in equation (3.8) will allow for a better understanding of capital flows.

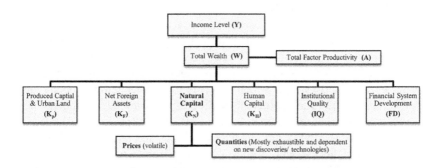

Figure 3.1   Sustainable development requires non-decreasing per capita total wealth over time

Rodriguez and Sachs (1999) also acknowledge that the unsustainable over-consumption explanation of the resource curse could be avoided if rents were invested in international assets that pay annuities. For them, relaxing the assumption of imperfect capital mobility across countries could turn the conclusion of the resource curse upside down. In addition, policy implications of the resource–growth relationship suggest the use of a policy mix of reserve accumulation and industrial policy (Polterovich et al., 2010). While the former helps protect the competitiveness of the existing tradable production, the latter puts emphasis on the modern or manufacturing sector, which generates sustainable higher growth rates. Therefore, accumulating reserves by resource-rich countries could be a major driver of the upstream capital flows phenomenon.

My main hypothesis, hence, is that a higher initial abundance of subsoil-type natural capital could explain much of the subsequent capital flows, as shown in Figure 3.2. That is, I expect a negative relationship between initial subsoil resource abundance and subsequent annualized average net capital inflows. The second hypothesis is about the persistent global imbalances phenomenon – countries with net external credit positions in 1995 tend to be associated with a subsequent annualized average of net capital *outflows*. The third hypothesis is that I do not expect the allocative efficiency hypothesis to hold.

Although the aforementioned is an extended supply-side framework, demand-side channels could be of great importance. Many previous studies illustrate that investment and savings have different degrees of responsiveness

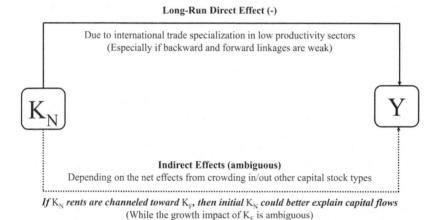

Figure 3.2   The direct and indirect effects of natural capital on income and international capital movements

to income increases. First, with habit formation in consumption preferences, Carroll et al. (2000) show that an increase in income growth can only cause increased savings. Second, Buera and Shin (2017) illustrate in a joint dynamic model that when economy-wide reforms correct for distortions (mainly, taxes and subsidies), TFP initially increases with a larger saving response than a muted investment response. Nevertheless, these complications are beyond the focus of the current study.

3.4   DATA AND EMPIRICAL APPROACH

3.4.1   Data Sources and Descriptive Statistics

In this chapter, I utilize different data sources for measures of net capital inflows during 1996–2015. Particularly, I rely on Alfaro et al.'s (2014) updated and extended database and Lane and Milesi-Ferretti's (2017) dataset. First, the data on CA balances are available in the IMF's International Financial Statistics (IFS) database but only reported for a short period based on the latest sixth edition of the *Balance of Payments and International Investment Position Manual* (BPM6). For a longer period of analysis, Alfaro et al. have supplemented the IMF BPM6's data with the previous data reported based on the BMP5, while considering sign convention changes between the two manuals. Second, official development assistance (ODA) aid flows are from the OECD-Development Assistant Committee (DAC). By adding the ODA net aid flows to the reverse sign of CA, I construct the aid-adjusted measure as in equation (3.5). Furthermore, the valuation-adjusted measure in equation (3.7) is constructed from the data on NFA estimated by Lane and Milesi-Ferretti (2007, 2017).

Data on wealth are from the World Bank-Wealth Accounts (WB-WA) database, which spans 1995–2014. Other data sources are as follows: population and real GDP from the World Bank-World Development Indicators (WB-WDI), sub-indicators of institutional quality from the Political Risk Services International Country Risk Guide (ICRG) database, a composite index of financial system development from Svirydzenka (2016) and a *de jure* capital account openness index from the updated dataset of Chinn and Ito (2006). The indexes range between zero and one, with greater values for higher degrees of developed financial systems and openness to foreign capital flows. Using the ICRG data, I similarly construct a composite institutional quality index using six sub-indicators.[13]

Table 3.2 reports the descriptive statistics.[14] Since I consider economies of different sizes, all variables are in per capita units. Moreover, the 1995 capital abundance measures are defined as the stock of each capital type divided by GDP.[15] First, the sample means of the alternative measures of net capital

Table 3.2   Descriptive statistics

Variable	N	Mean	SD	Min	Max
Measures of net capital inflows					
$-CA$ (%GDP), avg. 1996–2015	108	2.78	7.29	−28.48	18.88
ΔNFL (%GDP), avg. 1996–2015	108	−0.88	4.14	−21.73	10.95
$-CA+ODA$ (%GDP), avg. 1996–2015	108	6.27	11.07	−28.47	38.25
The set of explanatory variables					
Real per capita growth (%), avg. 1996–2015	108	2.18	1.69	−1.53	8.7
Population growth (%), avg. 1996–2015	108	2.35	2.7	−1.13	15.7
KA Openness Chinn-Ito Index, 1995	108	0.52	0.31	0	1
Initial wealth abundance measures					
Produced capital abundance, 1995	108	3.78	1.66	1.01	13.67
Net foreign assets abundance, 1995	108	−0.52	0.76	−3.42	1.78
Human capital abundance, 1995	108	8.17	2.75	1.16	16.6
Natural capital abundance, 1995	108	5.31	5.38	0	22.92
Subsoil resource abundance, 1995	108	0.53	1.14	0	6.13
Non-subsoil resource abundance, 1995	108	4.78	5.14	0	21.94
Additional explanatory variables					
Financial Development Index, 1995	107	0.32	0.24	0.05	0.87
Institutional Quality ICRG Index, 1996	96	0.64	0.15	0.32	0.93

Sources: the author's calculations using various datasets from International Monetary Fund, World Bank, OECD, the International Country Risk Guide (ICRG), Alfaro et al. (2014), Lane and Milesi-Ferretti (2017), Svirydzenka (2016) and Chinn and Ito (2006).

inflows show different signs, showing the important role of aid flows and valuation effects as discussed in section 3.2.1. Second, the data show large cross-country differences, especially for the initial natural capital abundance that ranges from zero to 22.92.[16] Furthermore, an average country in the sample associates with a capital openness index at 0.52 and a financial system development index at 0.32 in 1995. Similarly, the mean of the institutional quality index is at 0.64 in 1996. In addition, there could be seen remarkable variations in the other explanatory variables, including per capita real growth rates, population growth rates and the decomposed natural resource abundance measures along with other wealth measures. These variables capture country-specific conditions with regard to capital flows.

Following the natural resource–growth literature that emphasizes different implications of different types of resources, I also differentiate between different types of natural capital. Barbier (2007) demonstrates that some studies on the resource curse literature show that countries with a higher endowment of subsoil resources had on average slower economic growth rates than those with a higher endowment of other resources (p. 118). This study defines *subsoil* resources as fossil fuel energy, minerals and metals, while *non-subsoil* resources comprise agricultural land, pastureland, forests and protected areas.

Table 3.3 contrasts a set of main variables across different income and regional groups.[17] Data show that the mean values of the measures of net capital inflows have different signs, while different types of natural capital seem to play an important role. For instance, while high-income, *non-OECD* countries are associated with the highest *subsoil* abundance, they display the largest net capital outflows and slowest growth rates. While OECD countries lack natural capital, other low-to-middle-income countries are associated with the highest abundance of *non-subsoil* natural capital. In sum, it is important to investigate capital movements by comparing different measures of capital flows and disaggregated natural capital.

3.4.2   Empirical Approach

To investigate the long-run pattern of capital flows, I adapt an empirical specification, motivated by the growth accounting literature, as in Gourinchas and Jeanne (2013). They assume that returns to physical capital are equalized across countries if measured appropriately, relying on the findings of Caselli and Feyrer (2007), who correct for natural endowment and price differences. Caselli and Feyrer also support the argument of Lucas about endowment complementarity (as in human capital) rather than credit frictions in driving international capital movements. Drawing on the conclusions of development accounting literature that cross-country differences stem from the growth in TFP rather than factor supply, Gourinchas and Jeanne assert that the initial abundance measures are constant along the balanced growth path. Furthermore, countries with higher productivity growth should invest more, which implies higher returns to capital, and hence they should associate with net capital inflows. Thus, they focus on the association between net capital inflows and productivity growth, while controlling for capital openness, population growth and initial capital abundance measures. The latter only includes the initial physical capital-to-output ratio (k_p/y) and debt-to-output ratio (d/y). However, I emphasize that the initial capital abundance could still play a significant role, especially with the broad definition of total wealth.

I extend Gourinchas and Jeanne's (2013) empirical specification to consider six initial abundance measures of capital. I also attempt to mitigate

Table 3.3 *Country group comparison, selected variables*

Group	g_y	−CA (%GDP)	ΔNFL (%GDP)	−CA +ODA (%GDP)	$\dfrac{K_N}{y}$	Subsoil $\dfrac{K_N}{y}$	Non-subsoil $\dfrac{K_N}{y}$
		Annualized averages (1996–2015)				In 1995	
By income							
High income: OECD	1.78	−0.26	0.03	−0.25	0.63	0.12	0.51
High income: non-OECD	1.3	−7.76	−4.23	−7.59	2.16	1.77	0.39
Upper middle income	2.65	3.05	0.66	4.38	4.45	0.48	3.97
Lower middle income	2.35	3.69	−1.89	8.45	7.18	0.73	6.44
Low income	2.13	9.66	−1.12	20.22	10.85	0.19	10.66
By region							
East Asia and Pacific	3.43	−0.1	−0.64	3.58	5.53	0.38	5.15
Europe and Central Asia	2.02	0.46	0.54	0.7	0.94	0.08	0.85
Latin America and Caribbean	2.08	3.65	−0.39	5.66	4.64	0.54	4.1
Middle East and North Africa	1.07	−1.44	−1.74	−0.29	3.25	1.63	1.62
North America	1.49	2.01	−0.6	2.01	0.6	0.16	0.44
South Asia	3.6	3.31	−0.08	5.49	4.51	0.08	4.43
Sub-Saharan Africa	1.91	6.38	−2.08	14.1	9.54	0.6	8.94

Sources: the author's calculations using data from WB-WA, WB-WDI and LM (2017), following the World Bank's classifications by region and income as of 2014.

concerns over endogeneity, due to simultaneity bias, by lagging the initial capital abundance measures in 1995.[18] Instead of TFP growth, typically attributed to human capital in previous studies, I emphasize the role of endowment complementarity between all types of capital stock as argued by Caselli and Feyrer (2007), and hence focus on the real growth in per capita GDP. By doing that I could test the allocative efficiency hypothesis – a positive association between averaged net total capital inflows and per capita real growth. I also examine how cross-country differences in initial wealth composition (k_j/y) explain the subsequent annualized average of net capital flows. Accordingly, the main empirical specification is as follows:

$$
\left(\frac{\text{Inflows}}{y} \right)_{avg.1996-2015,i} = \alpha + \beta_1 \cdot \left(\frac{k_P}{y} \right)_{1995,i} + \beta_2 \cdot \left(\frac{k_F}{y} \right)_{1995,i} + \beta_3 \cdot \left(\frac{k_H}{y} \right)_{1995,i}
$$

$$
+ \beta_4 \cdot \left(\frac{k_N}{y} \right)_{1995,i} + \beta_5 \cdot \text{KAO}_{1995,i} + \beta_6 \cdot \left(g_n \right)_{avg.1996-2015,i} \tag{3.9}
$$

$$
+ \beta_7 \cdot \left(g_y \right)_{avg.1996-2015,i} + \varepsilon_i
$$

Next, I consider the inclusion of the composite wealth *indexes* of institutional quality and financial system development, the specification of which I call the *full* specification.[19] The reason for having two specifications is threefold. First, unlike the wealth *stock* measures by the World Bank, these are indexes calculated to range between zero and one. Second, data availability decreases the sample size from 108 to 95 economies. Third, and more importantly, because of the high correlations of these indexes with the abundance of natural resources, I could have a multicollinearity problem. Therefore, there is an unbiasedness–efficiency tradeoff that I must evaluate carefully.

I run equation (3.9) three times because of the three measures of net capital inflows, as discussed in section 2.2. This procedure allows us to disentangle any commonalities and differences across estimates. Besides, I adopt White's heteroscedasticity-consistent standard errors that address the potential heteroscedasticity. Because of some concerns, I then employ a battery of robustness checks.

3.5   RESULTS

3.5.1   Main Regression Results

This section reports the regression estimates using the whole sample.[20] Table 3.4 reports the *main* specification estimates using the three measures of net capital

Table 3.4   Estimates of the main specification

Variables	−CA (%GDP)	ΔNFL (%GDP)	−CA+ODA (%GDP)
Produced Capital Abundance, 1995	0.286	−0.102	0.393
	(0.396)	(0.459)	(0.500)
Net Foreign Assets Abundance, 1995	**−2.945***	**1.041**	**−4.674***
	(0.867)	(0.865)	(1.293)
Human Capital Abundance, 1995	−0.413	−0.340**	−0.391
	(0.256)	(0.136)	(0.307)
Subsoil resource abundance, 1995	**−3.171***	**−0.986**	**−4.062***
	(0.496)	(0.701)	(0.709)
Non-subsoil resource abundance, 1995	**0.268***	**0.0821**	**0.786***
	(0.091)	(0.117)	(0.142)
KA Openness Chinn-Ito Index, 1995	−4.469**	0.101	−4.833*
	(2.106)	(1.329)	(2.476)
Per capita real growth (%), avg. 1996–2015	**−0.460**	**0.165**	**−0.621**
	(0.406)	(0.249)	(0.574)
Population growth (%), avg. 1996–2015	0.103	−0.206	0.586*
	(0.171)	(0.169)	(0.297)
Constant	6.993**	3.029	6.403*
	(2.788)	(2.140)	(3.700)
Observations	108	108	108
R-squared	0.511	0.141	0.614

Notes:
1) Robust standard errors in parentheses.
2) *** $p < 0.01$, ** $p < 0.05$, * $p < 0.1$.

inflows.[21] First, the initial abundance of *subsoil* natural capital abundance enters with a significantly negative coefficient, whereas *non-subsoil* resource abundance associates with a positive coefficient (as in columns 1 and 3). Interestingly, the valuation-adjusted measure (as in column 2) shows that there is an important role of the valuation effects, as these two coefficients turn out to be no longer statistically significant. Moreover, while columns 1 and 3 show there is evidence of the negative association between the initial abundance of net foreign assets and subsequent net capital inflows, column 2 shows a reverse in sign and significance because of the role of valuation effects. Simply put, the valuation effects seem to mute these relationships. Results imply that only by ignoring the valuations effects do I find supporting evidence on the role of disaggregated natural capital and the persistence of global imbalance. Thus, countries with CA surpluses in the past (reflected by higher NFA positions) have continued to be associated with subsequent net capital *outflows* (or CA surpluses). Further, the estimates of the three measures show no evidence of the neoclassical allocative efficiency hypothesis, as captured by a statistically insignificant coefficient on the real per capita growth. In addition, human capital abundance enters with a negative sign and is only significant in the regression of column 2 of Table 3.4. Nevertheless, that raises concerns over the use of this measure of human capital in a cross-country context. That is, it is based on households' discounted lifetime expected earnings, which I have argued in section 3.2 could capture labour cost rather than skills in a cross-country context. Accordingly, I suggest interpreting the negative coefficient as follows: all else being equal, semi-industrialized countries with lower expected lifetime earnings could associate with a subsequent annualized average of net capital *outflows*.[22]

The estimates in column 1 suggest that an increase by one standard deviation (1.14) in the initial abundance of *subsoil* resources, *ceteris paribus*, associates with a reduction in the ratio of subsequent annualized average net capital inflows to GDP by 3.61 percentage points. Put differently, all else being equal, an increase in the initial abundance of subsoil resources from the 25th to 75th percentile associates with a reduction in the ratio of subsequent annualized average net capital inflows to GDP by about 1.29 percentage points. That is a decrease in net capital inflows equivalent to about 41 per cent of the sample median. By contrast, an increase by one standard deviation (5.14) in the initial abundance of *non-subsoil* resources associates with an increase in the ratio of subsequent annualized average net capital inflows to GDP by about 1.37 percentage points. In sum, estimate results validate the main hypothesis about the role of natural capital.

Next, I introduce two more components of wealth, following Gylfason's (2004) definition of wealth. These are social capital and domestic financial capital, proxied by the composite indexes of institutional quality and financial system development, respectively. The joint test for the inclusion of both variables results in a p-value for the F-test at 0.0375, suggesting the relevance of these variables to the model. Nevertheless, the regression estimates after the inclusion of these variables remain qualitatively unchanged with regard to our a priori hypotheses.[23]

In summary, the empirical findings validate the main hypothesis that there is a significantly negative association between initial *subsoil* natural capital and subsequent annualized average net capital inflows, except for specification 2

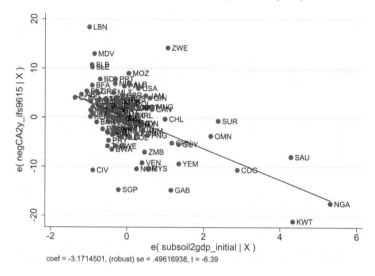

Figure 3.3   *A partial regression plot between the initial abundance of sub-soil resources and subsequent annualized average net capital inflows*

which adjusts for valuation effects. Figure 3.3 displays the partial regression plot of that negative association, which suggests that subsoil resource-rich countries largely affected the capital flow movements during 1996–2015. Conversely, findings show a positive association between initial *non-subsoil* natural abundance and subsequent net capital inflows. Moreover, there is evidence of persistent global imbalances. Interestingly, once valuation effects are incorporated, these relationships are muted, implying a stabilizing role in the global financial system. Finally, I found no evidence of allocative efficiency.

3.5.2   Robustness Checks

I now examine whether the main findings could be affected when considering a battery of robustness checks. First, the period of study during 1995–2015 is characterized by many volatile episodes of capital flows that might have caused a structural change in the allocative efficiency hypothesis. All of these episodes could have impacted *certain types* of capital flows, except for the 2008–2009 global financial crisis (GFC), which could cause a structural change to net *total* capital inflows. Therefore, I test for a structural change due to the 2008–2009 GFC, using a dummy-variable technique, known as a least absolute deviations (LAD) regression. Second, the allocation puzzle argument by Gourinchas and Jeanne (2013) is particularly about EMDEs, so I exclude OECD countries. Third, due to the special characteristics of China and India, I also drop them in one specification. Fourth, I identify and exclude potential influential observations using informal and formal statistical tests. That is, I employ a formal statistical test known as the DFBETA method to identify potentially influential observations and adopt an informal way by dropping countries with less than one million population. In addition, I consider both robust and quantile regression analyses. The robust regression analysis uses iteratively reweighted least squares based on Cook's distance method in which lower weights are assigned to observations with values greater than one. The quantile regression is based on minimizing the sum of *absolute* errors from the *median*, compared to the OLS regression which minimizes the sum of *squared* errors from the *mean*.[24] Next, I run an OLS regression with fixed effects for income and regional groups to control for any unobserved heterogeneity, so we could mitigate for potential omitted variable bias. Finally, due to our concern about the measure of human capital *wealth*, I test the robustness of the main findings when using the widely used proxy, which is the average years of schooling as constructed by Barro and Lee (2013).

Due to space limitations, the test results are not reported but could be shared upon request.[25] Briefly, the main findings remain overall qualitatively unchanged, specifically, with regard to the coefficients on the initial abundance measures of the *subsoil* natural resources and NFA. The only change is for the *non-subsoil* abundance where the statistical significance weakens or even disappears in some specifications, as when controlling for income-group fixed effects and replacing the proxy for human capital.

3.6   DISCUSSION AND CONCLUSION

Although the neoclassical growth theory suggests that low-income countries should be associated with faster economic growth and net capital *inflows*, the empirical literature shows evidence of the Lucas paradox or even the allocation puzzle. That is, fast-growing EMDEs associate with net capital *outflows* on average. In this chapter, I have examined the allocative efficiency of capital flows in the financial globalization era during 1995–2015, while emphasizing the role of initial wealth composition in general and natural capital in particular. I take advantage of a recently released database on wealth accounting, supplemented by wealth index proxies. Total wealth is defined as the sum of produced capital, human capital, natural capital, NFA, social capital and domestic financial capital (Gylfason, 2004). Moreover, I use three measures of net total capital inflows. The typical and aid-adjusted CA measures produce similar estimates, particularly with regard to natural capital. Findings indicate a negative association between the initial abundance of *subsoil* natural capital and net capital inflows. In addition, there is evidence of persistent global imbalances, as captured by a negative coefficient on the initial NFA abundance. On the contrary, there is no supporting evidence for the allocative efficiency hypothesis – the positive association between economic growth and net capital inflows. This could stem from the large sample size rather than the adopted productivity growth measure. Chinn and Prasad (2003) and Alfaro et al. (2014) find that as the sample size increases, the relationship becomes either insignificant or weakly and positively significant. Alfaro et al. also show that replacing the average per capita real growth with the catch-up productivity measure calculated by Gourinchas and Jeanne (2013) does not change much the regression estimates.

Interestingly, the valuation-adjusted measure alters the previous findings, implying the great importance of the valuation effects. The coefficient sign on initial NFA abundance changes although it is statistically insignificant. In this regard, Gourinchas and Rey (2005) demonstrate that the US has enjoyed an exorbitant privilege in which the total return on foreign assets exceeds that on foreign liabilities, despite being a debtor country from the post-Bretton Woods period until 2004. They conclude that valuation adjustment has played a stabilization role for the US. In a later study, Gourinchas and Rey (2015) also demonstrate that the valuation effects have played a crucial role in the current international financial system in which G7 countries were the largest winners while the BRICS countries were losers.

This chapter, therefore, demonstrates that the introduction of natural capital allows for the role of economic policy, unlike the standard neoclassical model. Policymakers in EMDEs can utilize the stock of natural capital, so they affect the GDP level and growth through liquidation rather than productive investment. With capital mobility, as in the financial globalization era that we live in, policymakers have the potential to mitigate the Dutch disease effects by ameliorating the appreciation pressure in the exchange rate. Besides, if the accumulation of NFA is implemented as suggested by PIH, smoothing both consumption and investments, then K_N could also crowd in K_F during the development process.

Particularly, this chapter finds statistical evidence that the accumulation in the form of NFA positions by subsoil-abundant economies explains much of the subsequent net capital *outflows* in EMDEs. The assumption of *imperfect* capital mobility is also critical to the seminal models of uneven development (Krugman, 1981) and the natural resource curse (Rodriguez and Sachs, 1999). Resource-rich countries can benefit from capital mobility to break the unsustainable overconsumption argument. Rodriguez and Sachs acknowledge the role of international capital markets in breaking out the unsustainable overconsumption. They state:

If an economy can invest its resource windfalls in international assets that pay permanent annuities, then the problem we are alluding to could not occur. Any economy experiencing a resource boom will invest it and permanently consume the interest it earns on that asset.

(p. 278)

Moreover, while Gourinchas and Jeanne (2013) call the allocation puzzle a saving puzzle and attribute that to a capacity constraint on investment, I could argue that the underlying cause could be the abundance of natural capital in EMDEs through the Dutch disease effects.[26] That is, the Dutch disease effects cause not only an appreciation of the exchange rates but also an expansion of the resource sector that crowds out investment opportunities in the modern sector which has a larger capacity for new investment and employment opportunities. In addition, EMDEs could use international capital markets to keep their real exchange rates manageable, through the accumulation of foreign reserves, in order to protect their exports' competitiveness and mitigate the Dutch disease effects. This could also be somehow linked to the argument of 'fear of floating' by Calvo and Reinhart (2002). Therefore, foreign reserve accumulation allows subsoil resource-abundant countries to stabilize their exchange rates and smooth the use of resource rents. In other words, policymakers could play a critical role in reducing their economies' foreign exchange constraints.

An important implication of these findings is the greater role of economic policy, unlike in the standard neoclassical growth theory adopted by the previous literature on capital flows. Results suggest that capital flows tend to be largely driven by foreign asset accumulation in *subsoil* resource-abundant countries. On the other hand, Table 3.3 shows that the high-income, non-OECD countries associate with the relatively highest subsoil abundance but slowest growth rates over the last few decades. Therefore, while subsoil resource-rich countries should adopt a policy mix of reserve accumulation and industrial policy, data suggest the need for assigning more weight to the latter to generate sustainably rapid growth. They should adopt an industrialization strategy by developing a *dynamic* comparative advantage, particularly through the role of economies of scale and scope (see e.g. Vasudevan, 2012). Besides the challenges of industrialization, any policy framework should consider creating employment opportunities that keep pace with the growing population. In addition, reserve accumulation allows for the use of exchange rates as a developmental policy tool as in the export-led growth strategy implemented by fast-growing emerging Asian countries. Shortly, studies demonstrate that an appropriate level of the exchange rate could be a key tool for real economic growth and for creating more employment opportunities (see e.g. Frenkel and Taylor, 2006; Rodrik, 2008).

Since this study does not empirically address all aspects that affect capital flows, future research avenues could be about linking wealth composition to the following: global real and financial factors, the dollar hegemony and financial deregulation and innovations in advanced economies.

In conclusion, this chapter extends an open-economy growth model by considering the role of initial wealth composition, while emphasizing natural capital, to explain net capital inflows. There is no evidence of the allocative efficiency, but findings indicate the following: 1) persistent global imbalances and 2) a negative (positive) association between the initial abundance of subsoil (non-subsoil) natural capital and subsequent net capital inflows, averaged over 1996–2015.

ACKNOWLEDGEMENTS

The development of this chapter owes a lot to Ramaa Vasudevan. I also extend my gratitude and appreciation to Edward Barbier, Stephan Weiler, Elissa Braunstein, Steven Pressman and Aleksandr V. Gevorkyan for their support and insightful feedback, along with participants in many seminars and conferences for their helpful comments.

NOTES

1. Disclaimer: The views in this chapter are the author's own and do not necessarily reflect those of the Saudi Central Bank.
2. This is due to the law of diminishing returns – a decreasing marginal productivity of capital.
3. That is, whether to examine the relationship between gross (net) capital inflows and income levels (growth rates).
4. See Table 3.1 of this chapter.
5. Table 3.1 shows that the average *total* wealth of high-income non-OECD countries is very low relatively due to their economy sizes. For a cross-country comparison, it is important to consider *per capita* units, as in the last row. That is, the average *per capita* total wealth increases monotonically with the level of development.
6. Only disaggregated capital flows are available in the data.
7. The financial account reports all transaction flows of foreign direct investment, equity and debt portfolio investment, other investment, IMF credit use and change in foreign exchange reserves.
8. Specifically, I refer to Official Development Assistance (ODA) grants that target humanitarian and economic development, rather than military assistance.
9. Also, there is a rich strand of the literature on the growth impact of foreign aid flows although empirical evidence is inconclusive (Rajan and Subramanian, 2008).
10. Recall the BOP identity ($B = -CA = FA = 0$) and note that net aid receipts are reported with a positive sign (credit in the CA) while all other types of capital inflows are reported with a negative sign (debit in the FA).
11. Gourinchas and Rey (2015) also demonstrate that while the G7 advanced countries have been the largest winners, BRICS countries have been losers in terms of the valuation effects.
12. The scaling by GDP level helps mitigate concerns on economy size differences.

13. Specifically, I calculate an equally weighted average index for institutional quality using the following sub-indicators: 1) voice and accountability, 2) political stability and absence of violence, 3) government effectiveness, 4) regulatory quality, 5) rule of law and 6) control of corruption.
14. A pair-wise correlation matrix is reported in a supplemental Online Appendix Table A3.3: https://sites.google.com/view/ubaqais/.
15. Since real per capita GDP data are in constant 2010 USD while wealth measures are in constant 2014 USD, I adjust the base year of the former to 2014 for consistency.
16. In fact, an influential country, Liberia, is dropped from the sample because of an initial value of natural capital abundance of 72.49.
17. The lists of country groups are reported in the Online Appendix Tables A3.1 and A3.2.
18. In other words, I attempt to avoid the reverse directional effect from capital flows to the accumulation of capital measures.
19. While data on a composite index of financial system development are available in 1995, data on institutional quality starts from 1996. I believe this data restriction would not be problematic since institutional quality changes slowly over time and, hence, using the year 1996 as initial year should not make a notable measurement error bias to the regression estimates.
20. Liberia is the only country that I have excluded. It seems an obvious influential observation as it could be identified by both informal and formal statistical checks.
21. Table 3.4 considers the decomposition of natural capital into two types. By contrast, using the *aggregate* natural capital abundance produces meaningless estimates as shown in a supplemental Online Appendix Table A3.4-2.
22. I validate the normality of residuals using a kernel density plot. I also find that there is no indication of multicollinearity in this main specification as suggested by the values of variance inflation factors (VIF) and condition indices (CI). Following the role of thumps discussed by Gujarati and Porter (2009, pp. 337–342), I find that no value of VIFs and CIs exceeds 5 and 20, respectively. All of which suggests that we could draw inferences from the estimates.
23. Due to space limitation, results are not reported but could be accessed at https://sites .google.com/view/ubaqais/. It should also be noted that the sample decreases due to the list-wise deletion of Burundi, Belize, Comoros, Cambodia, Lao PDR, Maldives, Mauritania, Mauritius, Nepal, Rwanda, Solomon Islands, Eswatini and Zimbabwe. This full specification also seems to suffer from a multicollinearity problem as the maximum value of the condition indices is about 32, exceeding the role of thump of 30 as discussed by Gujarati and Porter (2009, pp. 337–342).
24. That is why the quantile regression is known as a least absolute deviations (LAD) model.
25. They can also be accessed at https://sites.google.com/view/ubaqais/.
26. In this regard, Hausmann, Rodrik and Velasco (2005) explain growth diagnostics and emphasize that lower growth performance could be either from saving or investment binding constraints.

REFERENCES

Alfaro, L., Kalemli-Ozcan, S., and Volosovych, V. 2008. Why doesn't capital flow from rich to poor countries? An empirical investigation. *The Review of Economics and Statistics*, 90(2): 347–368.

Alfaro, L., Kalemli-Ozcan, S., and Volosovych, V. 2014. Sovereigns, upstream capital flows, and global imbalances. *Journal of the European Economic Association*, 12(5): 1240–1284. DOI: 10.1111/jeea.12106.

Barbier, E. B. 2007. *Natural Resources and Economic Development*. Cambridge: Cambridge University Press.

Barro, R. J., and Lee, J. W. 2013. A new data set of educational attainment in the world, 1950–2010. *Journal of Development Economics*, 104: 184–198. DOI: 10.1016/j. jdeveco.2012.10.001.

Buera, F. J., and Shin, Y. 2017. Productivity growth and capital flows. *American Economic Journal: Macroeconomics*, 9(3): 147–185.

Calvo, G. A., and Reinhart, C. M. 2002. Fear of floating. *The Quarterly Journal of Economics*, 117(2): 379–408.

Carroll, C., Overland, J., and Weil, D. 2000. Saving and growth with habit formation. *American Economic Review*, 90(3): 341–355. DOI: 10.1257/aer.90.3.341.

Caselli, F., and Feyrer, J. 2007. The marginal product of capital. *The Quarterly Journal of Economics*, 122(2): 535–568. DOI: 10.1162/qjec.122.2.535.

Chinn, M. D., and Ito, H. 2006. What matters for financial development? Capital controls, institutions, and interactions. *Journal of Development Economics*, 81(1): 163–192. DOI: 10.1016/j.jdeveco.2005.05.010.

Chinn, M. D., and Prasad, E. S. 2003. Medium-term determinants of current accounts in industrial and developing countries: An empirical exploration. *Journal of International Economics*, 59: 47–76.

Frenkel, R., and Taylor, L. 2006. *Real Exchange Rate, Monetary Policy and Employment: Economic Development in a Garden of Forking Paths*. Amherst, MA: Political Economy Research Institute.

Gourinchas, P.-O., and Jeanne, O. 2013. Capital flows to developing countries: The allocation puzzle. *Review of Economic Studies*, 80(4): 1484–1515. DOI: 10.1093/restud/rdt004.

Gourinchas, P.-O., and Rey, H. 2005. *From World Banker to World Venture Capitalist: US External Adjustment and the Exorbitant Privilege*. Working Paper No. 11563, Cambridge, MA. http://www.nber.org/papers/w11563.

Gourinchas, P.-O., and Rey, H. 2015. External adjustment, global imbalances, valuation effects. In Helpman, E., Rogoff, K., and Gopinath, G. (eds.) *Handbook of International Economics*. North Holland: Elsevier B.V.: pp. 585–645. DOI: 10.1016/B978-0-444-54314-1.00010-0.

Gujarati, D., and Porter, D. 2009. *Basic Econometrics*. 5th edn. Boston, MA: McGraw-Hill.

Gylfason, T. 2004. *Natural Resources and Economic Growth: From Dependence to Diversification, CEPR and CESifo*.

Hausmann, R., Rodrik, D., and Velasco, A. 2005. Growth diagnostics. http://www.tinyurl.com/y3y5zksu.

Jorgenson, D. W., and Fraumeni, B. M. 1989. The accumulation of human and non-human capital, 1948–1984. In Lipsey, R., and Tice, H. (eds.) *The Measurement of Saving, Investment, and Wealth*. Chicago: University of Chicago Press, National Bureau of Economic Research, pp. 227–282.

Jorgenson, D. W., and Fraumeni, B. M. 1992a. Investment in education and U.S. economic growth. *Scandinavian Journal of Economics*, 94 (Suppl.): S51–S70.

Jorgenson, D. W., and Fraumeni, B. M. 1992b. The output of the education sector. In Griliches, Z., Breshnahan, T., Manser, M., and Berndt, E. (eds.) *The Output of the Service Sector*, Chicago: National Bureau of Economic Research.

Krugman, P. 1981. Trade, accumulation, and uneven development. *Journal of Development Economics*. 8: 149–161.

Lane, P., and Milesi-Ferretti, G. M. 2007. The external wealth of nations mark II: Revised and extended estimates of foreign assets and liabilities, 1970–2004. *Journal of International Economics*, 73(2): 223–250. DOI: 10.1016/j.jinteco.2007.02.003.

Lane, P., and Milesi-Ferretti, G. M. 2017. International financial integration in the aftermath of the global financial crisis. *IMF Working Paper*, 17(115): 1–53.

Lange, G., Wodon, Q., and Carey, K. (eds.). 2018. *The Changing Wealth of Nations 2018: Building a Sustainable Future*. Washington, DC: World Bank Group.

Lucas, R. 1990. Why doesn't capital flow from rich to poor countries? *American Economic Association*, 80(2): 92–96.

Neumayer, E. 2004. Does the "resource curse" hold for growth in genuine income as well ? *World Development*, 32(10): 1627–1640. DOI: 10.1016/j.worlddev.2004.05.005.

Polterovich, V., Popov, V., and Tonis, A. 2010. Resource abundance: A curse or blessing? *United Nations Working Paper*, 93. DOI: 10.2139/ssrn.1814382.

Prasad, E., Rajan, R., and Subramanian, A. 2007. Foreign capital and economic growth. *Brookings Papers on Economic Activity*, 1: 153–230.

Rajan, R. G., and Subramanian, A. 2008. Aid and growth: What does the cross-country evidence really show? *The Review of Economics and Statistics*, 90(4): 643–665.

Rodriguez, F., and Sachs, J. D. 1999. Why do resource-abundant economies grow more slowly? *Journal of Economic Growth*, 4(3): 277–303.

Rodrik, D. 2008. The real exchange rate and economic growth. *Brookings Papers on Economic Activity*, 2.

Stauffer, T. R. and Lennox, F. H. 1984. Accounting for "wasting assets": income measurement for oil and mineral-exporting rentier states. Vienna: OPEC Fund for International Development.

Svirydzenka, K. 2016. Introducing a new broad-based index of financial development. *IMF Working Paper*, WP/16/5: 1–43.

Van der Ploeg, F. 2011. Natural resources: Curse or blessing? *Journal of Economic Literature*, 49(2): 366–420. DOI: 10.1257/jel.49.2.366.

Vasudevan, R. 2012. Terms of trade, competitive advantage, and trade patterns. *Review of Political Economy*, 24(2): 183–202. DOI: 10.1080/09538259.2012.664324.

4. Non-financial corporations as financial intermediaries and their macroeconomic implications: an empirical analysis for Latin America

Claudia de Camino, Esteban Pérez Caldentey and Cecilia Vera[1]

4.1 INTRODUCTION

The international bond market has become an important source of global liquidity and cross-border finance, outpacing bank-intermediated cross-border finance.[2] In emerging market economies, the non-financial corporate sector has made extensive use of the international bond market to finance its operations. There is growing evidence that apart from financing its operations, the non-financial corporate sector has been acting as a financial intermediary capturing liquidity from international capital markets and investing it in financial assets both at home and abroad.[3] Research has found that flows into emerging economies associated with non-financial corporations have indeed increased markedly over the years, and, to the extent that these flows are driven by financial investments rather than real activities, concerns have been raised over the potential implications for financial fragility and instability.[4]

This chapter complements the existing literature on this topic by focusing on Latin America (LAC) and presenting evidence for a selected group of countries in the region. The existing literature on the subject analyses emerging markets as a group with a few examples at the country level. In the case of Latin America, Brazil is the most cited case example. To our knowledge, this is the first study that analyses intercompany lending for the specific case of Latin America as a region with detailed information for selected countries within the region.

We present evidence that, as in the case of other emerging market economies, corporates non-resident in the region – in many cases foreign affiliates of Latin American firms – have been sending the proceeds of international bond issues to be invested in LAC through several channels. Although we review these channels, we centre our analysis on one type of flow, *intercompany loans*, that has gained importance in the past several years and that we argue poses potential instability risks for the countries receiving them.

Intercompany loans along with equity are classified as foreign direct investment (FDI) in the balance-of-payments accounting statistics. Since the 2000s intercompany loans have increased significantly both in US dollar value and as a percentage of FDI. Even though intercompany loans are considered a long-term financial flow, the evidence shows that their dynamics resemble those of short-term portfolio flows. The growing dependency on short-term flows can lead to situations of financial fragility and instability as these are driven by short-term gains rather than long-term economic development concerns. Short-term flows tend to be highly volatile and prone to sudden reversals. This makes economies more vulnerable to changes in external conditions. This fact also links intercompany loans with the behaviour of the foreign exchange market.

Intercompany loans have a high correlation with the business cycle in several Latin American countries, and in many cases this relationship becomes even more obvious during and following crisis periods. Intercompany loans are a key element in understanding to what extent the business cycle in Latin America is driven by internal/external factors and in understanding the transmission mechanisms linking external to internal conditions.

This chapter is divided into seven sections. Following the introduction, section 4.2 describes the growing importance of the bond market as a source of cross-border finance at the global level and, also, for developing regions including Latin America. Section 4.3 shows that the non-financial corporate sector is a major borrower in the international bond market, but that increasing debt has not been accompanied by a commensurate rise in investment, opening up the possibility that firms use the bond market as a financial vehicle. Building on this evidence, section 4.3 describes the alternative financial channels and operations through which non-financial sector corporates can use the proceeds of the bond issues. The section then goes on to detail how bond proceeds can be channelled as intercompany loan inflows and explains the rationale for including intercompany loans as FDI when, in fact, they are a short-term flow masked as FDI.

Section 4.4 documents the growing importance of intercompany loans since the 2000s, in absolute terms, and also as a percentage of FDI. Section 4.5 provides statistical and econometric evidence showing that intercompany loans tend to behave as short-term flows. Section 4.6 presents three motivations that can explain the behaviour of intercompany loans: fiscal (minimizing tax payable on profits), carry-trade (taking advantage of interest rate differentials) and business cycle motivations. The evidence presented provides support for the business cycle motivation. The implications and final reflections are provided in the last section.

4.2   THE INTERNATIONAL BOND MARKET AND CORPORATE SECTOR DEBT

Since the global financial crisis (2008–2009) the international bond market has become a major source of global liquidity and cross-border finance, outpacing bank-intermediated cross-border finance.

Between the fourth quarters of 2000 and 2020, outstanding debt security issues by non-bank borrowers expanded from US$1.5 to 8.6 trillion. This represented 47 per cent and 54 per cent of total liquidity at the global level. Developed economies are the main providers and beneficiaries of debt flows. Still, developing and emerging market economies borrowing through the international bond market account for roughly a quarter of the total and 47 per cent of global liquidity channelled to this group of economies (Table 4.1).

The decomposition of the amount outstanding of debt security issues for emerging market economies in the aggregate, by region (East Asia and the Pacific, Africa and the Middle East, Developing Europe and Latin America and the Caribbean) and by sector (banks, other financial corporations, non-financial corporations and general government) for the period 2000–2020 shows that the general government followed by the non-financial corporate sector are the largest borrowers in the international bond market (on average 51.6 per cent and 23.8 per cent of the total).

Table 4.1   Total credit to non-bank borrowers: bank loans and debt securities issued by non-bank borrowers, amounts outstanding, US$ trillion, 2000–2020

	2000	2007	2010	2020
	World			
International debt securities (bonds)	1.5	3.9	4.6	8.6
Cross-border loans	1.6	4.3	4.9	7.5
Bonds/liquidity (percentage)	47%	48%	48%	54%
	Developing and emerging market economies			
International debt securities (bonds)	0.4	0.7	0.8	2.2
Cross-border loans	0.6	1.2	1.6	2.5
Bonds/liquidity (percentage)	42%	36%	34%	47%

Note: The data includes bond issues and cross-border loans in US dollars, euros and yens. All the figures were converted to United States dollars, using the exchange rate for the relevant quarter, weighted by the size of debt and loans denominated in dollars, euros and yen. Liquidity refers to the sum of bonds and cross-border loans. The data for each year refers to the fourth quarter.
Source: On the basis of Bank for International Settlements (BIS), 2020.

Also, an analysis of the data for the same period reveals that the share of the general government in the stock of international issues has declined over time while that of the non-financial corporate sector has increased (64.2 per cent and 45.0 per cent; 19.9 per cent and 25.6 per cent of the total for 2000 and 2019).[5] In addition, the growth of non-financial corporate debt expanded significantly in the aftermath of the global financial crisis (2007–2009). In the case of developing and emerging market economies the debt stock of the non-financial corporate sector expanded by 117 per cent between 2000 and 2009 (US$108.2 and 235.4 billion respectively) and by 169 per cent between 2010 and 2020 (US$281.6 and 756.2 billion respectively). In the case of Latin America and the Caribbean, the debt stock of the non-financial corporate sector increased by 42 per cent between 2000 and 2009 (US$53.6 and 76.3 billion respectively) and by 225 per cent between 2010 and 2020 (US$103.3 and 336.6 billion respectively).

However, for the region, the extensive use of the international bond market by the non-financial corporate sector has not been accompanied by an increase in investment. In fact, the evidence points to the contrary: the coexistence between increasing debt and a decline in the rate of growth of the gross formation of fixed capital at both the aggregate and country levels. At the regional level, while the debt levels of the non-financial corporate sector more than doubled between 2010 and 2020, the rate of growth of the gross formation of fixed capital declined from 11.6 per cent to –10.4 per cent (Figure 4.1).

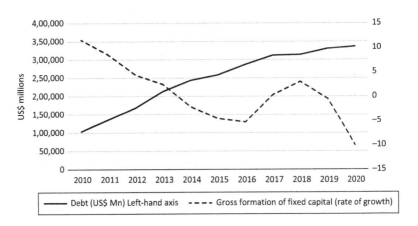

Source: On the basis of World Bank (2021) and BIS (2021b).

Figure 4.1   *Latin America and the Caribbean: amount outstanding of non-financial corporate debt (in US$ millions) and rate of change of the formation of gross fixed capital formation, 2000–2019*

The issuance of debt in the international capital market is an available option only to the largest and most well-established firms which concentrate a significant share of total fixed assets and investment. An analysis covering the total listed firms (2,241) for the larger economies of the region in 34 sectors of economic activity[6] for the period 2009–2016 shows that international bond-issuing firms account for a large share of total assets and especially of total expenditure on fixed assets and long-term investment. On average, bond-issuing firms represent 33.9 per cent of total assets, 35 per cent of expenditure on short-term investment and 40.8 per cent of expenditure on long-term investment (Table 4.2).[7]

This finding may indicate that, in line with recent research for other emerging market economies, the non-financial corporate sector does not use the international bond market to expand productive capacity or for improvements in productivity, but rather for financial purposes.[8] More precisely, non-financial corporates have been acting as financial intermediaries by capturing international liquidity and investing a growing amount in financial assets abroad (see Advjiev, 2014b). The growing capital flows from non-financial corporates into developing and emerging market economies' financial assets have given rise to concerns regarding their potential macroeconomic implications for financial fragility and instability in the receiving countries.[9]

4.3   NON-FINANCIAL CORPORATES AND CAPITAL FLOWS

The non-financial sector corporates that issue bonds in international markets can invest the proceeds in financial assets abroad through several channels and financial operations as illustrated in Figure 4.2. The different investment options can be described through a simple example. Suppose company C_b (belonging to emerging market country B) but located in developed country A issues bonds in international capital markets (Figure 4.2, column 1). The company C_b can afterwards choose to keep those proceeds in country A and invest them there, either in physical capital or in financial assets. But it can also choose to invest the proceeds abroad, buying financial assets from another country, including possibly its home country B (column 2).

In this latter case, the emerging market economy receives a financial inflow from a non-resident and will therefore show up in the financial account of the balance of payments (BoP) as a liability of economy B towards the developed country A. This inflow can appear as a direct investment, a portfolio investment or as another investment depending on the type of assets acquired by company A (column 4) and depending on who is the recipient of funds in the other country (column 5). The following subsections describe these three categories.[10]

Table 4.2 Number of total bond-issuing and non-bond-issuing firms: bond-issuing firms' share of total assets, short-term investment, expenditure on fixed assets and fixed investment and the total number of firms (2016)

Country	Bond-issuing firms				Total number of firms and number of firms issuing and not issuing bonds		
	Share of total assets	Share of expenditure of short-term investment	Share of expenditure on fixed assets and long-term investment	Share of total number	Number of bond-issuing firms	Number of non-issuing firms	Total number of firms
	(%)	(%)	(%)	(%)			
Argentina	38.8	30.5	47.7	4.7	23	469	492
Brazil	35.0	21.9	42.2	3.8	95	2,406	2,501
Chile	30.9	9.7	43.7	5.0	30	568	598
Colombia	39.6	62.6	45.2	3.2	11	333	344
Mexico	34.4	13.4	43.1	5.0	49	922	971
Peru	24.5	71.9	23.0	4.1	25	591	616
Average/total	33.9	35.0	40.8	4.3	189	5,415	5,604

Source: Pérez Caldentey et al. (2019).

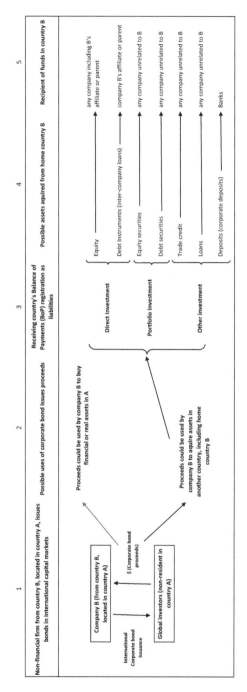

Source: Authors' own elaboration.

Figure 4.2   Investment options for non-financial corporations from the proceeds of international market bond issues

4.3.1   Direct Investment

An investment in a foreign firm's equity is considered a *direct investment (DI)* when it gives the investor control or a significant degree of influence on the management of such a firm. DI is normally founded upon a strategic long-lasting interest between a firm residing in a host country and a direct investor residing outside the firm's host country. By convention, the criterion to establish a long-lasting interest is provided by a benchmark of ownership by the direct investor of at least 10 per cent of the voting power of the firm. This benchmark provides the direct investor with a significant degree of influence in the management of the firm (Wacker, 2013).

The DI category in the balance of payments is composed of two flows: equity investment and debt instruments (or intercompany loans). Whereas equity investment gives place to the existence of a DI relationship – in the sense that it can provide 10 per cent or more of the voting power of a firm – all transactions between affiliated enterprises are also considered DI.[11]

This is the reason why loans between two affiliates (i.e. intercompany loans) are classified in the balance of payments within the DI category even though they are very different, in nature, from equity investment. This is worth emphasizing since the conventional approach views DI flows as being more stable than other types of flows – such as portfolio flows and other investment – which is normally associated with the equity investment component of DI rather than with its intercompany loan component.

Avdjiev et al. (2014) find that, although quantitatively, for most developing and emerging market economies, intercompany loan flows are still modest in comparison with direct investment equity flows, they have nevertheless experienced sizeable increases. This trend has coincided with a sharp rise in offshore issuance of international bonds by affiliates of emerging market enterprises, suggesting that the latter are indeed acting as financial surrogates who issue bonds offshore and then repatriate the funds to their home country company matrix through this channel.[12]

Insofar as the home country company matrix operates mainly in domestic currency, it will have a currency mismatch which can enhance its financial vulnerability when confronted with nominal exchange rate depreciation. The nominal exchange rate channel adds to debt service costs and increases the debt burden, thereby heightening credit risk. Available data for a range of countries in different developing regions suggest that since the global financial crisis, currency mismatches have trended up, owing to the behaviour of the non-financial corporate sector (Chui et al., 2018).

4.3.2   Portfolio Investment

The BoP portfolio investment category includes cross-border investment in debt or equity securities, other than those included in direct investment (or reserve assets). These can include the proceeds from a bond issuance by a corporation which can be invested in other countries' securities including debt securities (both public and private) as well as equity. As long as the receiving party is a non-related enterprise then the investments in question are considered portfolio flows and not part of direct investment.

4.3.3 Other Investment

Cross-border loans and deposits compose the largest part of this category, which the IMF defines as a residual one, including transactions other than those recorded in the previous ones listed. Although the majority of cross-border loans and deposits are from and towards the banking sector in different countries, the amount of external loan and deposit financing to emerging market economies provided by the corporate sector has been shown to be growing considerably since the global financial crisis of 2008–2009 (Avdjiev, 2014).

A second type of capital flow within the 'other investment' category is *trade credit*. In BoP accounts, this refers to credit extended directly by a foreign supplier of goods and services to a customer firm. Trade credit flows account for a small part of 'other investment' into emerging markets, as the extension of credit directly between exporters and importers can be seen as riskier than arranging trade financing through banks. Nevertheless, this flow has also shown a tendency to rise since the years of the global financial crisis.

4.4 THE CASE OF LATIN AMERICA: CAPITAL FLOWS FROM THE FOREIGN NON-FINANCIAL CORPORATE SECTOR

In this section we analyse flows from the foreign non-financial corporate sector into Latin American economies. We present evidence that, as has happened for the aggregate of emerging markets, LAC has been receiving increasing flows into financial assets arising from *corporates* outside the region. These flows have been channelled through trade credit and cross-border loans and deposits and intercompany loans.

An important issue to bear in mind in this section is that BoP accounting records the flows into the countries' asset and liability categories (direct investment, portfolio and other investment) but *does not* separate out the flows arising from the corporate sector from those coming from the financial or other sectors. For some flows, namely direct investment and trade credit, the very definition of the flow involves the corporate sector so that is not a problem. For cross-border loans and deposits, there exists a methodology that one can apply to estimate corporate flows separate from the rest. However, for portfolio investment, it is not possible to isolate the part arising from the corporate sector and so the analysis could not be undertaken. Nevertheless, the portion of

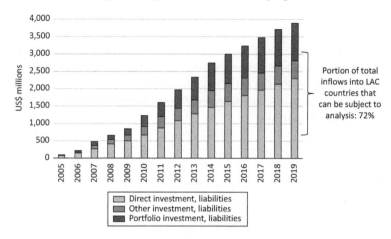

Note: Cumulative inflows starting from 2005; Latin America includes 18 countries.
Source: ECLAC on the basis of IMF Balance of Payments Statistics.

Figure 4.3   *Cumulative inflows (liabilities) towards Latin American
              countries by type of investment, in US$ millions*

inflows into LAC countries that can be subject to analysis is quite substantial
at 72 per cent of a total of almost US$4 trillion in cumulative flows since 2005
(Figure 4.3).

4.4.1   Trade Credit and Cross-Border Loans and
           Deposits from the Foreign Corporate Sector

Balance-of-payments data show that between the first quarter of 2005 and
2019 flows of corporate trade credit into Latin America expanded significantly, tripling from around US$6 billion per year to US$18 billion per year.
In spite of this growth, however, relative to other sources of foreign finance,
the importance of trade credit still remains limited, a trend similar to that
observed for the group of emerging countries as a whole.

Regarding cross-border loans and deposits originating from the foreign
corporate sector, although these are also still relatively small in comparison
with other flows, they also show an increasing trend, mostly since the aftermath of the global financial crisis (Figure 4.4)

4.4.2   Direct Investment Flows (Equity
           and Intercompany Loans)

Direct investment flows comprise the largest category when analysing cumulative inflows into Latin American countries. These flows have increased

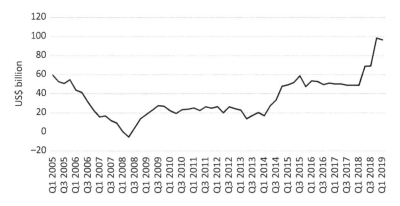

Note: Includes six Latin American recipient countries.
Source: On the basis of official data.

Figure 4.4   *Cross-border loans and deposits by foreign non-financial corporations towards LAC countries 2005q1–2019q1, in US$ billions*

markedly since the beginning of the 2000s. Available data for the periods 1990–2000, 2001–2009 and 2010–2019 show that FDI inflows increased on average from US$36.1 to 83 and to 172.5 billion representing 58 per cent, 72 per cent and 62 per cent of total inflows.[13]

The main component of FDI is equity investment. But the second component of FDI, intercompany loans, has also been on the rise. Available evidence for six Latin American countries for the period 1990–2019 including Argentina, Brazil, Chile, Colombia, Peru and Mexico shows that intercompany loans have increased since the 2000s (Figure 4.5). Also, the increase has been particularly significant following the global financial crisis (2008–2009). Between 2001–2009 and 2010–2019, intercompany loans increased by a factor of 25.7 for Colombia, 18.8 for Chile, 10.4 for Peru, 3.2 for Brazil, 1.5 for Argentina and 1.3 for Mexico.

The significant rise in the value of intercompany loans has been accompanied by an increase in the share of total foreign direct investment flows. At the regional level, intercompany loans represented roughly 18 per cent between 2005 and 2008, rising to 22 per cent between 2010 and 2014 and 24 per cent between 2015 and 2019 (Figure 4.6).

The fact that intercompany loans have been increasing their relative importance within DI flows towards Latin American economies raises potential instability concerns as these flows mostly respond to short-term considerations, similar to those driving portfolio flows and different from those guiding equity direct investment. Indeed, Avdjiev et al. (2014, p. 5) argue that intercompany loans can be seen as 'portfolio flows masked as FDI'.

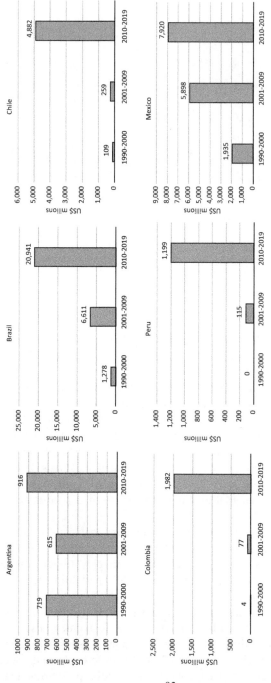

Source: ECLAC on the basis of IMF Balance of Payments Statistics.

Figure 4.5 Intercompany loans (gross inflows) for selected Latin American economies 1990–2000; 2001–2009; 2010–2019. Averages, US$ millions

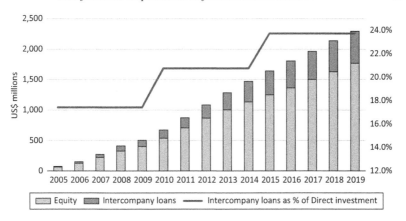

Note: Cumulative inflows starting from 2005; Latin America includes 18 countries.
Source: ECLAC on the basis of IMF Balance of Payments Statistics.

Figure 4.6   *Cumulative foreign direct investment flows towards Latin America: equity investment and intercompany loans, in US$ millions*

4.5   INTERCOMPANY LOANS AND THE BEHAVIOUR OF PORTFOLIO FLOWS: AN EMPIRICAL ANALYSIS

This view of intercompany loans as portfolio flows is corroborated in the case of Latin America and the Caribbean. Table 4.3 shows the correlation coefficients between intercompany loans and portfolio flows; intercompany loans and equity flows; and portfolio flows and equity flows for the period 2000q1–2019q1 and the pre- and post-global financial crisis subperiods (2000q1–2008q4 and 2010q1–2019q1 respectively). The correlation coefficients are computed using the filtered series of each of the aforementioned variables using three different filter methods (Christiano-Fitzgerald, Baxter-King and Hodrick-Prescott).

The results for the entire period under consideration show a statistically significant positive association in most cases between FDI-debt flows and portfolio flows and a negative association between FDI-debt flows and FDI-equity and between portfolio flows and FDI-equity. A decomposition of the entire period into two subperiods (the pre-crisis and post-crisis periods) shows that the results obtained predominate mainly in the post-crisis period.

These results point to the similarity in the behaviour of portfolio and FDI-debt flows, and to the dissimilarity in the behaviour of FDI-debt and equity

Table 4.3   Simple correlation coefficients of the cycle using the Christiano-Fitzgerald, Bexter-King and Hodrick-Prescott filters (2000q1–2019q1)

Variables/method	Christiano-Fitzgerald	Baxter-King	Hodrick-Prescott
Full period		**2000q1–2019q1**	
Intercompany loans and portfolio flows	0.29**	0.44**	0.02
Intercompany loans and equity flows	−0.55**	−0.55**	−0.04
Portfolio flows and equity flows	−0.18***	−0.18***	−0.13
Pre-crisis period		**2000q1–2008q4**	
Intercompany loans and portfolio flows	−0.01	−0.06	−0.05
Intercompany loans and equity flows	−0.29**	−0.54**	0.27
Portfolio flows and equity flows	0.14	0.10	−0.11
Post-crisis period		**2010q1–2019q1**	
Intercompany loans and portfolio flows	0.44**	0.65**	0.03
Intercompany loans and equity flows	−0.73**	−0.72**	−0.17
Portfolio flows and equity flows	−0.57**	−0.57**	−0.26

Note: The Christiano-Fitzgerald and Hodrick-Prescott filtered series start at 2000q1 and the Baxter-King filtered series begins at 2003q1. The statistical significance of the correlation coefficient was determined on the basis of the formula: $\rho = \dfrac{r(\sqrt{n-2})}{\sqrt{1-r^2}}$ where r is the simple correlation coefficient and n is the number of observations. ρ follows a student-t distribution with $n-2$ degrees of freedom. The degrees of freedom are 75 for the Christiano-Fitzgerald and Hodrick-Prescott filter and 63 for the Baxter-King filter for the period 2000q1–2019q1. For the pre-crisis period (2000q1–2008q4) the degrees of freedom are 34 for the Christiano-Fitzgerald and Hodrick-Prescott filter and 22 for the Baxter-King filter. For the post-crisis period (2010q1–2019q1) the degrees of freedom are 35 for all the filters. ** and *** denote significance at the 95% and 90% levels of confidence. The computations were carried out with the Grocer software (Version 1.81). See Dubois and Michaux (2020).

Source: The computations were carried out with the Grocer software (Version 1.81). See Dubois and Michaux (2020).

Table 4.4   *Cycles duration from peak-to-peak (measured in number of quarters) for portfolio, FDI-debt and FDI-equity flows and GDP, 2000q1–2019q1*

	Portfolio flows	FDI-debt (intercompany loans)	FDI-equity	GDP
Argentina	10.5	10.3	11.4	13.3
Brazil	15.4	11.6	17.2	15.2
Peru	11.5	9.5	17.6	17
Chile	9.6	15	17.2	35.5
Colombia	12.8	9.7	15.8	n.a.
Mexico	11.7	16	9.6	27

Note: The turning points (peaks and troughs) of a series are identified using the Bry-Boschan algorithm (1971) developed originally for monthly data and adapted to deal with quarterly observation by Harding and Pagan (2002a and 2002b). The algorithm consists of identifying local maxima and minima for a given series following a logarithmic transformation using specific censoring rules. These include the specification of two quarters for a minimum duration for a single phase, and a minimum duration of five quarters for a complete cycle (Harding and Pagan, 2002). The peak for a series y_t is found when y_t is greater than $y_{t\pm k}$ for $k=1,2$. Similarly, the trough for a series y_t is found when y_t is less than $y_{t\pm k}$ for $k=1,2$. The algorithm excludes the occurrence of two successive peaks or troughs.
Source: On the basis of official data.

flows. Another argument for distinguishing between FDI-debt and FDI-equity flows is the fact that the former exhibits a higher periodicity (frequency) than the latter.

On the basis of the Bry-Boschan statistical procedure which identifies the peaks and troughs of any given series, Table 4.4 shows the cycle duration (measured in terms of the number of quarters) from peak to peak of FDI-debt, FDI-equity and portfolio flows for the larger economies of Latin America (including Argentina, Brazil, Chile, Colombia, Peru and Mexico) for the period 2000q1–2019q1. In the majority of cases, the cycle duration tends to be higher for FDI-debt flows relative to equity flows, reflecting a higher-frequency cycle.

4.6   THE MOTIVATIONS EXPLAINING THE BEHAVIOUR OF INTERCOMPANY LOANS

There are at least three main motivations guiding the behaviour of intercompany loans which are different from those guiding the equity component: the fiscal motivation (profit-shifting), the carry-trade motivation and the business cycle motivation.

4.6.1   The Fiscal Motivation: Minimizing Tax Payable on Profits

Intercompany loans can be used by multinational enterprises (MNEs) not only to minimize the cost of capital[14] but also to shift profits from high-tax jurisdictions to lower-tax ones in order to minimize the total tax paid. If a parent company is a resident of a high-tax country and has a subsidiary in a low-tax country, the MNE can reduce the total tax paid by having the subsidiary issue a loan to the parent.

The issuing business unit would record interest income on the loan and therefore would be having a higher taxable income than if the loan had not existed. At the same time, the receiving unit would record interest expense on the loan and would therefore be having a lower taxable income than if the loan had not existed. In this way, the company managed to decrease profits in the country where they are taxed higher and increase profits in the country where they are taxed lower.

A further issue regarding this tax-minimizing strategy is the fact that many governments impose 'withholding taxes' on payments of interest income to non-residents. If this were the case, the benefits from using intercompany loans to minimize tax payments would be reduced and, as such, these taxes can be thought of as a means to combat tax evasion.[15]

4.6.2   The Carry-Trade Motivation

A carry-trade financial strategy takes advantage of interest rate differential and low volatility in exchange rates. It consists of borrowing funds at a low interest rate in one currency and investing the proceeds in a higher-yielding asset in another currency. A carry strategy is profitable, as long as the proceeds resulting from interest rate differentials are not offset by exchange rate movements (Galati et al., 2007).[16] For purposes of illustration, Figure 4.7 shows the evolution over time (December 2004 to December 2018) of a carry-trade return index and intercompany loans (both for gross inflows and net inflows) for Brazil, Colombia and Chile.

Investors wanting to take advantage of carry-trade strategies and invest in high-interest-rate countries may be subject to capital controls implemented by authorities precisely to discourage such yield-seeking/short-term volatile flows. On such an occasion, if controls are placed on fixed income and/ or equity portfolio investment, then intercompany loans can be a means to circumvent them as they are considered direct investments. A multinational enterprise could have its foreign affiliate issue bonds offshore in the international capital markets at a low interest rate and then loan the proceeds to the parent company for the latter to invest it in the home country at a higher domestic-currency interest rate.

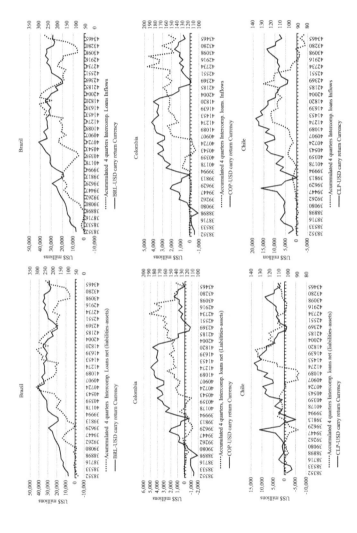

Note: The carry return is calculated by adding the spot return to the interest earned from the long-currency position and subtracting the interest owed from the short-currency position. The base date for the index is 1 January 1999 (Bloomberg, 2020).

Source: ECLAC on the basis of IMF Balance of Payments Statistics and Bloomberg (2020).

Figure 4.7 Carry trades (national currency vs USD) and intercompany loans (net flows and gross inflows for Brazil, Colombia and Chile) 2004q1–2019q4, in US$ millions

An example of the latter is provided by Brazil in the aftermath of the global economic and financial crisis of 2008–2009. The country was experiencing a surge in capital inflows and the Central Bank responded in late 2010 by tightening capital controls that had been adopted some months before. The capital controls in Brazil took the form of a tax on the exchange rate transaction when capital first entered Brazil but it was levied on only a subset of capital inflows, namely portfolio flows (both fixed income and equity). It is believed that it was as a result of this that there was a sevenfold increase in the intercompany loans component of DI when comparing the first half of 2010 with the first half of 2011. This effect later faded in the second half of 2011 as the government – suspecting that investors would be using this gateway to bring in funds without having to pay the tax – started taxing borrowing from abroad in addition to portfolio flows.[17]

As the example of Brazil indicates, a carry-trade strategy can explain the behaviour of intercompany loans in certain given episodes. In the same vein, Figure 4.7 shows that in some of the periods considered, intercompany loans and the carry-trade return index are positively associated. However, the empirical evidence for selected Latin American countries (Argentina, Brazil, Chile, Colombia, Mexico and Peru) over a longer time period (1999q1–2020q4) fails to detect a statistically significant correlation between intercompany loans (on a net basis) and the carry-trade index. Also, there is no causality (in the sense of Granger) between carry trade and intercompany loans (Table 4.5).[18]

4.6.3   The Business Cycle Motivation

A third explanation of the fluctuations in intercompany loans is what we term the business cycle motivation. The general idea is that intercompany loans tend to fluctuate with changes in economic activity.

Intercompany loans are often used as a means to adjust undesired exposure by a multinational company, for example, during the downward phase in the economic cycle and most importantly during and following a crisis in the host country. At such times, repaying loans to an affiliate is often easier and much quicker than selling off direct investment equity. As such, the intercompany loans component may show significant variation during and following a crisis while the equity component shows a more stable behaviour (World Bank GFSR, 2009, box 2.2).

The business cycle motivation can be illustrated with the examples of economic crisis exemplified by two interrelated crises at the beginning of the 2000s, which mark the start of the increase in intercompany loans in the Brazilian 1998–1999 and Argentinean 2001–2002 crises and more generally with the global financial crisis (2008–2009).

Table 4.5   Correlation coefficients and Granger causality test between intercompany loans and carry-trade index, 1999q1–2020q4

	Correlation coefficient	Granger causality H$_0$: carry trade does not Granger cause intercompany loans	
		F statistic	Number of observations
Argentina	−0.26	1.10	77
Brazil	0.14	0.15	76
Chile	−0.07	0.67	77
Colombia	−0.14	1.73	72
Mexico	−0.45	1.13	77
Peru	−0.04	2.20	49

Note: The series used in both intercompany loans and carry trade refers to the Hodrick-Prescott cycle component of both series to ensure that both tests are performed with stationary series. Carry trade refers to the return from borrowing the short currency (US dollar) to fund buying the long currency (national currency) and earning interest. The return is calculated by adding the spot return to the interest earned from the long-currency position and subtracting the interest owed from the short-currency position. The base date for the index is 1 January 1999.
Source: ECLAC on the basis of IMF Balance of Payments Statistics and Bloomberg (2020).

As a result of the Asian crisis (1996–1997), Brazil led its government to increase interest rates and implement an austere fiscal policy to maintain the value of its currency. These efforts failed and the Brazilian government decided in 1999 to float its currency leading to 35 per cent depreciation against the US dollar. This was followed by another round of fiscal austerity to secure a US$4.9 billion dollar loan from the IMF. The Asian and Brazilian crises had a direct impact on Argentina.

The Asian and Russian crisis (1998–1999) had a negative effect on Argentina that was compounded by the lack of policy space on its monetary regime implemented in 1991 which was a variant of a unilateral currency arrangement with the United States known as a currency board. The plan fixed the exchange rate at one peso per dollar and gave agents the possibility of freely using the dollar or the peso to settle monetary transactions. The Asian and Russian crises and the devaluation of the Brazilian real that followed in 1999 provoked a confidence crisis, a severe loss of competitiveness in Argentina *vis-à-vis* its main trading partner (Brazil) and a decrease in the terms of trade Argentina had implemented in 1991. The resulting recession was long-lasting and cast serious doubts on the ability of Argentina to confront its external debt obligations (US$14 billion) due in 2001. In addition, the government's margin of action was constrained by a deteriorating fiscal balance which left no choice but to pursue contractionary policies. These, in turn, compounded the expectations of a stagnant economy.

Figures 4.8 and 4.9 show the evolution of the cyclical component of GDP and net intercompany loans for these crisis episodes. The examples chosen for the global financial crisis include Argentina, Brazil, Colombia, Mexico, Paraguay and Peru.

Visual inspection shows a strong synchronicity between the decline in the cyclical component of GDP and net intercompany loans for most countries in these crisis episodes. Further empirical analysis of the global financial crisis for Argentina, Brazil, Chile, Colombia, Peru and Mexico using the cycle methodology used in section 4.4 shows that the decline in intra-company loans following the crisis, measured by the duration, amplitude and intensity was significantly larger than the decline in the equity component of FDI. The duration is longer for intercompany loans in most cases (Table 4.6).

The amplitude (the average rate of change from peak to trough) for intercompany loans exceeds that of equity by a factor of 6.4, 2.0, 10.6, 29.8 and 5.7 for Argentina, Brazil, Chile, Peru and Mexico. Similarly, the intensity of the contraction (the amplitude divided by the duration) is much larger for intercompany loans than for equity for all countries.

The evidence also shows that the positive association between the business cycle and the behaviour of intercompany loans is not only limited to crisis periods. In fact, it holds for longer periods as attested by the statistically positive correlation coefficient between both variables for the period 1999q1 to 2019q1 for selected Latin American countries (Argentina, Brazil Chile and Peru).

4.7   CONCLUSION

Two of the main stylized facts that have characterized the financial system in the aftermath of the global financial crisis are the rise in the international bond market as a major source of cross-border liquidity and the extensive use of the bond market by non-financial corporates to finance their operations. The evidence for emerging market economies including those of Latin America reveals that the proceeds of increased indebtedness in the international capital markets have not been used towards productive ends. This brings up the possibility that the non-financial corporate sector may be using the liquidity from the international bond market for financial operations including lending, speculative activities and short-term gains.

Favourable foreign exchange-rate conditions can act as an important incentive to issue debt in the international capital market. Similarly, expected and effective exchange-rate movements and their volatility can influence firms to engage in speculative activities.

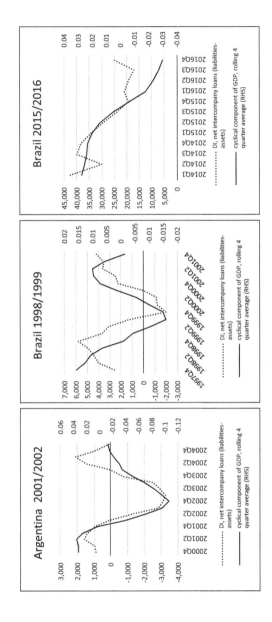

Note: The straight line corresponds to the cyclical deviation from GDP and the dotted line to net intercompany flows. The left-hand axis is millions of US$ dollars and the right-hand axis refers to rates of growth.

Source: ECLAC on the basis of IMF Balance of Payments Statistics.

Figure 4.8 *Cyclical component of GDP and net intercompany loan flows for Argentina (2001–2002) and Brazil (1998–1999; 2015–2016)*

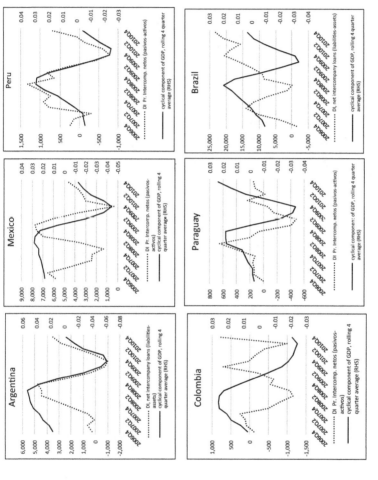

Note: The straight line corresponds to the cyclical deviation of GDP and the dotted line to net intercompany flows. The left-hand axis is millions of US$ dollars and the right-hand axis refers to rates of growth.

Source: ECLAC on the basis of IMF Balance of Payments Statistics.

Figure 4.9 Cyclical component of GDP and net intercompany loan flows for selected Latin American countries during the global financial crisis (2008–2009)

Table 4.6 *Cycle indicators and indicators for GDP, FDI equity and FDI intercompany loans for Argentina, Brazil, Chile, Colombia, Peru and Mexico*

	GDP		FDI equity		FDI intercompany loans	
	Peak	Trough	Peak	Trough	Peak	Trough
Argentina	2007q4	2009q2	2008q3	2008q4	2008q4	2009q4
Duration	6		1		4	
Amplitude	−8.86		−21.48		−137.6	
Intensity	1.48		21.48		34.25	
Correlations	GDP-intercompany loans = 0.41*				GDP-equity = 0.32*	
Brazil	2008q3	2009q1	2008q4	2009q4	2008q4	2010q2
Duration	6		4		6	
Amplitude	−2.41		−9.51		−19.77	
Intensity	0.40		2.38		3.29	
Correlations	GDP-intercompany loans = 0.33*				GDP-equity = 0.17*	
Chile	2008q1	2010q1	2008q4	2010q2	2008q4	2009q3
Duration	8		6		3	
Amplitude	−0.12		−4.66		−49.55	
Intensity	0.015		0.78		16.52	

(Continued)

Table 4.6 (Continued)

	GDP		FDI equity		FDI intercompany loans	
	Peak	Trough	Peak	Trough	Peak	Trough
Correlations	GDP-intercompany loans = 0.23*				GDP-equity = 0.31*	
Peru	2008q2	2009q2	2008q1	2009q1	2008q3	2009q4
Duration	4		4		5	
Amplitude	0.03		2.94		-87.61	
Intensity	0.01		0.73		17.52	
Correlations	GDP-intercompany loans = 0.21*				GDP-equity = 0.40*	
Mexico	2007q4	2009q2	2008q2	2009q3	2009q1	2010q2
Duration	6		5		5	
Amplitude	-1.22		-8.61		-49.09	
Intensity	0.20		1.72		9.82	
Correlations	GDP-intercompany loans = -0.08				GDP-equity = -0.011	

Note: The turning points (peaks and troughs) of a series are identified using the Bry-Boschan algorithm (1971) developed originally for monthly data and adapted to deal with quarterly observation by Harding and Pagan (2002). The algorithm consists in identifying local maxima and minima for a given series following a logarithmic transformation using specific censoring rules. These include the specification of two quarters for a minimum duration for a single phase and a minimum duration of five quarters for a complete cycle (Harding and Pagan, 2002). The peak for a series y_t is found when y_t is greater than $y_{t \mp k}$ for $k = 1,2$. Similarly, the trough for a series y_t is found when y_t is less than $y_{t \mp k}$ for $k = 1,2$. The algorithm excludes the occurrence of two successive peaks or troughs.

Source: Authors' own on the basis of IMF balance of payments statistics and official data. The correlation coefficient was computed for the period 1999q1 to 2019q1. The symbol * denotes statistically significant at the 95% level of confidence.

One of the main ways in which non-financial corporations channel the proceeds of bond issues is through intercompany loans. Due to accounting and statistical conventions, intercompany loans are classified as a long-term financial flow, as part of foreign direct investment along with equity. However, the empirical evidence shows that intercompany loans tend to behave as short-term flows and that, as argued in the literature on the subject, they are short-term flows 'masked as FDI'. In the case of Latin America, intercompany loans have significantly increased since 2000 and especially following the global financial crisis in absolute terms and as a percentage of FDI. One of the main motivations guiding intercompany loans besides tax avoidance and carry-trade financial strategies is the behaviour of the business cycles. This indicates that firms use intercompany loans as a means to shield themselves from the consequences of the fluctuations in economic activity. The significant co-movement between intercompany loans and the business cycle rises to the surface, especially in times of crisis.

However, while the use of intercompany loans may benefit individual firms, it may not benefit the economy, in the aggregate, especially when assets and investments are concentrated in a few firms, which are those that issue bonds in the international capital market. By using intercompany loans, firms contribute to the rising importance of short-term flows which are prone to sudden reversals and can generate greater volatility and also be a source of financial fragility and instability.[19]

Sudden reversals of financial flows impose depreciating pressures on the nominal exchange rate which can then affect the financial position of firms that are indebted in foreign currency. Depreciation not only raises debt service costs, and thence outgoings, but also swells liabilities by increasing the local-currency value of outstanding debt. If the collateral for the debt is likewise denominated in local currency, depreciation will also cause this asset to lose value. This can give rise to a mismatch such that the firm has to purchase currency to balance its accounts. Depending on its size and importance in the market and the number of firms behaving in this way, currency purchases can create further pressure for devaluation of the nominal exchange rate and increase the debt burden, especially in firms operating in the non-tradeable sector.

NOTES

1. The authors' names appear in alphabetical order. Claudia de Camino and Cecilia Vera are Economics Affairs Officers at the Economic Commission for Latin America and the Caribbean (ECLAC) in the Statistics and Economic Development Divisions respectively. Esteban Pérez Caldentey is chief of the Financing for Development Unit within the Economic Development Division at ECLAC.
2. Shin (2014) refers to this as the second wave of global liquidity. The first wave which took place prior to the global financial crisis was driven by global banks and their cross-border lending.

3. See Shin and Zhao (2013), Adjiev et al. (2014a and 2014b) and Caballero et al. (2016).
4. Ibid.
5. Corresponds to the last quarter of 2000 and the second quarter of 2019.
6. The countries included in this sample with the respective number of companies are Argentina (156), Brazil (1,281), Chile (279), Colombia (92), Mexico (228) and Peru (205).
7. Note that in Latin America and the Caribbean, investment is highly concentrated at the firm level. An exercise with the same dataset for 2008–2016 dividing all firms into 100 groups, at similar intervals and ordered by investment expenditures, shows that companies in the first, second and third percentiles on average accounted for 27.2 per cent, 56.7 per cent and 71.2 per cent of long-term gross fixed investment expenditure capital formation (ECLAC, 2018).
8. See Bastos et al. (2016) and Adjiev (2014b).
9. Note that increased indebtedness may be inversely related to investment as firms use the proceeds from bonds to increase their 'margins of safety'. An econometric estimation that relates investment in tangible assets to cash flow by degree of leverage for 270 firms in six Latin American countries (Argentina, Brazil, Chile, Colombia, Mexico and Peru) for the 2010–2016 period shows that when leverage exceeds a 0.77 threshold, a 1 per cent increase in cash flow to assets is associated with a reduction in investment of 0.25–0.24 per cent. See Pérez Caldentey et al. (2019).
10. In this simplified scheme we will not discuss derivatives nor other flows apart from the main categories presented in Figure 4.2.
11. 'Enterprises in a direct investment relationship with each other are called affiliates or affiliated enterprises. In addition, all enterprises that are under the control or influence of the same direct investor are considered to be in a direct investment relationship with each other' (IMF, 2007, p. 101).
12. See also Shin and Zhao (2013).
13. Total inflows include FDI, portfolio investment and other investment. Portfolio flows have also increased significantly since the 2000s decade, reaching US$28.7, 20.7 and 83.2 billion for the periods 1990–2000, 2001–2009 and 2010–2020 representing 46 per cent, 18 per cent and 30 per cent of total inflows (Table A4.1 of the appendix).
14. In general, as dividend payments are not tax deductible but interest payments are, firms would choose to increase the usage of debt to finance capital, relative to using the issuance of equity so as to minimize the company's cost of funds (capital).
15. The details of these mechanisms are, however, beyond the scope of our analysis.
16. This implies that the uncovered interest parity condition does not hold. See Galati et al. (2007).
17. See *Journal Do Comercio* (2011).
18. For a similar finding in the case of Latin America, see De Gregorio et al. (2017).
19. These effects can be compounded by recent evidence that show that bond flows are much more sensitive to changes in external interest rates than bank loans (Advdjiev et al., 2016).

REFERENCES

Avdjiev, S., Chui, M., and Song Shin, H. 2014. Non-financial corporations from emerging market economies and capital flows. In *BIS Quarterly Review*, December. Basel: Bank for International Settlements.

Avdjiev, S., Gambacorta, L., Goldberg, L. S., and Schiaffi, S. 2016. The shifting drivers of global liquidity. *BIS Working Papers No. 644.* Basel: Bank for International Settlements.

BIS. 2021a. *Global Liquidity Indicators.* Basel: Bank for International Settlements.

BIS. 2021b. *Debt Statistics.* Basel: Bank for International Settlements.

Bry, G., and Boschan, C. 1971. *Cyclical Analysis of Time Series: Selected Procedures and Computer Programmes.* New York: National Bureau of Economic Research.

Caballero, J., Panizza, U., and Powell, A. 2016. The second wave of global liquidity: Why are firms acting like financial intermediaries? *IDB Working Paper Series, No. 641.*

Chui, M., Kuruc, E., and Turner, Ph. 2018. Leverage and currency mismatches: Non-financial companies in the emerging markets. *Special Issue: Global Trade Policy 2018*, 41(12). The World Economy. http://wileyonlinelibrary.com/journal/TWEC.

De Gregorio, J., García, N., and Jara, M. 2017. *The Boom in Corporate Debt in Latin America: Carry Trade or Investment?* Mimeo.

Dubois, É., and Michaux, E. 2020. Grocer 1.82: An econometric toolbox for Scilab. http://grocer.toolbox.free.fr/grocer.html.

ECLAC. 2018. *Economic Survey of Latin America and the Caribbean.* Santiago: Economic Commission for Latin America and the Caribbean.

Galati, G., Health, A., and McGuire, P. 2007. Evidence of carry trade activity. *BIS Quarterly Review*, September: 27–41.

Harding, D., and Pagan, A. 2002a. A comparison of two business cycle dating methods. *Journal of Economic Dynamics and Control*, 27: 1681–1690.

Harding, D., and Pagan, A. 2002b. Dissecting the cycle: A methodological investigation. *Journal of Monetary Economics*, 49: 365–381.

Hardy, B., and Saffie, F. 2019. From carry trades to trade credit: Financial intermediation by non-financial corporations BIS. *BIS Working Papers No. 773*, August.

IMF. 2007. Balance of payments position and the international financial position. https://www.imf.org/external/pubs/ft/bop/2007/pdf/chap6.pdf.

IMF. 2021. Balance of payments statistics.

Journal Do Comercio. 2011. *Empréstimo de matriz externa para filiais no País pagará IOF*, 3 August. https://www.jornaldocomercio.com/site/noticia.php?codn=69297.

Pérez Caldentey, E., Favreau Negront, N., and Méndez Lobos, L. 2019. Corporate debt in Latin America and its macroeconomic implications. *Journal of Post Keynesian Economics*, 42(3): 335–362.

Rodrigues Bastos, F., Kamil, H., and Sutton, B. 2016. Corporate financing trends and balance sheet risks in Latin America: Taking stock of 'The Bon(d)anza.' *IMF Working Paper WP/15/10.*

Shin, H. S. 2014. The second phase of global liquidity and its impact on emerging economies. In Chung, K., Kim, S., Park, H., Choi, C., and Shin, H. S. (eds.) *Volatile Capital Flows in Korea.* New York: Palgrave Macmillan, pp. 247–257.

Shin, H. S., and Zhao, L. Y. 2013. *Firms as Surrogate Intermediaries: Evidence From Emerging Economies.* Mimeo.

Wacker, K. M. 2013. On the measurement of foreign direct investment and its relationship to activities of multinational corporations. *European Central Bank Working Paper Series No. 1614*, November.

World Bank. 2021. *World Bank Development Indicators.* Washington, DC: World Bank.

APPENDIX

Components of Financial Flows to Latin America

Table A4.1   Financial flows to Latin America by type: US$ and share of total 1990–2020

	1990–2000	2001–2009	2010–2020
FDI (millions of US$)	36,135	83,095	172,558
Portfolio flows (millions of US$)	28,658	20,659	83,256
Other investment (millions of US$)	–2,748	11,396	24,000
Total (millions of US$)	62,045	115,149	279,814
FDI share (%)	58	72	62
Portfolio share (%)	46	18	30
Other investment share (%)	–4	10	9

PART II

Currency and exchange rate

5. Currency relationships over time: a network analysis and case study of Mexico

Georgia Bush, Serafin Martínez-Jaramillo, Luis O. L. Escobar-Farfán and Erwin Flores-Tamés

5.1 INTRODUCTION

The exchange rate is a key macroeconomic variable for any open economy. The price of one's currency in the foreign exchange market links domestic activity with the global economy and is an important variable for economic decision-making for households and firms. In terms of macroeconomic policy, the famously named 'trilemma' articulates the importance of exchange rate fluctuations and the challenge of balancing domestic monetary policy, capital flows and the international price of one's currency. For many emerging and frontier economies, the development strategy has relied on export competitiveness and the ability to sell their products abroad. In addition, capital inflows, in the form of financial flows or foreign direct investment, have helped address capital scarcity in these economies during the recent era of globalization that began in the 1990s. In this context, the global economy has become more integrated, both in the goods markets and the financial markets. And, developing economies have managed their position by taking into account their policy mix and the dynamics of their exchange rate. The more integrated the economy, the more the currency is linked to the global foreign exchange market.

Consequently, an important question is how the foreign exchange market has evolved. In particular, given the globalization trend of the past couple of decades, have developing economy currencies become more integrated and less peripheral in the foreign exchange market? Are there some currencies that have become more central than others? Do financial crises affect these currency relationships? To answer these questions, first we must depict the global foreign exchange market. To do this we will exploit network analysis techniques. Networks are convenient representations of complex phenomena and network theory provides a comprehensive wealth of theoretical results and practical methods and algorithms to study complex systems. In particular, network models have been successfully applied in finance in the last two decades. Thus the goal of this chapter is to measure and better understand the global foreign exchange market using network analysis. We will study exchange rate correlations and the evolution of those relationships through the global financial crisis.

Correlation networks and their study have been applied in many disciplines such as biology, genetics, medicine and social networks to name a few. Finance is not an exception, and correlation networks have been well studied before; see, for example, Mantengna et al. (2000), Onnela et al. (2004), Boginski et al. (2005), Tumminello et al. (2005), Naylor et al. (2007), Fenn (2010), Pozzi et al. (2012), Massara et al. (2016) and Musmeci et al. (2017), to name just a few.

A distinguishing feature of financial networks is that most of the time series used to build them have non-zero correlations. As a consequence, heavily connected structures arise from this process, and there is a need to filter out some of the information (links). For this purpose, filtering techniques have been proposed ranging from threshold-based methods to some graph-based ones like the minimum spanning tree (MST) (Gower and Ross, 1969), which is a highly popular filtering technique for correlation networks. In particular, foreign exchange (FX) currency correlation networks have been investigated before; a non-exhaustive list of works includes McDonald et al. (2005), Naylor et al. (2007), Kwapien et al. (2009), Fenn (2010), Sharif et al. (2012), Wang et al. (2014), Wang and Xie (2016), Yang et al. (2019) and Hasbrouck and Levich (2020).

Despite the relatively good coverage of papers on FX correlation networks, most of them rely on the MST methodology. In contrast, the literature on stock market correlations includes papers that employ other filtering techniques, in particular the planar maximally filtered graph (PMFG) approach (Tumminello et al., 2005). In our view, the use of the MST loses important information about the relationships around nodes which have been already identified as important by the MST. Ignoring such information might lead to misleading measurements of centrality as by construction, tree structures have low centralization, a concept that we will be discussing in section 5.2. Therefore, the conclusions that you might draw about the centrality/relevance of specific currencies might not be adequate.

In this chapter, we construct dynamic currency networks using exchange rate correlations for 66 currencies for the period 1995–2018. We contrast the results from the MST and PMFG filtering techniques and argue that the MST is not sufficient to study centrality. Next, after filtering out the most irrelevant correlations, we use our foreign exchange network to 1) compare currency relationships before, during and after the global financial crisis (GFC); and 2) document and analyse currency centrality for emerging and frontier economy currencies, with a case study on the Mexican peso.

Our initial findings are that the centrality measures using the PMFG network show considerable and richer dynamics over the sample period, suggesting currency correlations are constantly evolving. We also find that on average, frontier currencies are less central in general, and developed currencies are more central until around 2013. Frontier and developed economy currencies experience greater variability in their centrality. And comparing pre-, during and post-GFC, we see developed economy currencies going from being interlinked mostly with each other to being spread throughout the network, meaning more and stronger correlations with emerging and frontier economy currencies.

The rest of the chapter is organized as follows: section 5.2 describes the data used to build the correlation networks and introduces the network concepts used in this study; section 5.3 presents the results obtained from the analysis of the FX networks; section 5.4 discusses the main results and analyses the dynamics of some centrality metrics by different types of economies; finally, section 5.5 concludes.

5.2   DATA AND METHODOLOGY

We construct dynamic currency networks using exchange rate correlations for a sample of 66 developed, emerging and frontier economy currencies for the period 1995–2018.

5.2.1   Data

A choice must be made regarding what variable to use for currencies in our network construction. We want each node to be a currency and each link to represent the relationship between one currency and the other.

We use daily market data on exchange rates during 1994–2018, which are publicly available and sourced from the Pacific Exchange Rate Service website.[1] The panel data is unbalanced and covers a maximum of 66 currencies over the sample period. Most currencies remain in the sample once they have entered.[2] The exchange rate data is used to calculate correlations between currencies over a rolling-window year-long period. We use a reverse exponential decay where the daily exchange rate for currency X, x_t, is weighted with $w_t = \left(1 - \left(\dfrac{1}{ws}\right)\right)^t$, where ws is the window size and t is the time passed.

Therefore, more recent data points receive greater weight. Then we define X^* as

$$X^* = \left(\frac{\sum_{t=1}^{ws} (w_t x_t)}{\sum_{t=1}^{ws} w_t} \right)$$

And the weighted correlation between currency X and currency Y is

$$\rho_{X^*,Y^*} = \frac{cov(X^*,Y^*)}{\sigma_{X^*} \sigma_{Y^*}}$$

We exclude all currencies that became part of the euro from our analysis.[3] To classify the currencies, we use the framework outlined by MSCI which categorizes economies as developed, emerging and frontier.[4] The advantage of this classification is that it is not only dependent on per capita income but also includes financial development criteria which may affect currency dynamics.

5.2.2 Network Approach

When we construct a dynamic currency network, where the network nodes are the currency exchange rate with respect to a base currency (US dollar) and the connections are the correlations between currency exchange rates, this results in a fully connected network. In theory, if the correlation between currencies is zero, there will be no connection between these two currencies in the network. However, in practice, many links exist because of low correlations that are not far from zero. Consequently, filtering methods must be applied to discard non-meaningful links. In our setting, a network is represented as an $N \times N$ matrix W, where N is the number of currencies, such that

$$W_{ij} = \begin{cases} w_{ij}, & \text{the non} - \text{zero correlation between currencies } i \text{ and } j, \\ 0, & \text{otherwise.} \end{cases}$$

Given that our networks are undirected (i.e. the links do not have a specific direction), we have $W = W^T$. From the previous definition, we can further describe the *adjacency matrix* of a network as:

$$A_{ij} = \begin{cases} 1, & if \ w_{ij} \neq 0, \\ 0, & if \ w_{ij} = 0. \end{cases}$$

It is on the W matrices that the filtering techniques are applied. A standard technique is the MST (Gower and Ross, 1969; Mantegna and Stanley, 1999). However, the MST was created in the context of electrical networks with the goal of finding the minimum distance of cable needed to connect all the nodes in the network. Because of this, the weight of a link can be interpreted as a distance while finding the MST, which is why we use the inverse of the correlations to perform the filtering, converting them back to their original scale after the filter has been applied. For financial networks, we are interested in a richer set of topological information that enables the inclusion of feedback loops and spillover effects and the calculation of centrality measures.

Other topological approaches have been proposed. These include the PMFG and the triangulated maximally filtered graph (TMFG). These techniques take into account the weights of the links, in other words, the magnitude of the correlations between currencies. They also cap the total number of links in the filtered graph.

We will argue that to study centrality one must use alternatives to the MST. Intuitively, the MST reduces the graph too much, eliminating all cliques (triangular-shaped connections between three nodes) and thus any local information about interconnectedness.

5.2.3   Node Centrality Metrics

Following are definitions of common node centrality measures used in network analysis.

Degree: the number of links from a given node v, $C_D(v) = \deg(v) = \sum_{j=1}^{N} A_{vj}$.
By this centrality measure, the 'most central' node will have the highest number of connections in the network, v^*. This is the simplest and most commonly used centrality measure. The average degree of the graph G with E edges or links and V vertices is defined as $D_A(G) = \dfrac{2 \times E}{V}$.

Strength: The sum of all link weights that node u has with the rest of the nodes in the network. It is noteworthy that some of the values in the sum can be zero, which means you do not have a link with every node. The strength for node u can be calculated as:

$$s_u = \sum_{j=1}^{N} W_{uj}$$

Betweenness: the number of times a node acts as a bridge among the shortest paths between two other nodes. More formally, for a network with the set of nodes V, it is the fraction of all shortest paths from node s to t, σ_{st}, that pass through a given node v, and this can be expressed as

$$C_B(v) = \sum_{(s \neq v \neq t \in V)} \left(\sigma_{st}(v) / \sigma_{st} \right)$$

Closeness: The overall distance (direct or indirect) between the given node and the rest of the nodes in the network. For a graph (network) with the set of nodes V comprising n nodes, the closeness centrality measure for node v can be expressed as:

$$C_c(v) = (N-1) / \sum_{\forall u \neq v} d(u,v)$$

where $d(u, v)$ is the distance in the network between nodes u and v.

Clustering: Measures the connectedness of a node's neighbourhood. This is not a centrality metric but it is useful to describe the density of connections around nodes. The more connections among neighbours, the higher the clustering coefficient. More formally, it is the ability of a node's neighbour to form a complete graph, which is defined as a graph with three edges or links and three vertices (a closed triangle). The clustering coefficient for node v can be expressed as:

$$C_{cl}(v) = \left(\Delta_G(v) \right) / \left(\lambda_G(v) \right)$$

where the numerator is the number of subgraphs G having three edges and three vertices including the vertex v, and the denominator is the number of subgraphs of G with three vertices, two edges and the vertex v between the two edges (an open triangle shape).

Page Rank: originally proposed in Brin and Page (1998), a node gains its importance from the importance of the nodes pointing to it. The Page Rank of node i can be written as:

$$x_i = \alpha \sum_{j \neq i} A_{ij} \frac{x_j}{k_j^{out}} + \beta$$

with $\alpha, \beta > 0$ and A the adjacency matrix. To avoid 0 in the denominator, one can set $k^{out} = 1$ for all nodes with no outgoing links.

5.2.4   Network Centralization

We can also analyse the centralization of the network as a whole. According to Freeman (1978), network centralization measures index the degree to which the centrality of the most central point exceeds the centrality of all other points. Centralization is thus expressed as a ratio:

$$C_X = \frac{\sum_{i=1}^{n}\left[C_x\left(v^*\right)-C_x\left(v_i\right)\right]}{\max \sum_{i=1}^{n}\left[C_x\left(v^*\right)-C_x\left(v_i\right)\right]}$$

where n is the number of nodes, $C_x\left(v_i\right)$ is the individual centrality measure x of node v_i and $C_x\left(v^*\right)$ is the largest value of $C_x\left(v_i\right)$ for any node in the network. The denominator is the maximum possible sum of differences in individual node centrality for a graph of n nodes. Thus, C_X will take values between 0 and 1. And, $C_X=0$ if and only if all individual centralities are equal. $C_X=1$, if and only if only one node, v^*, completely dominates the network.

To fix ideas, consider the two networks pictured (Figure 5.1), each with five nodes. First, on the left is an example of a star network. These by construction have one central node linked to all other nodes. Thus the degree of centrality of the central node is 4, and for all the other nodes it is 1. On the right is an example of a fully connected network, where all nodes are connected and thus have the same degree of centrality, here equal to 4. Intuitively, we can see that the star network is a highly centralized network. Applying the aforementioned centralization formula, the denominator for any five-node network will be 12. For the star network with five nodes $(4 - 1) + (4 - 1) + (4 - 1) + (4 - 1) + (4 - 4) = 12$, $12/12 = 1$, the highest possible value of degree centralization. For the fully connected network of 5 nodes, $5 * (4 - 4) = 0$, $0/12 = 0$.

In general, for any network of size n, the maximum degree of centrality a node can have is $(n - 1)$ and the minimum is 0. The maximum sum of differences is the sum of $(n - 1) - 1$ for $(n - 1)$ nodes, hence $(n - 2)(n - 1) = n^2 - 3n + 2$. The general formula for degree centralization of a network with n nodes is thus defined as:

$$C_D = \frac{\sum_{i=1}^{n}\left[C_D\left(v^*\right)-C_D\left(v_i\right)\right]}{n^2 - 3n + 2}$$

(a) *Star* type network   (b) Fully connected network

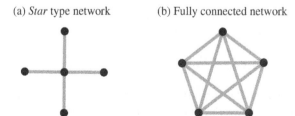

Figure 5.1   Network centralization examples

We will use these measures to analyse the centrality of the foreign exchange network and of various currencies over time.

5.3   NETWORK RESULTS

In this section, we report the results of constructing our foreign exchange network. We compare and contrast the network results using the two different filtering techniques. In particular, we provide evidence that the MST filters out important information about local connectedness and thus a key point is that the MST is not an optimal method to capture and analyse the dynamics of currency centralization.

First we assess the stability of the networks and the centralization of the networks. We show plots of our foreign exchange network for certain dates, and we report our centrality results for groups of currencies over the sample period.

5.3.1   Stability of the Network

We have constructed a dynamic network, which means for every date in our sample we have a network graph. The Jaccard index is a measure of the stability of the network over time and is defined as the number of links in common between the current period graph and the prior period graph. In Figure 5.2, we plot the Jaccard index for our foreign exchange networks using the MST and PMFG filtering approaches. They both show good stability. The moving average of the similarities across dates, the red horizontal line, is above 70 per cent for both networks.

5.3.2   Measuring Centrality of Currencies

In Figures 5.3 and 5.4, we present snapshot graphs for the MST and the PMFG, for illustrative purposes using 23 August 2017. The shape of the nodes

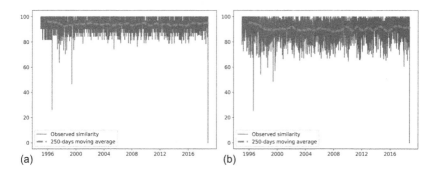

Figure 5.2   Jaccard index of network stability

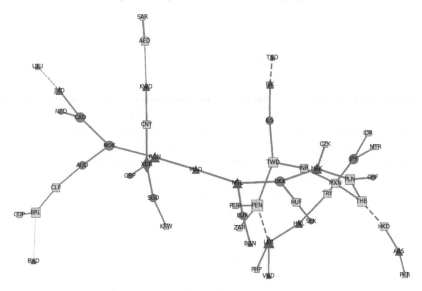

Figure 5.3   Foreign exchange network, minimum spanning tree (MST)

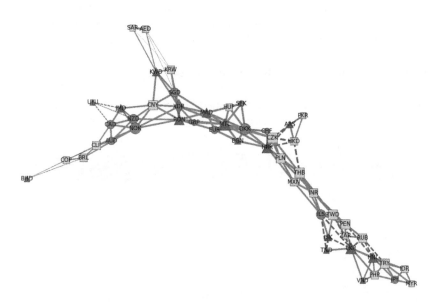

*Figure 5.4   Foreign exchange network, planar maximally filtered graph
             (PMFG)*

corresponds to developed (circles), emerging (squares) and frontier (triangles) economy status based on the current MSCI categorization. The size of the nodes corresponds to the degree of centrality of that node, the number of links between that node and others. The larger the node, the higher the degree of centrality. The width of the lines corresponds to the magnitude of the weight of the link, here the correlation between currencies. The wider the line, the higher the correlation. Finally, the type of the lines corresponds to the direction of the correlation, dashed if it's a negative correlation, and solid if it's a positive one.

Both the MST and PMFG retain the same 51 currencies. However, we can see the contrast between the MST and the PMFG graph. Many more local connections are captured in the more complex PMFG graph. For example, the Mexican peso (MXN) in the MST is a bridge between the Indian rupee (INR) and the Thai baht (THB). In the PMFG we can see more links, for example, between the Mexican peso and the Polish zloty (PLN) and the Israeli shekel (ISL). As a consequence, the degree of centrality measure will be the same or larger for the PMFG network, and the clustering centrality metric will be non-zero. In an MST, all nodes by construction have a clustering centrality of zero.

All but one of the average centrality measures for the PMFG are of greater magnitude than for the MST.[5] The two charts, Figure 5.5 and 5.6, show the evolution of the average value of two selected node centrality measures, averaged for a given date across the currencies in the specified group: developed (solid), emerging (dashed) and frontier (dash-dot). The left graphs (a) in Figures 5.5 and 5.6 show results using the MST technique, while the right graphs (b) show the results using the PMFG approach. Table A5.1 in the appendix lists the currencies in each group. The degree measure, shown in Figure 5.6, is much greater (note the different scales), and the clustering measure using the PMFG, shown in Figure 5.5, is non-zero. For every group of currencies, the PMFG is capturing more information about centrality and its dynamics than the MST.

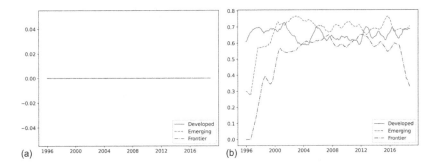

Figure 5.5   Clustering of currencies

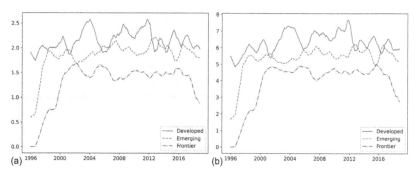

Figure 5.6   Degree centrality of currencies

5.3.3   Centralization of the Network Overall

Figure 5.7 compares the evolution of the degree of centralization for the two networks resulting from the two filtering techniques. On the left is the MST centralization and on the right the PMFG. These plots provide evidence that the PMFG filter generates a more centralized network. PMFG degree of centrality is as high as 0.3 and consistently above 0.1 versus the MST which is consistently below 0.1. A consistently higher value allows for more variation. The PMFG technique captures sharp changes in network centralization shown by the spikes in the black vertical lines. There are also periods when the 250-day moving average of degree centralization increases, shown by the solid line during the years 2000, 2008 and 2011. Centralization of the network peaks in late 1999, then declines and stays steady at around 0.15 for the 2002–2008 period. After the GFC, network centralization shows more variability than during the 2002–2005 period.

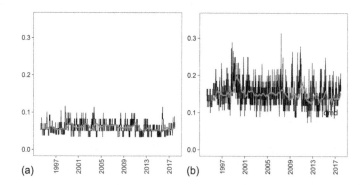

Figure 5.7   Degree centralization of the network

5.4   APPLICATIONS AND ANALYSIS

The first part of this chapter provides evidence that the network resulting from the PMFG filtering technique is better for the analysis of centrality because of the greater number of links retained in the graphs when compared to the MST approach. Thus the following analysis will be conducted using the PMFG foreign exchange network. First we will compare currency relationships at different dates, before, during and after the GFC.[6] Next, we will analyse individual emerging and frontier economy currencies, starting with the Mexican peso. We expect to see that developing economy currencies are more important in the foreign exchange network and that some emerging and frontier economy currencies have become more central.

5.4.1   The Global Financial Crisis

In this section we compare several snapshots, presented in chronological order from older to more recent. Our periods of interest are before the GFC, up until 2008, a period of globalization and relative calm in macroeconomic conditions known as the Great Moderation, and the period during the GFC that began in the US in the third quarter of 2008 and spread to Europe, with the peak of the European sovereign debt crisis during 2010–2012. Finally we generate a visualization snapshot for a period after the resolution of the GFC. Figures 5.8 and 5.9 show the foreign exchange network in 2005 and 2006, before the GFC period and during a period of globalization. Figures 5.10 and 5.11 depict the correlation network for the GFC period, between 2009 and 2012. Finally, Figure 5.12 shows the foreign exchange network in 2017.

The 2005 graph (Figure 5.8) shows the developed economy currencies (circles as nodes) grouped together with many correlations (links) among themselves. For example, the euro and the British pound are close neighbours in a core group. Emerging (square nodes) and frontier (triangular nodes) currencies are linked together mostly in a separate branching area on the left of the figure. The graph includes 24 of 29 frontier currencies and all 24 emerging currencies. By 2006, we see in Figure 5.9 a more complex graph with regional groupings, and developed currencies spread out throughout the network. The graph still includes 24 frontier currencies and 24 emerging currencies. Notably, there is no longer a core grouping of currencies. The British pound is farther from the euro and on its own branch with the Israeli sheqel. On the opposite side of the graph, the Singapore dollar is connected to the New Zealand dollar and a grouping of emerging and frontier currencies, as well as to another branch that includes the Australian dollar. These graphs provide evidence that in the lead-up to the GFC, emerging and frontier economy currencies were becoming less peripheral in the foreign exchange market.

At the beginning of the crisis period, Figure 5.10 has lost some of the branching complexity and developed economy currencies have grouped almost

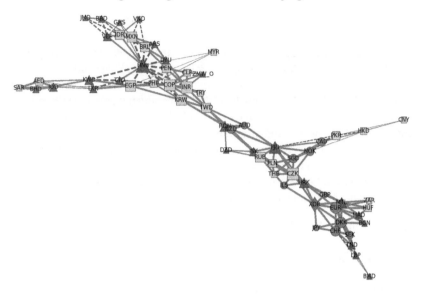

Figure 5.8   Foreign exchange graph (PMFG), 2005

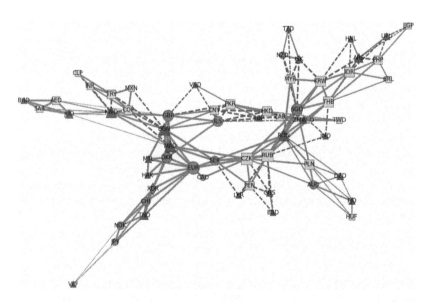

Figure 5.9   Foreign exchange graph (PMFG), 2006

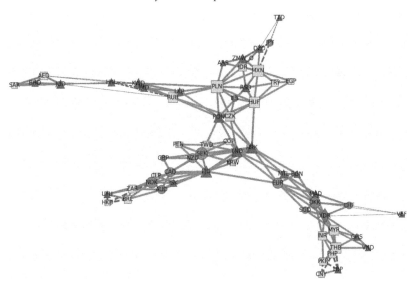

Figure 5.10   Foreign exchange graph (PMFG), 2009

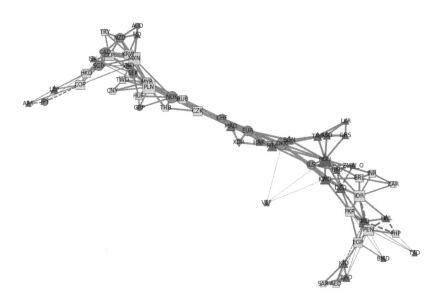

Figure 5.11   Foreign exchange graph (PMFG), 2012

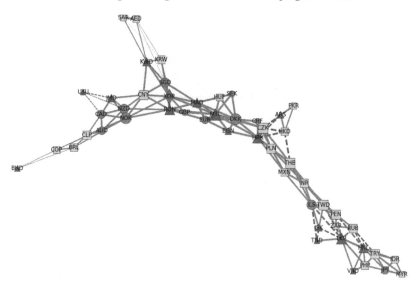

Figure 5.12   Foreign exchange graph (PMFG), 2017

entirely into two of the four branches with the notable exception of the Japanese yen. The lower left branch of the figure includes the British pound, the Swedish and Norwegian kroners and the New Zealand, Australian and Canadian dollars. The euro bridges to a grouping of the Danish kroner, Swiss franc and Singaporean dollar, which in turn connect to a group of emerging and frontier currencies. The graph still includes 24 frontier currencies and 24 emerging currencies. The 2009 network does not have the same clear core-periphery structure as in the early 2000s, but nevertheless, circle nodes dominate the core.

By 2012 (Figure 5.11), the network has become a thick and long central branch with developed currencies spread throughout three-quarters of the graph. The filtered graph retains 25 frontier currencies and 24 emerging currencies. The Japanese yen at one end is linked to the Singapore dollar through a group of emerging economies. Further along, a grouping of the Australian, New Zealand and Canadian dollars are linked via the Mexican peso to a group of other emerging economy currencies. A grouping of frontier economy currencies (triangles) are linked to the Israeli sheqel, Danish kroner and then the euro. The lower quarter is a mix of emerging and frontier currencies. Thus while the structure in 2012 is less complex with fewer branches than pre-crisis, the developed currencies are again no longer a dominating core, with more correlations between developed and both emerging and frontier currencies.

Figure 5.12 shows the graph of the correlation network for 2017. Some of the features of the 2012 graph are maintained, for example, the Australian, New Zealand and Canadian dollars grouping, the euro bridging role and the

Japanese yen in a distinct part of the graph. Of note, the Japanese yen in the post-crisis graph is linked to a larger group of emerging and frontier currencies. This may be related to the use of the yen as a funding currency for higher-yielding investments in emerging market currencies. Also, post-crisis, there are only 15 frontier currencies retained in the graph, which are spread throughout the network. This evidence suggests that post-crisis, some frontier currencies lost centrality, while others maintained their correlation links.

5.4.2   Centrality Dynamics

To analyse the evolution of the centrality of currencies over the entire sample period, we plot the evolution of our centrality measures. The incline at the start of the period for these measures is related to the unbalanced nature of the panel; fewer currencies are observed prior to 2000. Also, currencies may enter the data set as their use and trading activity are increasing, thus their centrality measures are on the rise. We have calculated six different measures for all currencies, for the dynamic foreign exchange network constructed using the PMFG filtering technique. In this section we will discuss average metrics for the three economic groupings and then discuss a single currency example.

5.4.2.1   Developed, Emerging and Frontier
Figure 5.13 shows the average centrality measures for the specified group of currencies, developed (solid), emerging (dashed) and frontier (dash-dot). Table A5.1 in the appendix lists the currencies classified into these groups. Figure 5.14 shows the standard deviation of centrality for these groups. Except for closeness and clustering, the centrality of the developed economy currencies is greater than for emerging and frontier currencies. In particular, the number of links to other currencies, and the strength of these correlations, are consistently higher for developed economy currencies until around 2013. For all of the measures, frontier currencies are less central. In terms of the variability of currency centrality, the frontier economies experience higher standard deviations for closeness and clustering. And developed and frontier experience generally higher volatility in degree and strength than emerging economy currencies.

5.4.2.2   The Mexican Peso
The centrality measures for the Mexican peso are plotted in Figure 5.15. For most of the centrality measures, we can observe a change from before 2008 to the period after. The after-period is characterized by higher volatility with dramatic peaks.

One explanation for the shift could be a pre- and post-crisis effect similar to the general changes analysed in section 5.1. However, we would also like to highlight two important events relevant to the Mexican peso and its place in the foreign exchange market.

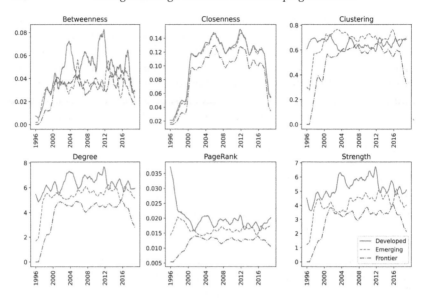

Figure 5.13   Centrality 1995–2018 (PMFG), average for groups of currencies

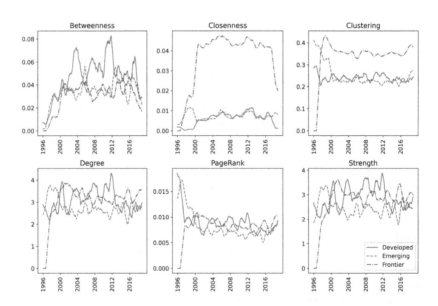

Figure 5.14   Centrality 1995–2018 (PMFG), standard deviation for groups of currencies

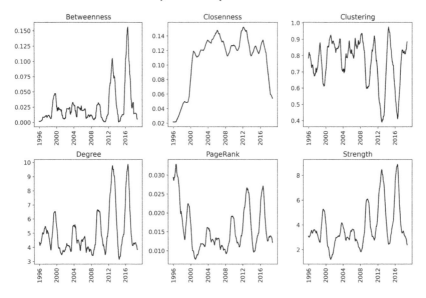

Figure 5.15   Centrality 1995–2018 (PMFG), Mexican peso (PMFG)

First, on 27 May 2008, the Mexican peso, along with Israel's sheqel, was accepted into the CLS payments system, originally known as Continuous Linked Settlement (CLS Bank). This simultaneous global, multi-currency settlement system handles foreign exchange transactions and was launched in 2002 with 39 members and seven currencies. At the time of Mexico's acceptance, CLS was already handling the following other 15 currencies: the Australian dollar, Canadian dollar, Danish krone, euro, Hong Kong dollar, Japanese yen, Korean won, New Zealand dollar, Norwegian krone, Singapore dollar, South African rand, Swedish krona, Swiss franc, UK pound sterling and US dollar. On 16 November 2015, the Hungarian florin joined, bringing the number of currencies to 18.

Second, in March 2010 Citibank announced that Mexico, in particular Mexican peso-denominated sovereign debt, would be the first Latin American country to enter the World Government Bond Index (WGBI). The WGBI is a key investment benchmark that can affect investment flows, particularly when countries are added to the index. Around the time of Mexico's entrance in October, inflows were notable, in particular from Japanese investors. These events would have facilitated the tradability and liquidity of the Mexican peso, leading to a shift in the centrality dynamics of the currency. In particular, increasing integration into the global financial system could lead to correlations with a broader set of currencies.

5.5   CONCLUSION

In terms of the network approach, it is important to move beyond the MST filtering technique when the goal is to analyse the centrality of the foreign exchange network. This technique is useful to explore the important relationships among currencies but ignores important information regarding the neighbourhoods of the nodes in such networks. As a result, resorting to the MST when measuring centrality could be misleading.

Our initial findings are that the centrality measures using the PMFG network show considerably richer dynamics over the sample period, suggesting currency correlations are constantly evolving. We also find that on average, frontier currencies are less central in general, and developed currencies are more central until around 2013. Frontier and developed economy currencies experience greater variability in their centrality. And comparing pre-, during and post-GFC, we see developed economy currencies going from being interlinked mostly with each other, to being spread throughout the network, meaning more and stronger correlations with non-developed economy currencies. Finally, the case study of the Mexican peso suggests changes in a currency's payment system, and financial developments such as the investability of the local currency-denominated bond market can affect centrality dynamics.

Future work on this topic could follow several avenues. An analysis could focus on developed market currencies' role in the FX market, in which case different underlying currencies could be used instead of the US dollar in order to incorporate this currency into the study. With respect to network techniques, the further development of new filtering strategies such as the Pólya filter could allow for alternative filtering methods to be used for the FX market. Finally, given appropriate FX market centrality metrics, these could be related to domestic and foreign macroeconomic phenomena.

NOTES

1. http://fx.sauder.ubc.ca/data.html.
2. Please see Figure A5.1 in the appendix for more details for each currency.
3. The following currencies are excluded from our analysis because they were replaced by the euro: Belgian francs, Cypriot pounds, Dutch gilders, Estonian kroons, Finish markkas, French francs, German marks, Greek drachmas, Irish punts, Italian liras, Luxembourg francs, Portuguese escudos, Slovakian korunas, Slovenian tolars and Spanish pesetas.
4. Please see the appendix and Table A5.1 for more detail.
5. See Figure 5.13 for the plots for all six currency centrality measures.
6. The exact dates of the snapshot graphs are 13 July 2005, 13 October 2006, 18 March 2009, 22 October 2012 and 23 August 2017. Each graph captures the correlation over the prior 250 business days, equivalent to a year-long period, as described in section 5.2.

REFERENCES

Boginski, Vladimir, Sergiy Butenko, and Panos M. Pardalos. 2005. Statistical analysis of financial networks. *Computational Statistics & Data Analysis*, 48(2): 431–443.

Brin, Sergey, and Lawrence Page. 1998. The anatomy of a large-scale hypertextual web search engine. *Computer Networks and ISDN Systems*, 30(1): 107–117.

Fenn, Daniel. 2010. *Network communities and the foreign exchange market*. PhD Dissertation, University of Oxford.

Freeman, Linton C. 1978. Centrality in social networks conceptual clarification. *Social Networks*, 1(3): 215–239.

Gower, John C., and Gavin J. S. Ross. 1969. Minimum spanning trees and single linkage cluster analysis. *Journal of the Royal Statistical Society: Series C (Applied Statistics)*, 18(1): 54–64.

Hasbrouck, Joel, and Richard M. Levich. 2020. Network structure and pricing in the FX market. *SSRN*, January.

Kwapien, Jaroslaw, Sylwia Gworek, Stanislaw Drozdz, and Andrzej Gorski. 2009. Analysis of a network structure of the foreign currency exchange market, *Journal of Economic Interaction and Coordination*, 4.

Mantegna, R. N. Cross-correlation between stock prices in financial markets.

Mantegna, Rosario N., and H. Eugene Stanley. *Introduction to Econophysics: Correlations and Complexity in Finance*. Cambridge: Cambridge University Press, 1999.

Massara, Guido Previde, Tiziana Di Matteo, and Tomaso Aste. 2016. Network filtering for big data: Triangulated maximally filtered graph. *Journal of Complex Networks*, 5(2): 161–178.

McDonald, Mark, Omer Suleman, Stacy Williams, Sam Howison, and Neil F. Johnson. 2005. Detecting a currency's dominance or dependence using foreign exchange network trees. *Physical Review E*, 72: 046106.

Musmeci, Nicolo, Vincenzo Nicosia, Tomaso Aste, Tiziana Di Matteo, and Vito Latora. 2017. The multiplex dependency structure of financial markets. *Complexity*, 2017.

Naylor, Michael J., Lawrence C. Rose, and Brendan J. Moyle. 2007. Topology of foreign exchange markets using hierarchical structure methods. *Physica A: Statistical Mechanics and Its Applications*, 382(1): 199–208.

Onnela, J.-P., Kimmo Kaski, and Janos Kert'esz. 2004. Clustering and information in correlation based financial networks. *The European Physical Journal B*, 38(2): 353–362.

Osman, Ibrahim H., Baydaa Al-Ayoubi, and Musbah Barake. 2003. A greedy random adaptive search procedure for the weighted maximal planar graph problem. *Computers & Industrial Engineering*, 45(4): 635–651.

Pozzi, Francesco, Tiziana Di Matteo, and Tomaso Aste. 2012. Exponential smoothing weighted correlations. *The European Physical Journal B*, 85(6): 1–21. ʃ

Sharif, Shamshuritawati, Nur Syahidah Yusoff, and Maman A. Djauhari. 2012. Network topology of foreign exchange rate. *Modern Applied Science*, 6(11): 35.

Tumminello, Michele, Tomaso Aste, Tiziana Di Matteo, and Rosario N. Mantegna. 2005. A tool for filtering information in complex systems. *Proceedings of the National Academy of Sciences*, 102(30): 10421–10426.

Wang, Gang-Jin, and Chi Xie. 2016. Tail dependence structure of the foreign exchange market: A network view. *Expert Systems With Applications*, 46: 164–179.

Wang, Gang-Jin, Chi Xie, Peng Zhang, Feng Han, and Shou Chen. 2014. Dynamics of foreign exchange networks: A time-varying copula approach. *Discrete Dynamics in Nature and Society*, May 2014, 170921.

Yang, Xin, Shigang Wen, Zhifeng Liu, Cai Li, and Chuangxia Huang. 2019. Dynamic properties of foreign exchange complex network. *Mathematics*, 7(9): 832.

APPENDIX

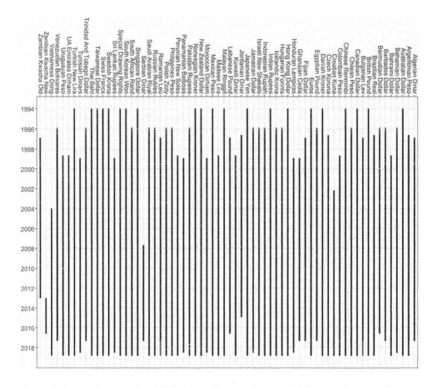

Note: This plots the dates for which we have the currency correlations data. For network construction, gaps of one to three days were filled by interpolation.

Source: Pacific Exchange Rate Service website, http://fx.sauder.ubc.ca/data.html and authors' calculations.

Figure A5.1   Currency sample 1995–2018

Currency Categorization

Quoted from the MSCI Market Classification Framework report published at www.msci.com/market-classification. The framework consists of the following criteria:

- Economic development: considers the sustainability of economic development and is only used in determining the classification of developed markets, given the wide range of development levels within emerging and frontier markets.
- Size and liquidity requirements: determines those securities that meet the minimum investability requirements of the MSCI Global Standard Indexes.
- Market accessibility criteria: aims to reflect international institutional investors' experiences of investing in a given market and includes five criteria: openness to foreign ownership, ease of capital inflows/outflows, efficiency of operational framework, availability of investment instruments and stability of the institutional framework.

Table A5.1   Currency categorization, according to MSCI as of 2018

Developed	Code	Emerging	Code	Frontier	Code
Australian dollar	AUD	Brazilian real	BRL	Algerian dinar	DZD
British pound	GBP	Chilean peso	CLP	Argentine peso	ARS
Canadian dollar	CAD	Colombian peso	COP	Bahamian dollar	BSD
Danish krone	DKK	Czech koruna	CZK	Bahraini dinar	BHD
Euros	EUR	Egyptian pound	EGP	Barbados dollar	BBD
Israeli new sheqels	ILS	Hong Kong dollar	HKD	Bermudian dollar	BMD
Japanese yen	JPY	Hungarian forints	HUF	Bulgarian lev	BGN
New Zealand dollar	NZD	Indian rupees	INR	Croatian kuna	HRK
Norwegian kroner	NOK	Indonesian rupiah	IDR	Fijian dollar	FJD
Singapore dollar	SGD	Malayan ringgit	MYR	Ghanaian cedis	GHS
Swedish krona	SEK	Mexican peso	MXN	Honduran lempiras	HNL
Swiss francs	CHF	Pakistani rupees	PKR	Icelandic krona	ISK
Special drawing rights	XDR	Peruvian new soles	PEN	Jamaican dollar	JMD
		Philippines peso	PHP	Jordanian dinar	JOD
		Polish zloty	PLN	Kuwaiti dinar	KWD
		Russian rubles	RUB	Lebanese pound	LBP
		Saudi Arabian riyal	SAR	Maltese lira	MTL
		South African rand	ZAR	Moroccan dirham	MAD
		South Korean won	KRW	Panamanian balboas	PAB
		Taiwanese dollar	TWD	Romanian new leu	RON
		Thai baht	THB	Serbian dinar	RSD

(*Continued*)

Table A5.1   *(Continued)*

Developed	Code	Emerging	Code	Frontier	Code
		Turkish lira	TRY	Sri Lankan rupees	LKR
		Trinidad and Tobago dollar	TTD	Jamaican dollar	JMD
		UAE dirham	AED	Tunisian dinars	TND
		Yuan renminbi	CNY	Uruguayan peso	UYU
				Venezuelan bolivares	VEF
				Vietnamese dong	VND
				Zambian kwacha new	ZMW N
				Zambian kwacha old	ZMW O

Source: MSCI Market Classification Framework, www.msci.com/market-classification.

6. On the limits of real exchange-rate targeting under foreign exchange constraint

Eduardo F. Bastian[1]

6.1 INTRODUCTION

Foreign exchange constraint has been a frequent macroeconomic problem in the world at least since the end of the First World War and the collapse of the gold standard. As a result, there have been sundry theoretical formulations and policy proposals on this problem and its consequences. In the 1920s, Germany's balance-of-payments difficulties — stemming from the war reparation payments – gave rise to the so-called German Balance of Payments School (GBP School henceforth), which claimed that Germany's 1920s hyperinflation was due to the need of constantly devaluing the exchange rate as a means to pay the reparations.

After the Second World War, in the late 1940s, there was a kind of global foreign exchange constraint: whilst for Europeans it came under the form of *dollar shortage*, for developing countries its incarnation was in the form of the *external strangulation* of the development process (Bacha, 1984, p. 263). In the two following decades, foreign exchange constraint was fundamentally a developing country problem. As a result, the most interesting discussions came from developing countries – like the Latin American structuralist school – or were based on developing countries' dilemmas, as was the case with the dual-gap model.

However, foreign exchange constraint regained worldwide interest in the 1970s after the First Oil Shock and again in the early 1980s after the Second Oil Shock and developing countries' external debt crisis. This renewed interest gave rise to a new round of contributions, for instance, Thirlwall's (1979) balance-of-payments constrained growth model, new developments on the dual-gap approach by Latin American *neo-structuralists* and even some interesting reflections by Sraffian economists (De Vivo and Pivetti, 1980) on developed countries' balance-of-payments problems.

This chapter develops a simple neo-Kaleckian analytical framework to analyse the consequences of foreign exchange constraint in a small open economy. More specifically, it extends Bastian and Setterfield (2020) – who developed a conflicting-claims inflation model for an open economy – as a means to incorporate the foreign exchange constraint into the analysis. Therefore, this chapter introduces a trade balance curve in the real exchange rate/real wage space, allowing for a combined analysis of a steady-state inflation equilibrium and an external equilibrium based on the hypothesis that a country under foreign exchange constraint cannot attract foreign capital by means of increasing domestic interest rates, meaning that it constantly needs to run a trade surplus.

As regards policy options, the combination of inflation targets and flexible exchange rates has been a fad in mainstream macroeconomic thinking since the late 1990s. However, some dissenting ideas have appeared outside the mainstream. In this chapter, we focus on the policy proposal of a stable and competitive real exchange-rate target as suggested by famous Argentinean economist Roberto Frenkel in the 2000s and endorsed by other economists in Argentina, Latin America and abroad. This case is especially interesting because Argentina at the time of Frenkel's writing was employing a stable and competitive real exchange-rate target regime and was under foreign exchange constraint. Hence, we use our analytical framework to discuss the short-term limits of a stable and competitive real exchange-rate targeting regime. For this purpose, we analyse the short-term impacts of three different policies and a shock: 1) progressive wage policies; 2) public consumption increase; and 3) industrial policies. Finally, we also analyse the impacts of positive terms of trade shocks.

The chapter is divided into two sections, besides the Introduction and the Conclusion. Following this discussion in the Introduction, section 6.2 provides an overview of some of the non-mainstream literature on foreign exchange constraint in the post-Second World War. In this context, we briefly present the main ideas concerning foreign exchange constraint of the Latin American structuralist school plus the dual-gap model, the balance-of-payments constrained growth and the propositions of Sraffian economists in the face of Italy's balance-of-payments problems in the late 1970s. Section 6.3 is the analytical part. It presents the Bastian and Setterfield (2020) model and extends it by developing the trade balance curve. It then explains the functioning of a stable and competitive real exchange-rate regime in such a model. Finally, it discusses the four cases listed earlier.

6.2   BRIEF NOTES ON THE LITERATURE ON FOREIGN EXCHANGE CONSTRAINT[2]

As previously noted in the Introduction, foreign exchange constraint became – in the first two decades after the Second World War – fundamentally a developing world challenge. Therefore, not surprisingly some of the most interesting works on the issue were written in developing countries or about their situation.

A key example of a contribution coming from the developing world consists of the work of the so-called Latin American Structuralist School (LASS), which evolved after the Second World War around the United Nations Economic Commission of Latin America (ECLAC) in Santiago, Chile. Starting with his 1949 *Latin American Manifesto*, Raúl Prebisch – LASS leading economist and ECLAC's general secretary – argued that there was a trend towards the deterioration of Latin American countries' terms of trade. This was due to their productive structure and their exports and imports basket, meaning a structure specialized on the production of commodities for the foreign market and a huge dependency of manufacturing imports. This structural profile was a characteristic of the *periphery* and was in sharp contrast with the *centre* wherein the productive structure was diversified (Prebisch, 1949). As Rodriguez (1977) observes, things got even worse for Latin American countries when the United States became the world's *leading cyclical centre* in the 1920s: whilst Britain used to be a heavy commodity importer, the US had a low imports coefficient (Rodríguez, 1977, pp. 212–213). Hence, Latin American countries were doomed to face chronic external deficits, meaning that foreign exchange constraint was a constant concern. As a result, industrialization by means of planning and development policies was ECLAC's recommendation for Latin American countries to overcome their structural fragilities.[3]

One problem of the structuralist school was the absence of formalized analysis of the problems it was discussing. In this sense, the dual-gap model approach did not face the same issue. The dual-gap model was developed in the Northern Hemisphere academia starting with the pioneering work of Chenery and Bruno (1962) on the Israeli economy. In a nutshell, dual-gap models 'discuss the interactions of the foreign exchange constraint and the savings constraint in the determination of the economic growth rate of a developing country' (Bacha, 1989, p. 214). Hence, they explicitly admit the foreign exchange constraint as a relevant factor impacting developing countries' growth rates. In this analysis, the foreign exchange constraint is a function for instance of the country's import share of investment and the highest predetermined export level, which depends on the world's demand growth (Bacha, 1989, p. 217).

Dual-gap models also found their way among a new generation of Latin American economists, sometimes referred to as *neo-structuralists*. They became to some extent popular in Latin America in the context of the external debt crisis of the early 1980s. A leading scholar in this group was Brazilian economist Edmar Bacha.[4] In the 1984 *Festschrift* in honour of Hollis Chenery, he presented for instance a formal two-gaps model of a *semi-industrialized* economy[5] wherein he extends Chenery and Bruno's (1962) model to include capital movements assuming the form of interest-bearing foreign debt (Bacha, 1984, pp. 264–265). Later, he proposed a three-gap model, wherein the third gap is a fiscal gap stemming from the government's budget constraint (Bacha, 1989).[6]

During the same period that neo-structuralist economists were employing and developing Chenery's original contribution, Thirlwall's (1979) paper gave rise to the so-called balance-of-payments constrained growth model literature. The paper's focus was on growth rate differences between developed countries, but Thirlwall himself believed that the points he raised were even more important to developing countries (Thirlwall, 1979, p. 46). In that paper, Thirlwall claimed a demand-driven economic system and argued that in an open economy the dominant constraint on demand expansion was the balance of payments. Accordingly, he observed that in the face of balance-of-payments difficulties, a country would need to curtail demand. Hence, this could prevent demand from expanding up to the existing productive capacity thus discouraging productive investment (Thirlwall, 1979, pp. 45–46). The overall consequence – which became known as Thirlwall's law – was that 'if a balance of payments equilibrium must be maintained, a country's long run growth rate will be determined by the ratio of growth of its exports to its income elasticity of demand for imports' (Thirlwall, 1979, p. 46). The main policy conclusion was that countries could increase their balance-of-payments equilibrium rate by means of increasing exports and/or reducing their income elasticity of demand for imports.

As previously noted, Thirlwall's paper gave rise to a broad literature on balance-of-payments constrained growth.[7] There were sundry papers testing empirically the validity of Thirlwall's law for many different countries. There were also theoretical extensions to Thirlwall (1979), for instance, the inclusion of financial flows in the original analysis.[8]

Finally, around the same period, De Vivo and Pivetti (1980) – two Sraffian economists[9] – analysed foreign exchange constraint in the case of a developed country, namely Italy. Their main concern was the limits to full employment due to balance-of-payments problems, arguing that 'the obstacles to full employment presented by a high import content of demand depend on the *form* of specialization as well as its overall level' (De Vivo and Pivetti, 1980, p. 2). Hence, they complained about Italy's productive specialization that emerged in the decades following the Second World War wherein exports grew at high rates, but in a context of rapid trade liberalization in which 'no efforts were made to check the rise in the import content of final demand' (De Vivo and Pivetti, 1980, p. 3).

According to De Vivo and Pivetti (1980), specialization makes a country's economic growth rate increasingly dependent on the rise in exports. Moreover, the type of specialization also matters in the sense that the more the country's exportable goods are subject to intense competition in the foreign market and/ or the more its imports are essential wage goods and means of production, then the more its economic growth rates are constrained by demand limits which the country can't overcome by means of domestic economic policy.

In the face of high imports share and balance-of-payments difficulties, the authors recommended, in the case of Italy, a combination of policies. On the one hand, they recommended selective and temporary import controls following criteria towards maximizing the reduction of the external constraint and simultaneously minimizing the negative impacts on real wages (De Vivo and Pivetti, 1980, pp. 16–18). On the other hand, they recommended direct industrial policies aimed at imports substitution, namely 'public investments in those sectors where domestic production currently supplies a low share of the domestic market' (De Vivo and Pivetti, 1980, p. 16). They regarded devaluations as deleterious due to their negative impact on real wages and the restrictive policies that usually follow them, which tend to reduce economic growth rates and employment levels.

In sum, there are differences within this sample of non-mainstream contributions on foreign exchange constraint. Whilst some offer a formal analysis of foreign exchange constraint, others are descriptive. There are examples of studies wherein the focus is on developed economies (Thirlwall, 1979; De Vivo and Pivetti, 1980), whereas others focus on developing economies (structuralist school, dual-gap model). Whilst most authors discuss the impact of the balance of payments on economic growth, De Vivo and Pivetti's (1980) focus is on employment levels. In any case, there is, though, one point that seems to be common to all of them: the importance of industrial policies as a means to overcome the problem of foreign exchange constraint. Although just a few explicitly recognize this point, it is a corollary that directly or indirectly stems from all the contributions in the sample, be it the reduction of the imports share by direct import substitution policy, the change in the composition of imports towards reducing the income elasticity of the demand for imports or the reduction of the imports share of investment. Hence, it is a matter of *how* to adopt industrial policies and not a matter of *if* industrial policies are a way of dealing with the constraining impacts of the balance of payments.

6.3   POSSIBILITIES AND LIMITS OF REAL EXCHANGE-RATE TARGETING UNDER FOREIGN EXCHANGE CONSTRAINT

6.3.1   Conflicting-Claims Inflation and Trade Balance

This chapter follows Bastian and Setterfield's (2020) open-economy conflicting-claims inflation model, which adapts and extends a model first developed by Blecker (2011) and Lavoie (2014). There are some advantages of following this way instead of the contributions discussed in section 6.2. The first is that it builds from a handbook model, namely Lavoie (2014). Non-mainstream economists usually have a *language* problem due to the diversity of approaches and models. Hence, building from a relatively well-known model makes it easier to communicate the ideas and thus advance the analysis. Secondly, Bastian and Setterfield (2020) already provide a framework for an open-economy conflicting-claims inflation analysis. Therefore, the inclusion of balance-of-payments issues gives a broad perspective since it allows a simultaneous short-term comparative static analysis of the inflation rate, the real wage, the real exchange rate and the trade balance.

In Bastian and Setterfield's (2020) model (BS henceforth), wage inflation and price inflation depend on workers' and firms' bargaining power and on their respective target real wages. Moreover, BS's model abstracts from productivity growth, meaning that real wage equals the wage share.[10] BS's model starts with:

$$w = \mu_1(\omega_w - \omega) \tag{6.1}$$

$$p = \varphi_2(\omega - \omega_f) \tag{6.2}$$

where w is wage inflation, ω is the current real wage, ω_w and ω_f are workers' and firms' target values of the real wage, respectively, and p is price inflation. The parameters μ_1 and φ_2 represent workers' and firms' bargaining power. Whilst workers' target real wage means the real wage that workers would like to receive, firms' target real wage indicates the real wage that firms would like to pay, which is associated with a certain target mark-up.[11] Workers' bargaining power indicates how much of their desired real wage workers can obtain by means of bargaining. The same holds for firms' bargaining power as regards the real wage they would like to pay. Equations 6.1 and 6.2 show that workers are pushing for real wage increases, whereas firms are pushing for real wage reductions. Unless firms or workers have absolute bargaining power, the actual real wage is always something in between workers' and firms' target real wage.[12]

Equations 6.1 and 6.2 describe a closed economy. As regards an open economy model, wage and price inflation also depend on how workers and firms incorporate the real exchange rate in their claims. According to Bastian and Setterfield (2020), 'workers and firms can be thought of as seeking to protect their preferred claims on total real income from the encroachment of the external sector' (Bastian and Setterfield, 2020, p. 1280). Hence, equations 6.3 and 6.4 show that firms' and workers' target real wages depend on an exogenous component (ω_{w0} and ω_{f0} respectively), and the value of the real exchange rate (e_R).

$$\omega_w = \omega_{w0} + \mu_2 e_R \tag{6.3}$$

$$\omega_f = \omega_{f0} - \varphi_2 e_R \tag{6.4}$$

By substituting equations 6.3 and 6.4 into equations 6.1 and 6.2, BS obtain their open-economy conflicting-claims model.

$$w = \mu_1([\omega_{w0} + \mu_2 e_R] - \omega) \tag{6.5}$$

$$p = \varphi_1(\omega - [\omega_{f0} - \varphi_2 e_R]) \tag{6.6}$$

As Figure 6.1 shows, there is a steady-state equilibrium real wage wherein wage inflation and price inflation curves intersect. This point also defines the equilibrium inflation rate. The model permits static comparative analyses, meaning that it is possible to compare two different periods, as regards the steady-state equilibrium point, after changes in one or some of the key variables in the model.[13]

Let us now extend BS's analysis to get some balance-of-payments insights. We start by defining a trade balance curve (TB curve) in the real wage/ real exchange rate space, representing combinations of real wages and real exchange rate levels wherein the trade balance equals zero ($tb = 0$). The TB curve is an upward sloping curve, meaning that higher real wages increase

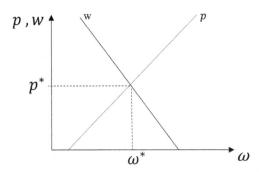

Source: author's elaboration based on Lavoie (2014) and Bastian and Setterfield (2020).

Figure 6.1   Conflicting-claims inflation

imports thus requiring a higher (devalued) real exchange rate to keep the trade balance equal to zero. In other words, we are implicitly assuming that this is a wage-led economy. Equation 6.7 represents the TB curve (see the appendix for technical details on how we derive the TB curve):

$$e_R = \tau + \left(\frac{\beta_u}{\beta_e}\right)\left(\frac{f_0}{\left[\theta(1-\omega)-f_2\right]}\right) \tag{6.7}$$

where: $\tau = \dfrac{-\left(\beta_0 + \beta_{uf}\,u_f\right)}{\beta_e}$

and: $\theta = s_r - f_1$

wherein the variables represent: the sensibility of the trade balance to changes in the domestic rate of capacity utilization (β_u), the sensibility of the trade balance to changes in the real exchange rate (β_e), exogenous factors affecting investment (f_0), the sensibility of investment to changes in domestic capacity utilization (f_2), the foreign rate of capacity utilization (μ_f), the sensibility of the trade balance to changes in the foreign rate of capacity utilization (β_{uf}), capitalists' propensity to save (s_r) and the sensibility of investment to changes in the profit rate (f_1).

The TB curve's slope depends on structural factors, for instance, the country's imports and exports' elasticities due to the parameter β_e. In this respect, we assume that the Marshall-Lerner condition holds, meaning that an increase in the real exchange rate improves the trade balance. More importantly, equation 6.7 makes sure that increasing real wages (ω) demand a higher real exchange rate (e_R) as a means to keep the trade balance equal to zero.

Figure 6.2 shows the positively sloped trade balance curve in the real wage/real exchange rate space. It also shows that points above the TB curve represent situations wherein there is a trade balance surplus, whereas points below it represent a trade balance deficit.

Combining Figures 6.1 and 6.2, Figure 6.3 defines the equilibrium levels of the real wage, the inflation rate and the real exchange rate that simultaneously guarantee a steady-state inflation rate and a balanced TB. The equilibrium rates are represented in Figure 6.3 by ω^*, p^* and e_R^*.

However, keeping the trade balance in equilibrium is not enough for countries under foreign exchange constraint. These countries – which are mostly developing countries – are usually exposed to a combination of external vulnerabilities: 1) low levels of international reserves and/or high levels of external debt; 2) huge external deficits in services and income; and 3) short access to foreign finance, meaning that keeping high domestic interest rates is almost useless as regards attracting foreign capital.[14] As a result, these countries need

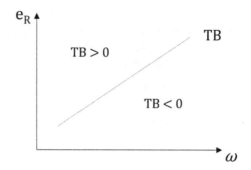

Source: author's elaboration.

Figure 6.2   Trade balance curve

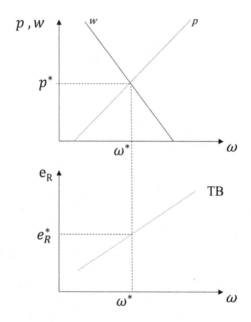

Source: author's elaboration.

Figure 6.3   External equilibrium

to run trade surpluses to generate current account surpluses or at least to pre-vent large current account deficits. This condition is mandatory for reducing the likelihood of a balance-of-payments crisis. Hence, their only sustainable combinations of real wage and real exchange rate are the ones above the TB curve.[15]

What is the best exchange rate regime for a country under these circumstances? Exchange rate anchoring – which is a kind of regime that developing countries have tried from time to time in the past – lost most of its appeal within the mainstream after the sequence of currency crises in the developing world in the 1990s. After these crises, inflation-targeting regimes became increasingly popular. The inflation targets were accompanied by an exchange rate policy based on dirty floating.[16]

In any case, there was a recent example of a developing country under foreign exchange constraint that opted for a kind of exchange rate anchor – namely a real exchange-rate targeting regime – with relative success. This country was Argentina, which used it during the first decade of the 2000s after the collapse of the convertibility regime in 2001–2002.[17] During this period, famous Argentinean economist Roberto Frenkel wrote a series of articles defending a *stable and competitive real exchange-rate targeting regime*, for instance Frenkel (2006), Frenkel and Ros (2006) and Frenkel and Taylor (2009).[18]

According to Frenkel (2006), 'a competitive real exchange rate leads to higher net exports and, consequently, to higher demand on local activities and higher output and employment levels' (Frenkel, 2006, p. 579). Besides the direct impacts of an increase in the tradable sector output and employment, Frenkel observed indirect positive effects, notably productivity growth acceleration thanks to the higher tradable sector output plus positive externalities to the non-tradable sector stemming from this higher productivity growth, including higher job generation (Frenkel, 2006, p. 579). Moreover, he argued that there was a strong case for real exchange-rate targeting when it comes to inflation control. Accordingly, he observed that the exchange rate is usually the trigger of inflation acceleration in Latin America. Hence, a regime wherein the monetary policy aims at avoiding fluctuations that affect the nominal exchange rate (and thus the real exchange rate) was supposed to be a good mechanism to prevent inflation spirals (Frenkel, 2006, p. 587).

The problem with Frenkel (2006) is that he apparently assumes that the economy is export-led. His analysis ignores the effects of a devalued real exchange rate on real wages and thus on domestic consumption. Frenkel and Ros (2006) provide a formal analysis of the effects of the real exchange rate on employment. In this paper, they defend the positive employment effects of the real exchange rate. However, they recognize the potential contractionary effects of an exchange rate devaluation due for instance to its negative impacts on real wages and thus on consumption. In this regard, they argue that 'the real devaluation should be implemented together with fiscal and monetary expansionary policies' (Frenkel and Ros, 2006, p. 635). The problem is that a country under foreign exchange constraint may not have the degrees of freedom to adopt expansionary policies. Hence, Frenkel and Ros's (2006) solution to prevent the regressive effects of the regime may not hold.[19]

What are then the challenges of real exchange-rate targeting in the context of a country under foreign exchange rate constraint? What are the likely outcomes in the face of external shocks and after the adoption of specific policies? Based on this neo-Kaleckian framework and on simple comparative static examples, the next section examines some short-run caveats of real exchange targeting in a country under foreign exchange constraint.

6.3.2   Real Exchange Rate Targeting

We propose here that real exchange-rate targeting means fixing the level of the real exchange rate, so that there is just one value of the real wage (ω^*) wherein the trade balance equals zero.[20] More importantly, a real exchange-rate targeting under foreign exchange rate constraint means sustaining the real exchange rate at a *competitive* rate,[21] so that the country runs a trade surplus.[22] Figure 6.4 shows that the equilibrium real wage corresponds to an equilibrium real exchange rate e_R^*, which is the level wherein the trade balance equals zero.

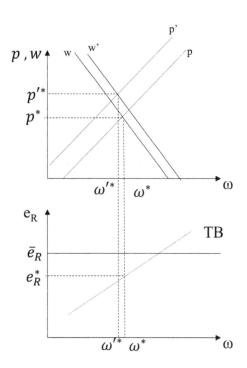

Source: author's elaboration.

Figure 6.4   Real exchange-rate targeting under foreign exchange constraint

Aiming at trade surplus, policymakers control the exchange rate to keep the real exchange rate devalued as regards this equilibrium real exchange rate e_R^*, meaning that the monetary authorities intervene in the nominal foreign exchange to keep the real exchange rate at a level $\bar{e}_R$ which is higher than e_R^*. At this competitive and stable real exchange rate $\bar{e}_R$, it would be in theory possible to increase real wages above ω^* up to the level wherein the trade balance equals zero. However, policymakers don't allow this wage increase due to the need to run a trade surplus. Moreover, such a policy of wage increase would not be free of side effects: the simultaneous rise in the real exchange rate and the real wage would increase the inflation rate. If inflation rates are too high there is the risk of an indexation process or more importantly the risk of a wage-price spiral.[23]

Based on this simple analytical framework, we now evaluate the real exchange-rate targeting regime in four different cases: 1) progressive wage policies; 2) public consumption increase; 3) positive terms of trade shock; and 4) industrial policies. The aim here is to develop some simple comparative static exercises, which can provide some stylized facts regarding the possibilities and limits of real exchange-rate targeting under foreign exchange constraint in the short term.

6.3.3 Policies and Shocks

6.3.3.1 Progressive wage policies

Progressive wage policies can be for instance rising minimum wages. As minimum wages are a reference for other wages within the economy, workers are likely to increase their target real wage in the face of a minimum wage increase. In our framework, this means an increase in the exogenous component of workers' target real wage ω_{w0}, thus leading them to increase their target real wage ω_w.

In a context of an economy facing foreign exchange constraint and adopting a real exchange rate target, this policy can be unsustainable, depending on the magnitude of the wage growth. The increase in real wages from the initial equilibrium real wage ω_0 to ω_1 would decrease or eliminate the country's trade surplus, exposing it to the risk of a short-term balance-of-payments crisis (see Figure 6.5). Hence, policymakers would have to give up the progressive wage policy or adjust the real exchange rate target, thus accepting a higher inflation rate and the risk – as previously noted in the last section – of a retaliatory dynamic between workers and capitalists, thus leading to a wage-price spiral in the way proposed by Bastian and Setterfield (2015).[24]

These results show the difficulty of adopting progressive wage policies in the face of a competitive real exchange rate regime. This is clearly the case in the context of foreign exchange constraint. In fact, most countries under such

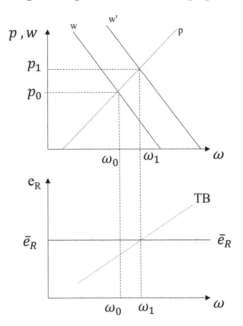

Source: author's elaboration.

Figure 6.5   Progressive wage policies

circumstances adopt regressive wage policies to help increase trade surplus or reverse trade deficits.[25] However, the situation is not radically different in normal times: if generating a large trade surplus is policymakers' purpose, then they are likely to keep the real wage undervalued.

In any case, it is worth noting that this is not an inescapable situation. Bastian and Setterfield (2020) observed that a *social pact* between classes is a strategy that can reduce losses for the working class and prevent wage-price spirals in the face of exchange rate devaluations. They called it a *social democratic model* in an obvious analogy to the experience of Western European countries during the so-called *Golden Age* following the Second World War. Nevertheless, they conceded that building such a pact is no easy task, especially when it comes to the developing world. In fact, such a partnership model demands a mature political debate and some previous developments as regards social institutions. Strong trade unions may be particularly mandatory to force the pact. As trade unions are increasingly weaker worldwide, models of this type may be getting less likely to succeed today than they were in the past.

6.3.3.2 Public consumption increase

Let's now analyse the impact of an expansionary fiscal policy in our model. However, as a starter, we shall clarify what we mean by it. In this chapter, we only take into consideration an expansionary fiscal policy that truly means a demand increase. Therefore, by expansionary fiscal policy, we mean public consumption or public investment increases, meaning that we exclude policies like tax reductions. Furthermore, we abstract the mid to long-term effects of increases in public expenses. As a result, we opt here to exclusively focus on public consumption increases because they are not capacity-creating expenses.

Starting from the analysis of the previous sections, a public consumption increase has indirect effects on the balance of payments in the context of the neo-Kaleckian framework applied in this study. For the sake of exemplifying, let's follow Setterfield (2006, p. 49) and suppose for instance that workers' bargaining power (μ) depends on one exogenous factor (β_μ) and on two endogenous factors, namely the unemployment rate (U) and institutions (I).[26] Hence, we define workers' bargaining power as follows:

$$\mu = \varphi_\mu - \varphi_U U - \varphi_I I \tag{6.8}$$

The idea that the bargaining power depends on unemployment rates in the way described here is controversial because it is in many ways unrealistic: it means that *any* increase or decrease in unemployment rates affects workers' bargaining power, whatever the current level of the unemployment rate. For instance, it is very unlikely that this relation holds in a depressed economy. A possible solution would be to suggest that below some unemployment level workers' bargaining power starts to increase. However, this would mean admitting a kind of NAIRU, which is something that most post-Keynesians would dislike.[27] There are some alternatives like considering that *falling* unemployment rates affect workers' bargaining power (Cassetti, 2003 *apud* Marie, 2010, p. 286). In other words, the bargaining power depends on the rate of change of the unemployment rate instead of its level. Finally, it is possible to define *corridors of stability* in the sense of different intervals of unemployment rates wherein the bargaining power is stable, so that it only increases when unemployment rates move beyond certain thresholds.[28] In sum, there is no easy fix as regards this issue, but the important message is that – in some way – unemployment rates affect workers' bargaining power.

Let's now consider a public consumption increase that reduces the unemployment rate in a way that increases workers' bargaining power. Figure 6.6 shows that the effect of this increase in workers' bargaining power is a change in the slope of the wage inflation curve and an increase in real wages. The

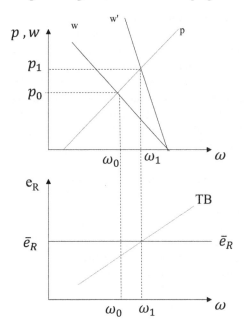

Source: author's elaboration.

Figure 6.6   Public consumption increase

final effect in Figure 6.6 is the same as in the previous case: the increase in workers' real wage eliminates the trade surplus.

The analysis shows that the combination of real exchange rate target and foreign exchange constraint limits the short-term use of public consumption increases. This limit depends though on the relation between public consumption effects on unemployment rates and workers' bargaining power, which is something out of the scope of this chapter. In any case, as previously observed, it questions Frenkel's suggestion of using expansionary fiscal policies as a means to compensate for real wage losses stemming from exchange rate devaluation. This is so at least in the case of countries facing foreign exchange constraint. However, it is worth noting that even in the absence of foreign exchange constraint, public consumption increases tend to reduce trade surplus which is one of the core targets of policymakers when they keep the real exchange rate at a stable and competitive level. Hence, if the target is obtaining a large trade surplus, then policymakers tend to keep real wages undervalued. The other (and more desirable) option would be to build a social pact in the way described in the last section, but as previously noted, this is a rather difficult task. In other words, a stable and competitive exchange rate policy usually comes in the short run with undervalued real wages.

6.3.3.3 Positive terms of trade shock

A positive shock in the terms of trade moves the TB curve to the right (see Figure 6.7).[29] This move opens the possibility of an expansionary wage policy since it becomes possible to sustain the initial trade surplus and simultaneously increase the real wage. There are in fact two possibilities: policymakers can either 1) opt for progressive wage policies and/or expansionary fiscal policies; or 2) keep the real wage rate as it is at ω_0 – by means of regressive income policies – as a means to generate a bigger trade surplus.[30] The decision depends on the country's external vulnerability level and on how sensitive policymakers are in relation to progressive policies and/or expansionary policies, which depend on political aspects concerning the conflicting claims between workers and capitalists over the gains stemming from the positive terms of trade shock.

For instance, in the first decade of the 2000s, there was a boom in commodity prices that increased the terms of trade of many developing countries,

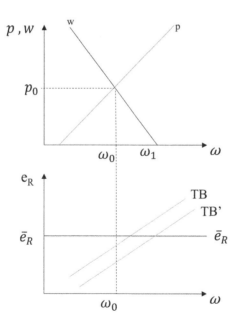

Source: author's elaboration.

Figure 6.7 Positive terms-of-trade shock

opening the space for progressive wage policies without risking balance-of-payments problems. Although not all of them had a real exchange-rate targeting regime, it is remarkable that many developing countries reduced poverty and income inequality during this decade. This was very much the case in Latin America wherein a series of left-wing coalitions were in power during this period and adopted policies towards reducing poverty and income inequality. This period of the first decade of the 2000s became known in Latin America as *post-neoliberalism* or *pink tide*.

The benefits of a positive terms-of-trade shock contrast with the deleterious effects of a negative shock in the terms of trade. Such a shock exacerbates the country's external vulnerability by reducing or eliminating its trade surplus. As a result, policymakers may opt for regressive wage policies as a means to preserve the trade surplus and avoid a balance-of-payments crisis.

6.3.3.4 Industrial policies

As previously noted in section 6.2, the non-mainstream literature on foreign exchange constraint usually suggests – directly or indirectly – that industrial policies play a decisive role when it comes to policies to overcome the problem. Up to this point, we have analysed different policies and shocks for a given productive structure. Let's now evaluate the impact of industrial policies in our analytical framework. Unlike the other policies addressed earlier, industrial policies are not short-term policies: they are aimed at fostering structural change, which is a long-term target. In any case, the framework proposed here provides some insights from comparative static analysis on how these policies can impact the economy in the long term and thus help improve the prospects of a country facing foreign exchange constraint.[31] Many developing countries are commodities exporters, which are mostly inelastic products as concerns the real exchange rate. Manufacturing products tend to be in general more responsive to the exchange rate than primary products. Therefore, industrial policies that for instance reduce the country's dependence on commodity exports tend to increase export elasticity to the exchange rate and trade balance elasticity to the exchange rate. In terms of the equations, it means increasing the value of the parameter β_e, thus making the TB curve flatter as Figure 6.8 shows (see also equation 6.7). Hence, industrial policies open the space – for a given real exchange rate – for higher real wages in the long term or, alternatively, to obtain a higher trade surplus for a given real wage and a given real exchange rate.[32] The opposite happens in the case of a *deindustrialization* process wherein the TB curve becomes more vertical thus calling for a reduction in the real wage.

There are, though, some important notes as regards the potential of industrial policies nowadays. In a world of global value chains, countries' exports depend increasingly more on imported inputs and their imports

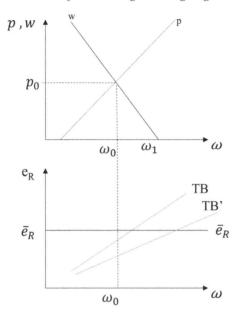

Source: author's elaboration.

Figure 6.8   Industrial policies

incorporate more of their own exports. In such a context, traditional industrial policies – based on import substitution or export promotion – are less likely to succeed (Milberg et al., 2014, p. 173). Furthermore, a process of industrial concentration has been happening in all relevant sectors and their sub-sectors, meaning that smaller firms from developing countries will find it increasingly harder to catch up and compete for markets against the world's top multinationals (Nolan, 2012, p. 17). Finally, there are challenges regarding climate change and a probable new wave of automation due to artificial intelligence. In sum, there are new challenges and demands, meaning that countries need to develop new forms of industrial policy for the 21st century.[33]

In any case, it is worth emphasizing that industrial policies have not lost their importance. Industrial policies are still mandatory as many countries indicate by their initiatives regarding Industry 4.0 and/or proposals of a *Green New Deal*. The COVID-19 pandemic also showed the importance of depending less on imported inputs and technology, especially as concerns the health care sector. In sum, industrial policies are changing, but they remain important, and for developing countries under foreign exchange constraint, they are still a key asset if they are to overcome or at least reduce their external vulnerability.

6.4   CONCLUSION

This chapter developed a simple analytical framework to deal with conflicting-claims inflation and balance-of-payments issues in a country under foreign exchange constraint. For this purpose, it built on the previous work by Blecker (2011), Lavoie (2014) and especially Bastian and Setterfield (2020). The analytical framework was used to analyse the limits of a stable and competitive real exchange-rate targeting regime in a country under these circumstances. More specifically, it evaluated the regime – by means of comparative static exercises – in four different cases: 1) progressive wage policies; 2) public consumption increase; 3) positive terms of trade shock; and 4) industrial policies.

The exercises showed that such a regime limits – at least in the short term – the space for progressive wage policies and public consumption increase. This is so because it needs *ceteris paribus* to prevent real wages from rising as a means to guarantee trade surplus, taking into account that wage changes affect the trade balance. In other words, other things being equal, the only way to sustain in the short term a competitive real exchange rate target and a trade surplus is by keeping real wages undervalued.

The exercises showed, though, that a positive terms-of-trade shock – which is an exogenous shock – can open room for these expansionary policies because it reduces the foreign exchange constraint. Furthermore, they showed that the type of policy that is under government control and that it can employ to increase the space for real wage increases is industrial policy. There seems to be an implicit consensus in this regard when it comes to the literature on foreign exchange constraint discussed in section 6.2 of the chapter, though current industrial policies ought to be different from the models of the past due to changes in industrial organization and contemporary challenges like climate change. In sum, the chapter concluded that the elimination of the constraints on real wage increases – due to the combination of real exchange-rate targeting and/or foreign exchange constraint – depends on:

1) *good luck* in the form of positive terms-of-trade shocks or
2) *good policy* by means of industrial policies.

NOTES

1.   The author would like to thank Caio Vilella, Carlos Pinkusfeld Bastos, Ítalo Pedrosa, Jonathan Marie, Mark Setterfield, Nicolás Burotto Ravanal and Numa Mazat for their helpful comments. Any remaining errors are my own.
2.   This section does not intend to provide a complete list of contributions on the foreign exchange constraint debate. The purpose is to pick a sample of heterodox contributions on the topic, containing contributions of authors from different schools of thought from

within the broad group of non-mainstream economists, whose analyses offer interesting insights on the issue.

3. According to Rodríguez (1977), there was a sort of spontaneous industrialization in the periphery in the 1930s due to the huge crisis in the centre and the change in the leading cyclical centre. However, balance of payments reappeared in the midst of the spontaneous industrialization process. Hence, only by means of planning and developing policies could Latin American countries overcome these balance-of-payments structural barriers.

4. Bacha (1986) provides what is perhaps the best definition of what *neo-structuralism* is about. In the Introduction of this 1986 book – which consists of a selection of his essays – he acknowledges the structuralist roots of his ideas and adds that 'I would like these essays to be regarded as exercises in the art of using modern analytical techniques as a means to elaborate the view on Latin American economy proposed by Prebisch, Furtado, Noyola and Pinto' (Bacha, 1986, p. 7).

5. According to Bacha, a 'semi industrialized economy is an economy which exports the same product that it consumes domestically. A newly industrializing country fits this conception better than a primary economy' (Bacha, 1984, p. 264).

6. From a Keynesian perspective, assuming the existence of a *fiscal constraint* is a rather disputable idea.

7. McCombie and Roberts (2002) termed Thirlwall (1979) as the *standard* balance-of-payments constrained growth model.

8. Setterfield (2011) praises Thirlwall's law's *remarkable durability* and provides an overview of the the theoretical extensions and the empirical literature on it.

9. By Sraffians, we mean the followers of the theoretical approach that combines the classical theory of value and prices – after Sraffa's (1960) reappraisal – plus the theory of output based on effective demand as proposed by Keynes and Kalecki in the 1930s.

10. If labour productivity grows faster than the real wage, then there is the possibility of a simultaneous rise in real wages and fall in the wage share. As there is no change in productivity growth in this model, an increase (fall) in the wage share always means an equivalent fall (increase) in the profit share.

11. Lavoie (2014) observes that 'a target set in terms of real wages can always be made equivalent to a target set in terms of a mark-up. Provided there is no change in productivity, it is thus indifferent to assume that both firms and workers set real-wage targets, or that they both set mark-up targets' (Lavoie, 2014, p. 549). In this chapter, we follow Lavoie (2014) and Bastian and Setterfield (2015, 2020), so that we assume that firms and workers set targets in terms of a real wage.

12. In case workers have absolute bargaining power, then the actual real wage equals workers' target real wage. The contrary is valid in case firms have absolute bargaining power, meaning that the actual real wage equals firms target real wage.

13. Unlike other analyses of conflicting-claims inflation – for instance, Lavoie (2014) – this study ignores the possibility of deflation. Hence, Figure 6.1 shows no negative values for price inflation.

14. Serrano (1998) observed that this was for instance the case in Brazil in the 1980s during the debt crisis.

15. As higher domestic interest rates are practically useless as regards attracting foreign capital to compensate current account deficits, we abstract the interest rate from our analysis.

16. For a list of arguments in favor of inflation-targeting regimes and against exchange rate anchoring from a mainstream perspective, see Mishkin (2007).

17. For an account of Argentina's performance in the five first years of the *stable and competitive real exchange rate regime*, see Frenkel and Rapetti (2008). For a critical review of the regime's performance in Argentina until the early 2010s, see Bastian and Soihet (2012).

18. At the same time in Brazil, a group of economists led by former Finance Minister Luiz Carlos Bresser Pereira started defending similar ideas. They call themselves *new developmentalists*.

19. There is a further negative impact of devaluations, namely their effects on the external debt in domestic currency, which may affect domestic consumption.

20. BS's model 'treats the nominal exchange rate as a residual adjusting variable that accommodates an equilibrium configuration comprising a determinate real wage and rate of inflation and a given real exchange rate' (Bastian and Setterfield, 2020, p. 1282). In the context of a real exchange rate regime, the adjustment results from the central bank acting in the foreign exchange market.
21. A competitive rate can have different meanings. We follow Frenkel (2006), who argues that "a competitive real exchange rate involves the distortion of relative prices in favor of tradable activities against non-tradable activities" (Frenkel, 2006, p. 579), thus leading to higher net exports. Moreover, the idea of a competitive rate here refers to policy-makers' perceptions and preferences. For an interesting analysis dealing with societal perceptions regarding the sensitivity to exchange rate devaluations and appreciations, see Gevorkyan and Khemraj (2019).
22. Depending on the country's international reserves levels, it can for instance run trade deficits for some time without risking an immediate balance-of-payments crisis. We abstract from these cases for the sake of simplicity.
23. For a discussion on the likelihood of a wage-price spiral and its consequences, see Bastian and Setterfield (2015).
24. It is worth noting that the trigger of the retaliatory dynamic can stem from both workers and capitalists.
25. In Argentina, the huge trade surplus of the first years of the stable and competitive real exchange rate targeting regime faded in the face of increasing real wages and inflation in the late 2000s. For details, see Bastian and Soihet (2012).
26. According to Setterfield (2006), the variable *Institutions* (I) 'captures the effects of institutional features of the labor market that create employment and/or income insecurity among workers' (Setterfield, 2006, p. 49).
27. Stockhammer (2008) may be an exception because he argues that NAIRU is compatible with heterodox theories.
28. Lavoie (2010) proposes a similar hypothesis, but in relation to levels of capacity utilization.
29. The terms-of-trade shock does not need to be a temporary shock, whose effects rapidly disappear. It can be a shock representing a lasting change like the one stemming from the commodities boom in the 2000s, which kept commodity at high and increasing levels for years, due for instance to China's emergence as a giant commodity importer.
30. As policymakers need to keep the real exchange rate stable and competitive, this means that – in the face of a positive terms of trade shock – the central bank needs to act in the foreign exchange market by means for instance of the accumulation of international reserves.
31. Industrial policies can have short-term fiscal impacts. We abstract this issue from the analysis here since the purpose is simply to evaluate the long-term comparative static impact of industrial policies.
32. As previously noted in the case of a positive terms-of-trade shock, there is a *potential* for progressive wage policies, but it all depends on policymakers' choices, which depend on the political dimension of the conflicting claims between workers and capitalists.
33. See Bastian and Setterfield (2020, pp. 1289–1290) for these points and some additional issues regarding industrial policies, especially in regard to new forms of industrial policy for the present and future. Medeiros (2019) provides a deep and updated analysis of historical and contemporary industrial policies.

REFERENCES

Bacha, E. 1984. Growing with limited supplies of foreign exchange: A reappraisal of the two-gap model. In: Syrquin, M., Taylor, L., Westphal, L. E. (eds.). *Economic Structure and Performance – Essays in Honor of Hollis B. Chenery*. Orlando: Academic Press, pp. 263–280.

Bacha, E. 1986. *El milagro y la crisis: economia brasileña y latinoamericana – ensayos de Edmar L. Bacha*. Ciudad de Mexico: Fondo de Cultura Económica.

Bacha, E. 1989. Um modelo de três hiatos. *Pesquisa e Planejamento Econômico*, 19(2): 213–232.

Bastian, E. F., and Setterfield, M. 2015. A simple analytical model of the adverse real effects of inflation. *Journal of Post Keynesian Economics*, 38(4): 637–665.

Bastian, E. F., and Setterfield, M. 2020. Nominal exchange rate shocks and inflation. *Cambridge Journal of Economics*, 44: 1271–1299.

Bastian, E. F., and Soihet, E. 2012. Argentina y Brasil: desafíos macroeconómicos. In *Problemas del Desarrollo*, 43(171). México: iiec-UNAM, octubre-diciembre, pp. 83–109.

Blecker, R. A. 2002. Distribution, demand and growth in neo-Kaleckian macro-models. In: Setterfield, M. (ed.). *The Economics of Demand-Led Growth Challenging the Supply-Side Vision of the Long Run*. Cheltenham: Edward Elgar.

Blecker, R. A. 2011. Open economy models of distribution and growth. In: Hein, E., and Stockhammer, E. (eds.). *A Modern Guide to Keynesian Macroeconomics and Economic Policies*. Cheltenham, UK: Edward Elgar, pp. 215–239.

Cassetti, M. 2003. Bargaining power, effective demand and technical progress: A Kaleckian model of growth. *Cambridge Journal of Economics*, 26: 449–464.

Chenery, Hollis B., and Bruno, M. 1962. Development alternatives in an open economy: The case of Israel. *Economic Journal*, 72: 79–103.

De Vivo, G., and Pivetti, M. 1980. International Integration and the balance of payments constraint: The case of Italy. *Cambridge Journal of Economics*, 4: 1–22.

Frenkel, R. 2006. An alternative to inflation targeting in Latin America: Macroeconomic policies focused on employment. *Journal of Post Keynesian Economics*, 28(4): 573–591.

Frenkel, R., and Rapetti, M. 2008. Five years of competitive and stable real exchange rate in Argentina, 2002–2007. *International Review of Applied Economics*, 22(2): 215–226.

Frenkel, R., and Ros, J. 2006. Unemployment and the real exchange rate in Latin America. *World Development*, 34(4): 631–646.

Frenkel, R., and Taylor, L. 2009. Real exchange rate, monetary policy and employment: Economic development in a garden of forking paths. In: Epstein, Gerald A., and Yeldan, Erinc (eds.). *Beyond Inflation Targeting*. Cheltenham: Edward Elgar.

Gevorkyan, A., and Khemraj, T. 2019. Exchange rate targeting and gold demand by central banks: Modeling international reserves composition. *Emerging Markets Finance and Trade*, 55(1): 168–180.

Hein, E., and Vogel, L. 2008. Distribution and growth reconsidered: Empirical results for six OECD countries. *Cambridge Journal of Economics*, 32(3): 479–511.

Lavoie, M. 2010. Taming the new consensus: Hysteresis and some other post Keynesian amendments. In: Fontana, Giuseppe, and Setterfield, Mark (eds.). *Macroeconomic Theory and Macroeconomic Pedagogy*. New York: Palgrave Macmillan.

Lavoie, M. 2014. *Post-Keynesian Economics: New Foundations*. Cheltenham: Edward Elgar.

Marie, J. 2010. Inflation in Argentina during the second peronist period (1973–76): A post-Keynesian interpretation. *Review of Political Economy*, 22(2): 281–299.

McCombie, J., and Roberts, M. 2002. The role of the balance of payments in economic growth. In: Setterfield, M. (ed.). *The Economics of Demand-Led Growth Challenging the Supply-Side Vision of the Long Run*. Cheltenham: Edward Elgar.

Medeiros, C. 2019. Industrial policies and international division of labor. *Brazilian Journal of Political Economy*, 39(1): 71–87.

Milberg, W., Jiang, X., and Gereffi, G. 2014. Industrial policy in the era of vertically specialized industrialization. In Salazar-Xirinachs, J. M., Nubler, I., and Kozul-Wright, R. (eds.). *Transforming Economies: Making Industrial Policy Work for Growth, Jobs and Development*. Geneva: International Labour Office, pp. 151–178.

Mishkin, F. 2007. *Monetary Policy Strategy*. Cambridge: The MIT Press.

Nolan, P. 2012. *Is China Buying the World?* Cambridge: Polity Press.

Prebisch, R. 1949. *El desarrollo económico de la América Latina y algunos de sus principales problemas*. Santiago: CEPAL, 1949.

Rodriguez, O. 1977. Sobre la concepción del Sistema centro-periferia. *Revista de la Cepal*, 1st semester: 203–247.

Serrano, F. 1998. Tequila ou Tortilha? Notas sobre a Economia Brasileira nos 90. *Archétypon*, 6: 18.

Setterfield, M. 2006. Balancing the macroeconomic books on the backs of workers: A simple analytical political economy model of contemporary US capitalism. *International Journal of Political Economy*, 35: 46–63.

Setterfield, M. 2011. The remarkable durability of Thirlwall's law. *PSL Quarterly Review*, 64(259): 393–427.

Stockhammer, E. 2008. Is the NAIRU theory a Monetarist, New Keynesian, Post Keynesian or a Marxist theory? *Metroeconomica*, 59: 3.

Thirlwall, A. P. 1979. The balance of payments constraint as an explanation of international growth rates differences. *Banca Nazionale del Lavoro Quarterly Review*, 128: 45–53.

APPENDIX

Deriving the TB Curve

We start by writing equation 6.5, which comes from Lavoie (2014) based on Hein and Vogel (2008) and Blecker (2011). It shows that the trade balance (tb) 'is a linear function of the real exchange rate (e_R), the domestic rate of capacity utilization μ and the foreign rate of domestic utilization μ_f with parameters β_u and β_{uf} assumed to be positive' (Lavoie, 2014, p. 532). The parameter β_e depends on the price elasticities of imports and exports.

$$tb = \beta_0 + \beta_e\, e_R - \beta_u\, u + \beta_{uf}\, u_f \tag{6.9}$$

In the TB curve, $tb = 0 \Rightarrow \beta_e e_R = \beta_u u - \left(\beta_0 + \beta_{uf} u_f \right)$

$$e_R = \tau + \left(\frac{\beta_u}{\beta_e} \right) u \tag{6.10}$$

where $\tau = \dfrac{-\left(\beta_0 + \beta_{uf} u_f \right)}{\beta_e}$

Following Blecker (2002), we know that the investment function (g^i) in the neo-Kaleckian canonical model depends on the profit rate (r) and capacity utilization (u), whereas the savings function depends on capitalists' propensity to save (s_r) and the profit rate (r).

$$g^i = f_0 + f_1 r + f_2 u \tag{6.11}$$

$$g^s = s_r r \tag{6.12}$$

And the profit rate depends on the profit share (Π) and capacity utilization (u):

$$r = \Pi u \tag{6.13}$$

Substituting 6.9 in 6.8 and setting $g^i = g^s$, we come to equation 6.9, which links capacity utilization with the profit share. It reflects goods market equilibrium. Blecker (2002) calls it neo-Kaleckian 'IS curve' (Blecker, 2002, p. 133)

$$u = \frac{f_0}{\left[\left(s_r - f_1 \right) \Pi - f_2 \right]} \tag{6.14}$$

As previously noted, productivity growth equals zero in this model, meaning that the wage share equals the real wage (ω). As the profit share (Π) equals $(1 - \omega)$, one reaches the TB curve by substituting equation 6.14 in 6.10.

$$e_R = \tau + \left(\frac{\beta_u}{\beta_e}\right)\left(\frac{f_0}{\left[\theta(1-\omega)-f_2\right]}\right)$$

where $\theta = s_r - f_1$.

7. Optimal foreign-exchange reserves in small open economies: the case of the Caribbean

Dave Seerattan

7.1   INTRODUCTION

The recent international financial crisis highlighted the need to hold adequate reserves to help countries deal with the fallout from negative international shocks. Indeed, much of the focus of the international community in the wake of the crisis was focused on crafting liquidity mechanisms to help countries deal with problems related to sudden stops in capital flows to many developing countries. Adequate reserves serve as a buffer to help smooth consumption during these turbulent periods and help prevent output losses that can significantly damage a country's development trajectory.

In fact, Dominguez et al. (2012) found that countries that pursued robust reserve accumulation prior to the crisis achieved higher levels of post-crisis growth. Feldstien (1999) also concluded in the aftermath of the Asian financial crisis, that countries could not rely on the IMF or reforms to the international financial architecture to protect them from crises. Even prudent macroeconomic policies could not protect countries since such policies did not prevent contagion from other markets because of increasing financial integration. Feldstien (1999) argued that self-protection through increased international liquidity in the form of adequate levels of foreign reserves was the best way to protect countries from the impact of financial crises and reversals in capital flows during periods of extreme risk aversion in international financial markets.[1]

The small open economies of the Caribbean are vulnerable to a variety of economic shocks including terms-of-trade volatility and sudden stops in capital flows. Additionally, they are exposed to frequent natural disasters which cause huge dislocations in their productive capacity given their small land masses. They also face structural weaknesses such as high levels of sovereign debt, low international competitiveness and underdeveloped financial markets. These countries are also predominantly fixed exchange rate regime countries which require them to have adequate international reserves to help deal with temporary imbalances on the external accounts while maintaining the peg. This has resulted in a situation where the region not only faces more frequent shocks but their capacity to respond to these shocks is compromised by structural weaknesses.

Moreover, many countries in the region do not have ready access to private foreign capital and have to rely on official development finance which takes time to access and is often not sufficient to meet the financing needs of these countries. In this context, an adequate level of international reserves is of paramount importance since it offers immediate access to hard currency in a crisis which helps avoid large decreases in consumption and growth. Indeed, it could be argued that the level of international reserves that is deemed optimal in the Caribbean may in all likelihood be higher relative to more resilient countries. Another important consideration is that amassing reserves ad infinitum can be a problem since holding reserves involve costs related to productive investment forgone to hold low-yielding reserve assets. The higher the level of reserves above the optimal level the greater the costs countries have to bear.

An optimal level of reserves to address contingencies created by their unique vulnerabilities is, therefore, a critical development policy issue in the Caribbean. Many countries in the region have, however, struggled to meet even the popular three-month import cover rule of thumb benchmark (see Figures 7.1 and 7.2). Most countries have only managed to achieve levels above this benchmark in the wake of the 2007–2008 international financial crisis when there was a concerted effort in the region to increase international reserve buffers to help mitigate the effect of the crisis, but this was achieved mostly through significant increases in foreign debt. This implies that the levels of reserves in the region may not be optimal in the context of their high levels of vulnerability to shocks and structural weaknesses.

This chapter, therefore, seeks to determine the optimal level of reserves for the small open economies in the Caribbean using a cost-benefit approach predicated on the insurance role of reserves. The study provides data-driven estimates of the benefit of reserves in terms of the mitigation of the impact of negative shocks, as well as the opportunity cost in terms of growth forgone by holding excessive reserves. The cost-benefit approach argues that the optimal reserve level is the point where the marginal cost of holding reserves equals its marginal benefit (Dabla-Norris et al., 2011; Calvo et al., 2012; Moore and Glean, 2016). Moreover, the chapter seeks to take explicit account of how structural features impact the amount of international reserves that is optimal to provide the necessary insurance against shocks while minimizing the costs associated with holding reserves.

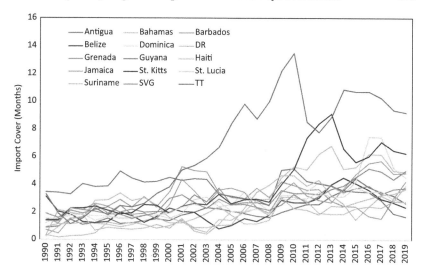

Source: World Bank, World Development Indicators.

Figure 7.1   Caribbean import cover

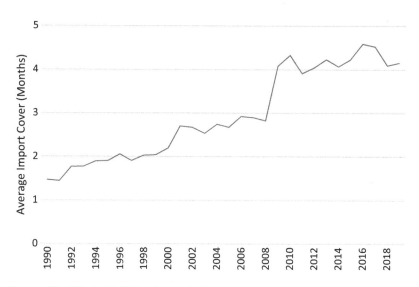

Source: World Bank, World Development Indicators.

Figure 7.2   Caribbean average import cover

7.2   LITERATURE REVIEW

There is an ongoing debate in the literature on the factors, as well as the weight of the factors that determine the optimal level of international reserves. There is also evidence that the determinants of optimal reserves change over time and may have a non-linear relationship (Delatte and Fouquau, 2011; Ghosh et al., 2017). As a result, there is no consensus on the best approach to measuring reserve optimality (Mwase, 2012). Aizenman and Lee (2007) argue that the reasons for holding reserves can be divided into precautionary and mercantilist motives.

The mercantilist motive[2] is driven by the need to weaken the domestic currency to promote export-led growth (Dooley et al., 2007). It is argued that this is a motive amongst Asian countries. There are a number of studies seeking to determine the degree to which mercantilist or precautionary motives account for international reserve accumulation. This literature generally finds that both motives have some influence (Aizenman and Lee, 2007; Jeanne, 2007). However, the evidence for the relative importance of the mercantilist motive is not very strong (Ghosh et al., 2014).

The precautionary motive is motivated by the need to insure against negative international shocks, especially sudden stops in capital flows (Jeanne and Rancière, 2011) or capital flight by domestic agents (Obstfeld et al., 2010). Under the rubric of the precautionary motive, a large stockpile of reserves can also serve to deter currency speculation (De Gregorio, 2014) including when it is linked to rivalry amongst countries, the so-called *Joneses effect* (Cheung and Qian, 2009), where a high level of reserves compared to regional peers can deter currency speculation. This is likely to be the motive when reserves are high but not used intensively.

A further extension under the precautionary motive framework involves the policy trilemma challenge where central banks are faced with trying to maintain financial stability while limiting excessive currency volatility in an environment of increasing international financial integration (Obstfeld et al., 2010). Under this framework, reserves help to protect the domestic financial system while limiting currency volatility in the context of increasingly open financial systems, leading to a tight correlation between reserves and measures of financial openness, financial development and exchange rate policy (exchange rate regime indicator).

In terms of the literature on the Caribbean, Dehesa et al. (2009) utilized the optimal reserve model that was developed by Jeanne (2007) to measure the optimal reserve levels in the Eastern Caribbean Currency Union (ECCU). Recent trends indicate that these countries may have held reserves above the necessary level but they argue that given the types of shocks that these islands are exposed to they can be considered adequate. Also, what seemed to be an excessively high level of reserve holdings by countries prior to the international financial crisis does not appear to be as sub-optimal in the aftermath of the crisis. They also argue that the liberalization of the capital account is a key factor in the determination of optimal reserves since reserves now not only have to insure against adverse current account shocks but also adverse capital account developments. They concluded that while the current holdings of the ECCU would be an effective buffer against current account and very small capital account shocks, the possibility of severe capital outflows would not. Hence, with increased global financial interconnectedness and deepening through the liberalization of the capital account it may become necessary for the Eastern Caribbean Central Bank to increase its reserve holdings to cover unfavourable capital flows. Nevertheless, the opportunity cost associated with this approach may be too costly to insure against an event that has such a small tail risk.

Carasco et al. (2013) utilized four methods to assess reserve adequacy in the Caribbean. These included simple ratio analysis, combined factor ratio analysis (Mwase, 2012; IMF, 2011), estimation and forecasting of reserve demand (Edison, 2003; Gosselin and Parent, 2005), as well as a rational optimizing behaviour modelling approach applying optimization frameworks developed by Jeanne and Ranciere (2006), Jeanne (2007) and Barnichon (2009). They found that different methods generated different optimal reserve results with optimal reserve levels changing across countries and time. They did find that there was significant evidence of reserves being below optimal reserve levels to be of concern for policymakers.

Barnichon (2009) used an optimizing heterogeneous-agents model to determine optimal reserves as insurance against natural disasters and terms-of-trade shocks. The calibration of optimal reserves using this model was sensitive to the choice of different parameters. He concluded that the optimal reserve level to adequately cover both risks was approximately two months of imports which is below the historical average for the region of 2.95 months of import cover.

Moore and Glean (2016) used a cost-benefit approach where the benefit of reserves is its insurance against shocks which helps prevent output losses and the costs related to domestic investments forgone to hold foreign low-yielding reserve assets. Their analysis suggests that the average optimal reserve level for the region was 6.25 months of import cover.

It should be noted that these estimates of optimal reserves for the region constitute a lower bound of optimal reserves since most studies assume risk neutrality but many countries are risk-averse, especially during crisis periods and, more importantly, many countries accumulate reserves for reasons above and beyond insurance against external shocks such as to defend pegged exchange rate regimes, to increase the confidence of foreign agents in the domestic economy (which helps boost foreign investments and lower borrowing costs), supporting liquidity in the local foreign exchange market and for intergenerational savings (Dabla-Norris et al., 2011).

7.3   METHODOLOGY AND DATA

This chapter adopts the cost-benefit approach to the estimation of optimal reserves used in other studies such as Dabla-Norris et al. (2011), Calvo et al. (2012) and Moore and Glean (2016). The benefit of reserves is the insurance it provides against shocks to avoid these events causing significant reductions in economic growth. The opportunity cost of reserves in this framework is the financial costs related to the differential between lower-yielding reserve assets and higher-yielding financial assets available to the monetary authorities, as well as the domestic investments forgone and therefore the lower growth implications of holding these low-yielding foreign reserve assets. Countries have to find the optimal balance between the opportunity costs of holding reserves and the benefit of the buffer that reserves provide in the event of a large shock. Following Calvo et al. (2012), the monetary authority is seeking to minimize the following loss function:

$$L(R) = P(S = 1 \mid R)OC(R \mid S = 1) + \rho R$$

where R is international reserves, P is the probability of a shock conditional on reserves, OC is the output cost conditional on a shock and ρR is the opportunity cost of reserves. In this framework, the probability of a shock and the output costs are both conditional on reserves; therefore, optimal reserves can be defined as:

$$R^* = arg \min_{R>0} L(R) = P(R)OC(R) + \rho R$$

Optimal reserves are therefore dependent on the balance between the marginal benefit reserves confer in terms of the minimization of output losses when large shocks occur and the opportunity costs of holding too many reserves.

As noted earlier, the opportunity cost of reserves is not only the financial cost related to investing in lower-return reserve assets rather than higher-return alternative financial assets available to the monetary authorities but also the costs related to not using more of these reserves for growth-enhancing public domestic investments. In Caribbean countries where there are significant infrastructural gaps that restrain growth, the latter component of the opportunity cost of reserves is likely to be much greater than the former component.

Moreover, Dabla-Norris et al. (2011) argued that developing countries that have limited access to financial markets and depend on concessional financing may have negative financial costs associated with reserves since the average interest rate on concessional financing may be lower than the return on the reserve portfolio. In this context, the growth forgone by investing in reserve assets rather than the growth-enhancing public investments is the proxy used for the opportunity costs of reserves in this study (Moore and Glean, 2016).

In the empirical work, the study, therefore, estimates the benefits of reserves using a probit model of the probability of crises conditional on the level of reserves. This is then combined with estimates for expected losses in growth from crises to determine the benefit reserves conferred on countries. The expected losses for growth due to crises and the cost of reserves on growth from public investments forgone to hold reserves are estimated through a fixed-effects panel growth model (Moore and Glean, 2016). This study improves on the previous literature by focusing on Caribbean countries which have unique vulnerabilities, especially the frequency of natural disasters,[3] which would affect the accuracy of estimates of optimal reserves since other countries have less vulnerability in this area and therefore would bias the average optimal reserve holding for this larger group of developing countries downward.

This chapter uses annual data spanning the period 1990–2019 for 15 Caribbean countries.[4] The relevant data such as foreign reserves, per capita GDP growth, FDI, remittances, openness, population growth, sovereign debt, capital formation, government expenditure, global growth, M2 and exchange-rate regime were sourced from the World Bank World Development Indicators Database, the IMF World Economic Outlook Database, the UNECLAC Database and regional central banks. The data on natural disasters were sourced from the EM-DAT database.

7.4　EMPIRICAL ANALYSIS

7.4.1　Identification of Crisis Events

An important element of this section is the identification of crisis events. In this regard, the methodology adopted by Dabla-Norris et al. (2011) is followed with some modifications.[5] In particular, shocks are first identified based on the percentage change in one or more of country-specific variables which tend to mirror crises, such as FDI, remittances, gross capital formation and natural disasters. Common global shocks identified using global growth are also included. Shocks are identified as values that fall below the 10 percentile in the left tail of country-specific distributions in the case of FDI, remittances and gross capital formation. The same applies to the common shocks from global growth. In the case of natural disasters (where we only include hurricanes and major earthquakes) we modify the way shocks are defined by including each event as a shock due to their general destructive impact. Identifying shocks this way leads to shocks being 26.2 per cent of all observations.[6] Crisis events are then identified from these shocks when they are accompanied by negative growth. Defined this way crisis events constitute 19.1 per cent of all observations.

7.4.2   Probit Model: Estimation of the Probability of Crisis

We use a probit model to estimate the probability of crisis for 15 Caribbean countries over the period 1990 to 2019. The crisis variable is the dependent variable and takes on a value of 1 in crisis years and 0 otherwise. The final model[7] included explanatory variables critical to our analysis such as reserves (as a percentage of GDP), natural disasters and per capita economic growth. Reserves and economic growth are expected to be negatively related to the probability of crises while natural disasters should increase the probability of crises. It also includes economic fundamentals which impact the probability of crisis such as FDI inflows, trade openness (imports plus exports of goods and services), increases in sovereign debt and broad money (M2) all included as a percentage of GDP (Dabla-Norris et al., 2011; Moore and Glean, 2016). FDI inflows and trade openness[8] are expected to be negatively related to the probability of crisis while debt and M2 (the size of domestic financial liabilities that can be converted into foreign currency and therefore negatively impact financial stability; Obstfeld et al., 2010) variables are expected to be positively related to the probability of a crisis. Global growth and a measure of external sector weakness (imports/exports – increases in this proxy denote greater external sector weakness or lower trade competitiveness) are also included given the highly open nature of these countries and their dependence on international trade, commodity prices and financial markets for growth. Global growth is expected to be negatively related to the probability of crisis while the external sector weakness variable is expected to be positively related to the probability of a crisis.

The results outlined in Table 7.1 largely conform to *a priori* expectations. Reserves and economic growth are strongly and statistically negatively related to the probability of crises while natural disasters increase the probability of crises. The openness variable was positive but not significantly related to the probability of crises. The debt and financial stability (M2) variables are significantly positively related to the probability of crises while FDI is significantly negatively related to the probability of crises. Higher global growth significantly lowers the probability of crises while external sector weakness increases the probability of crises. It is worth noting that global growth and

Table 7.1 Caribbean probability of crises models

Variable	Probit1	Logit	Probit2	Probit3	Probit4
C	-0.8467*	-1.4512*	-0.9215*	-0.7630	-0.8749*
	(0.4957)	(0.8574)	(0.5167)	(0.5553)	(0.4918)
Lagged reserves/GDP	-2.3816**	-4.4095**	-2.6472**	-2.2448**	-2.5241**
	(1.1272)	(2.1111)	(1.2418)	(1.2004)	(1.1125)
Natural disaster	0.4134***	0.7207***	0.4170***	0.4150***	
	(0.1129)	(0.2068)	(0.1130)	(0.1131)	
Lagged per capita growth	-0.0669***	-0.1163***	-0.0669***	-0.0671***	-0.0618***
	(0.0220)	(0.0396)	(0.0220)	(0.0220)	(0.0217)
FDI/GDP	-0.0456***	-0.0802***	-0.0467***	-0.0468***	-0.0437***
	(0.0181)	(0.0321)	(0.0181)	(0.0185)	(0.0177)
M2/GDP	0.0137***	0.0251***	0.0131***	0.0130***	0.0135***
	(0.0043)	(0.0078)	(0.0044)	(0.0048)	(0.0043)
Growth of debt	0.0195***	0.0359***	0.0192***	0.0195***	0.0193***
	(0.0051)	(0.0098)	(0.0051)	(0.0051)	(0.0050)
External weakness	0.2698*	0.4800*	0.2789*	0.2716*	0.2340
	(0.1481)	(0.2533)	(0.1491)	(0.1482)	(0.1561)

(*Continued*)

157

Table 7.1 (Continued)

Variable	Probit1	Logit	Probit2	Probit3	Probit4
Global growth	−0.3389***	−0.6093***	−0.3393***	−0.3391***	−0.3077***
	(0.0686)	(0.1231)	(0.0686)	(0.0687)	(0.0671)
Trade openness	0.0029	0.0052	0.0028	0.0027	0.0034
	(0.0030)	(0.0051)	(0.0029)	(0.0031)	(0.0029)
Lagged government exp.			0.006137		
			(0.0119)		
Exchange rate regime				−0.0743	
				(0.2229)	
Natural disaster2					0.1702**
					(0.0755)
Pseudo R-squared	0.2005	0.2002	0.2011	0.2007	0.1816

Notes:
1) Standard errors are in parentheses.
2) *, ** and *** denote significance at the 10, 5 and 1 per cent levels, respectively.

external weakness have the largest impact on the probability of crises so the external economic environment has a huge bearing on the probability of crises. Reserves were also shown to significantly lower the probability of crises in all formulations.

To test for the robustness of the probit specification, a logit specification was also estimated to see if the results of the preferred model held. As can be seen from Table 7.1 this produced very similar results. Further tests of the robustness involved including sequentially lagged government expenditure as a percentage of GDP (probit2), an exchange-rate regime dummy where floating rates are 1 and fixed rates 0 (probit3) and the use of a natural disaster variable where all disasters such as floods and pandemics are included (probit4). The results are robust to these checks with the only significant change being that the external weakness variable becomes insignificant when the broader definition of natural disasters is used. The government expenditure and exchange rate regime variables, while they had the correct sign, proved to be insignificant in this study contrary to other studies (Dabla-Norris et al., 2011; Moore and Glean, 2016).

7.4.3   The Growth Consequence of Crises

The next step is estimating the direct growth consequences of crises and the indirect opportunity costs in terms of growth forgone from investing in reserve assets rather than public investments, using the same sample from the estimation of the probability of crises. This is done by augmenting the basic economic growth model with the crisis variable. Gross capital investment (our proxy for public investment) is also included as this provides an estimate for the opportunity costs of holding reserves.

Models of economic growth in small open economies also include variables such as the growth in population, the global economic environment, capital formation, FDI, some measures of international competitiveness and openness. In the Caribbean, this should also include some structural features such as government expenditure because of the large footprint of the government in the economy, the propensity for financial instability since financial crises have been very detrimental to growth in the region given the relative size of the financial sector relative to the size of the economy, sovereign debt because of the highly indebted nature of many countries in the region and remittances because of the importance to the supply of hard currency and growth in some countries. Natural disasters should have been included because of their frequency and the significant negative impact on infrastructure and economic activity in the Caribbean (Fuentes et al., 2015; Strobl, 2012) but their impact is subsumed in the crisis variable because of the way it's identified.

Using a general-to-specific modelling approach, the final model included the crisis dummy variable, FDI, gross capital formation (our proxy for public investment), global growth, external sector weakness, the growth of sovereign debt, M2 as a percentage of GDP (to capture the propensity for financial instability as discussed earlier), population growth and remittances. Our dependent variable growth is measured as per capita GDP growth.

Crises, external sector weakness, the growth of debt, M2/GDP and population growth are expected to be negatively related to growth. FDI, global growth and gross capital formation are expected to be positively related to growth. The impact of remittances can be positive if the increase in foreign exchange liquidity effect overshadows the negative effects of brain drain on human capital development associated with migration. Remittances can also have negative consequences in terms of labour market participation. If these negative influences dominate, then remittances can be negatively related to growth (Beaton et al., 2017). The model is estimated using panel fixed effects to account for any unobserved differences across countries. The most important coefficients include the coefficient on the crises dummy and gross capital formation. The size and significance of these coefficients will drive our estimates of the expected loss from the crises and the growth forgone to hold reserves rather than using the resources for investment respectively.

The results from the panel fixed effects (pooled OLS and random effects are included to check the robustness of the results) are outlined in Table 7.2. The results are similar across the different panel models implying that the results are robust so we discuss the results from the fixed-effects model. The results indicate that crises are very significantly negatively related to growth while gross capital formation is significantly positively related to growth. All other coefficients are significant and have the expected sign except remittances which are marginally insignificant. Of note is that the natural disaster variable did not end up in the final model as it was never significant in any of the test models, ostensibly because the crises variable subsumed much of its impact. External sector factors dominate in terms of the determinants of growth in the Caribbean with global growth, FDI and external sector weakness having the largest impacts on growth. Financial stability issues are also an important determinant of growth in the Caribbean with all proxies for financial instability having significant negative impacts on growth in all specifications.

7.4.4   Optimal Cost-Benefit International Reserves

Using the results from the probability of crises model in section 7.4.2 and the panel growth model in section 7.4.3 it is possible to estimate the optimal level of reserves in the cost-benefit framework. The results from these two models allow us to generate empirical estimates of the expected loss in growth

Table 7.2   Caribbean panel growth model

Variable	Pooled OLS	Panel fixed effects	Panel random effects
C	4.7359 ***	6.7026 ***	5.7295 ***
	(0.6761)	(0.9824)	(0.8545)
Crises	−4.2009 ***	−3.9700 ***	−4.0599 ***
	(0.3589)	(0.3544)	(0.3509)
FDI	0.1458 ***	0.1296 ***	0.1341 ***
	(0.0240)	(0.0284)	(0.0265)
Gross capital formation	0.0226 ***	0.0269 ***	0.0250 ***
	(0.0078)	(0.0077)	(0.0076)
Global growth	0.3752 ***	0.4395 ***	0.4113 ***
	(0.1132)	(0.1114)	(0.1102)
External sector weakness	−1.0017 ***	−1.5282 **	−1.2284 ***
	(0.2659)	(0.4675)	(0.3643)
Growth in sovereign debt	−0.0335 ***	−0.0289 ***	−0.0308 ***
	(0.0086)	(0.0086)	(0.0085)
M2/GDP	−0.0407 ***	−0.0531 ***	−0.0483 ***
	(0.0061)	(0.0087)	(0.0075)
Population growth	−0.4161**	−0.8688 **	−0.6192 **
	(0.1885)	(0.4388)	(0.2974)
Remittances	−0.0398	−0.0891	−0.0621
	(0.0362)	(0.0561)	(0.0467)
Observations	450	450	450
R-squared	48.9	54.1	48.1

Notes:
1) Standard errors are in parentheses.
2) *, ** and *** denote significance at the 10, 5 and 1 per cent levels respectively.

from the crisis conditional on reserves (the benefit of reserves) and the growth forgone from investing in reserve assets rather than growth-enhancing public investments (the cost of reserves). The optimal level of reserves in this framework is the point at which the expected loss from crises just balances the growth forgone from investing in reserves rather than growth-inducing public investments.

Using this approach, the optimal level of reserves was estimated at 6.9 months of import cover. This estimate could be criticized on the grounds that it does not include the financial costs related to the difference between the return on low-yield reserve assets and the return on alternative assets available to the monetary authorities.[9] The average bond spread for Caribbean sovereigns for which data was available in 2019[10] was approximately 7.5 per cent and the respective average return on international reserves of respective central banks was 2.5 per cent, implying the financial cost of reserves was 5 per cent. If this cost is included in the simulation then the optimal reserve holding falls to 5.0 months of import cover. The region's actual average reserve cover for the period under review was approximately 3.0 months of import cover which is the common rule of thumb used but significantly below the optimal level of reserves for the region, implying that many countries in the region have been holding reserves at levels below what is adequate and this coupled with the considerable risks they are exposed to in the form of natural disasters and terms-of-trade shocks means that they are very vulnerable to economic reversals.

There is, however, considerable heterogeneity in the region so there was a wide range in reserve holdings over the period under review meaning that the optimal level of reserves differed significantly amongst individual countries and over time. In fact, although the average import cover for the region over the period was 2.96 months of import cover, the standard deviation was 1.92 months of import cover with minimum and maximum values of 0.15 and 13.48 months of import cover respectively. The optimal level of reserves is also not absolute but conditional on a number of structural features and economic fundamentals.

Based on the empirical models estimated in sections 7.4.2 and 7.4.3 the optimal reserves can be simulated conditional on different fundamental values. This is highlighted by conducting simulations assuming different scenarios such as a 10 per cent increase in hurricanes due to global warming, as well as policy measures to increase FDI by 10 per cent and reduce debt by 10 per cent. In the first scenario, optimal reserves increase from 6.9 months to 7.3 months of import cover when financial costs are not incorporated while increasing from 5.0 to 5.2 months of import cover when financial costs are included. In the second scenario where policymakers adopt policies to increase FDI by 10 per cent, optimal reserves fall from 6.9 to 3.9 months of import cover when financial costs are excluded and from 5.0 to 2.7 months of import cover when financial costs are included. In the third scenario where the authorities are able to reduce debt by 10 per cent, optimal reserves fall from 6.9 to 5.6 months of import cover when financial costs are excluded or from 5.0 to 3.9 months of import cover when financial costs are included (see Table 7.3). This demonstrates that the insurance that reserves provide can be substituted for by policies that reduce vulnerabilities.

7.5   CONCLUSIONS

This chapter presented an empirically based cost-benefit approach for the determination of optimal reserves for the Caribbean. This approach is based

Table 7.3 *Optimal reserve conditional on events and policy (months of import cover)*

Scenarios	Historical average	10% increase in natural disasters	10% increase in FDI	10% decrease in debt
Optimal reserves without financial cost	6.9	7.3	3.9	5.6
Optimal reserves with financial cost	5.0	5.2	2.7	3.9

Source: author's calculation.

on the insurance motive for reserves to smooth disruptions to economic growth caused by economic shocks. The study demonstrated that economic crises in the Caribbean are driven by natural disasters and structural economic vulnerabilities but the probability of crises is significantly lowered by international reserves. Crises are shown to have a significant negative impact on economic growth while growth is also hampered by too many reserves being invested in low-return assets instead of growth-inducing public investments. Using these empirically grounded relationships, the study estimated that the optimal reserve level for the Caribbean was 6.9 months of import cover but could be as low as 5.0 months of import cover if the financial opportunity cost of investing in low-return reserve assets instead of higher-yielding alternative financial assets is included in the analysis.

The average level of international reserves for the region over the period under review was 2.96 months of import cover which suggests that the region on average does not have adequate levels of reserves to deal with the frequency and magnitude of shocks to which they are exposed. There is also a lot of heterogeneity in the holding of reserves by individual countries in the region so some may have an adequate level of reserves given how their risk exposure and economic structure have evolved over time. This suggests that studies to determine the optimal level of reserves should be more country-centric. The approach to shock and crisis determination adopted in this study which focused on country-specific distributions was, therefore, a step in the right direction. All countries have also been making concerted efforts to increase their levels of reserves. Of the 15 countries covered by this study, only Trinidad and Tobago, Jamaica, St. Kitts and Nevis and Haiti have demonstrated any ability to maintain reserves above the 5.0 months of import cover benchmark and only for the latter part of the period under review.

The analysis also demonstrated that the determination of the optimal reserve level is not only conditional on the level of reserves and the probability of crises but also on the structural features of these economies. Economic realities such as high and unsustainable levels of sovereign debt, low FDI inflows, low levels of international competitiveness and financial instability risks can influence the optimal level of reserves. The ability of these countries to successfully address these vulnerabilities can lower the level of reserves that are deemed optimal. Policy measures to lower excessive debt levels and increase the inflows of FDI can therefore be seen as substitutes for higher levels of reserves in this optimality framework which can bring the level of optimal reserves closer to the actual levels of reserves held by the region.

NOTES

1. Countries could also bolster their international liquidity by reducing short-term debt and developing swap arrangements.
2. See Magud and Sosa (2010) for a recent review of the literature.
3. The impact rate for natural disasters is 26.2 per cent in the review period in the Caribbean. Indeed, some countries have been impacted more than once in a year; for example, in 2005 Haiti was impacted by five hurricanes. The level of destruction also tends to be higher. According to Barnichon (2009) a category 3 hurricane struck Grenada in 2004 and the destruction was estimated at US$800 million or 200 per cent of Grenada's GDP.
4. Antigua and Barbuda, the Bahamas, Barbados, Belize, Dominica, the Dominican Republic, Grenada, Guyana, Haiti, Jamaica, St. Kitts and Nevis, St. Lucia, St. Vincent, Suriname and Trinidad and Tobago.
5. The variables used for the identification of shocks are fewer and for natural disasters each hurricane and major earthquake is considered as a shock because of the devastating impact of these events.
6. If we include all disasters such as floods, droughts and epidemics listed in the EM-DAT database, the proportion of shocks rises to 48.4 per cent of observations, similar to the 47.8 per cent shock proportion identified by Dabla-Norris et al. (2011) for low-income countries when all natural disasters are included.
7. The general-to-specific modelling approach was adopted.
8. The relationship between trade openness and growth can be ambiguous since greater efficiency often leads to higher growth but market imperfections may lead to differences in resource endowments becoming more acute. In this context, although much of the literature would suggest a negative link between openness and economic crises, it could also be positive in many circumstances (Huchet et al., 2018).
9. Dabla-Norris et al. (2011) had argued that since the rate on concessional financing for a developing country was below the average return on reserves then this was negative or negligible.
10. Belize, Jamaica and Trinidad and Tobago.

REFERENCES

Aizenman, Joshua, and Jaewoo Lee. 2007. 'International Reserves: Precautionary Versus Mercantilist Views, Theory and Evidence.' *Open Economies Review*, 18(2): 191–214.

Barnichon, Regis. 2009. 'The Optimal Level of Reserves for Low-Income Countries: Self Insurance Against External Shocks.' *IMF Staff Paper*, 56(4): 852–875.

Beaton, Kimberly, Svetlana Cerovic, Misael Galdamez, Metodij Hadzi-Vaskov, Franz Loyola, Zsoka Koczan, Bogdan Lissovolik, Jan Kees Martijn, Yulia Ustyugova, and Joyce Wong. 2017. 'Migration and Remittances in Latin America and the Caribbean: Engines of Growth and Macroeconomic Stabilizers?' *IMF Working Paper, No. 144.*

Calvo, Guillermo, Alejandro Izquierdo, and Rudy Loo-Kung. 2012. 'Optimal Holdings of International Reserves: Self-Insurance Against Sudden Stop.' *NBER Working Paper, No. 18219.*

Carasco, Skeeta, Roland Craigwell, and Darrin Downes. 2013. 'An Assessment of Reserve Adequacy in Caribbean Economies.' *Central Bank of Barbados Working Papers No. 4.*

Cheung, Y.-W., and X. Qian. 2009. 'Hoarding of International Reserves: Mrs Machlup's Wardrobe and the Joneses.' *Review of International Economics*, 17(4): 824–843.

Dabla-Norris, Era, Jun Il Kim, and Kazuko Shirono. 2011. 'Optimal Precautionary Reserves for Low-Income Countries: A Cost-Benefit Analysis.' *IMF Working Paper, No. 249.*

De Gregorio, J. 2014. *How Latin America Weathered the Global Financial Crisis.* Washington, DC: Peterson Institute for International Economics.

Dehesa, Mario, Emilio Pineda, and Wendell Samuel. 2009. 'Optimal Reserves in the Eastern Caribbean Currency Union.' *IMF Working Paper, No. 77.*

Delatte, Anne Laure, and Julien Fouquau. 2011. 'The Determinants of International Reserves in the Emerging Economies: A Non-Linear Approach.' *Applied Economics*, 48(28): 4179–4192.

Dominguez, Kathryn M. E., Yuko Hashimoto, and Takatoshi Ito. 2012. 'International Reserves and the Global Financial Crisis.' *NBER Working Paper, No. 17362.*

Dooley, Michael P., Peter M. Garber, and David Folkerts-Landau. 2007. 'The Two Crises of International Economics.' *NBER Working Paper, No. 13197.*

Edison, H. 2003. 'Are Foreign Reserves in Asia Too High?' In *World Economic Outlook September.* Washington, DC: International Monetary Fund.

Feldstein, Martin. 1999. 'A Self-Help Guide for Emerging Markets.' *Foreign Affairs*, March/April.

Fuentes, Rodrigo, Karl Melgarejo, and Valerie Mercer-Blackman. 2015. 'Understanding Economic Growth in the Caribbean Region: A Conceptual and Methodological Study.' *IADB Working Paper, No. 595.*

Ghosh, A. R., M. S. Qureshi, and C. G. Tsangarides. 2014. 'On the Value of Words: Inflation and Fixed Exchange Rate Regimes.' *IMF Economic Review*, 62(2): 288–322.

Ghosh, A. R., J. D. Ostry, and C. G. Tsangarides. 2017. 'Shifting Motives: Explaining the Buildup in Official Reserves in Emerging Markets Since the 1980s.' *IMF Economic Review*, 65: 308–364.

Gosselin, M., and N. Parent. 2005. 'An Empirical Analysis of Foreign Exchange Reserves in Emerging Asia.' *Bank of Canada Working Paper, No. 38.*

Huchet, Marilyne, Chantal Le Mouël, and Mariana Vijil. 2018. 'The Relationship Between Trade Openness and Economic Growth: Some New Insights on the Openness Measurement Issue.' *The World Economy*, 41(1): 59–76.

Jeanne, Olivier. 2007. 'International Reserves in Emerging Market Countries: Too Much of a Good Thing?' *Brookings Papers on Economic Activity*, 1: 1–79.

Jeanne, Olivier, and R. Rancière. 2006. 'The Optimal Level of Reserves for Emerging Markets: Formulas and Applications.' *IMF Working Paper, No. 229.*

Jeanne, Olivier, and Romain Rancière. 2011. 'The Optimal Level of International Reserves for Emerging Market Countries: A New Formula and Some Applications.' *The Economic Journal*, 121(555): 905–930.

Magud, Nicolás, and Sebastián Sosa. 2010. 'When and Why Worry About Real Exchange Rate Appreciation? The Missing Link Between Dutch Disease and Growth.' *IMF Working Paper, No. 271.*

Moore, Winston, and Adrian Glean. 2016. 'Foreign Exchange Reserve Adequacy and Exogenous Shocks.' *Applied Economics*, 48(6): 490–501.

Mwase, Nkunde. 2012. 'How Much Should I Hold? Reserve Adequacy in Emerging Markets and Small Islands.' *IMF Working Paper, No. 205.*

Obstfeld, Maurice, Jay C. Shambaugh, and Alan M. Taylor. 2010. 'Financial Stability, the Trilemma, and International Reserves.' *American Economic Journal: Macroeconomics*, 2(2): 57–94.

Strobl, Eric. 2012. 'The Economic Growth Impact of Natural Disasters in Developing Countries: Evidence From Hurricane Strikes in the Central American and Caribbean Regions.' *Journal of Development Economics*, 97(1): 130–141.

8. Two sides of a currency crisis in emerging economies: economic and behavioural side of currency risk derivatives

Elżbieta Kubińska, Joanna Wyrobek, Łukasz Faryj and Anna Macko

8.1 INTRODUCTION

This chapter aims to present the economic and behavioural aspects of currency crises in emerging economies with the example of Poland in the second half of 2008. From an economic point of view, this chapter discusses the critical factors of the Polish economy's exposure to currency risk on a macroeconomic scale. The analysis of the crisis in 2008[1] allowed us to examine the reaction of the relatively small Polish economy to strong disturbances in the currency market. In response to the sharp depreciation of the zloty, as expected, a significant part of foreign portfolio investments withdrew from the country, imports and exports decreased, and the GDP growth rate dropped. At the same time, however, the depreciation of the Polish zloty resulted in a faster decline in imports than in exports, which slowed down the decline in GDP (it remained positive) and levelled the trade balance. This remarkable resistance to the crisis, however, could have been partially achieved through the German programmes to activate the German economy at that time, which due to the lack of certain cars at German resellers, involved purchases of cars in showrooms in neighbouring Poland. Generally speaking, on the macroeconomic scale, the country underwent the crisis relatively unscathed, but this does not apply to the microeconomic scale, where a large part of exporters suffered losses on options contracts, which instead of closing exposure to currency risk, only reversed its profile.

On a microeconomic scale, therefore, there was a huge crisis in the enterprise sector, many of which later went bankrupt. Abrupt depreciation of PLN in the second half of 2008 resulted in immense losses for Polish exporters; for example, the total amount of liabilities of the DUDA company (listed at WSE) amounted to PLN 300 million. Such senseless actions of exporters are hardly backed by any economic calculations (only the conviction that the Polish złoty would keep appreciating for eternity), which raises the question of the behavioural aspects of this phenomenon. The behavioural side of the currency crisis is therefore connected with the vast losses noted by Polish exporters who were involved in 'toxic' currency options. Those derivatives, which were also called 'I will kill you later', offered with zero-cost strategies an attractive exchange rate for exporters on the OTC market. Instead of taking a position in plain vanilla currency option or forward contract, exporters decided to take a position in options strategies with very positive short-term characteristics (zero cost and attractive exchange rate) but very risky in the long term (less attractive exchange rate, double volume in the case of negative payoffs).

To explain the popularity and willingness to take positions in toxic options rather than in traditional hedging securities, we carried out the survey. The research presented in this chapter are results of the survey among entrepreneurs, that is, micro, small and medium-sized enterprises operating in Poland (in the Podkarpackie voivodeship). Entrepreneurs were asked about their involvement in currency options strategies in 2008. The goal was to explain the entrepreneurs' involvement in toxic options by examining the degree of motivational and cognitive inclinations discussed in behavioural finance; for example, the propensity to succumb to the conservatism or availability heuristics, risk attitudes and overconfidence effect were examined. The questionnaire survey examines the economic and behavioural side of the decision to engage in loss-making option strategies

The remaining chapter proceeds as follows: we start by elaborating on foreign-exchange risk in Poland, and then, in section 8.2, we discuss currency options strategies. In section 8.3, we present behavioural aspects of decisions on involvement in currency option strategies. In section 8.4, we report the results of the survey carried out among small and medium-sized enterprises, and the last section 8.5 contains conclusions and implications of the findings for potential actions aiming at preventing engagement in toxic options.

8.2   FOREIGN-EXCHANGE RISK IN POLAND

Poland has been a member of the European Union since 2004 but still maintains its own currency, which is the Polish zloty. It is believed that Poland's staying outside the euro area helped the Polish economy to survive the subprime crisis without a significant decline in GDP (Carlson et al., 2016). In fact, Poland was the only country in European Union which did not notice a recession during the financial crisis in 2008 (based on Eurostat data, the GDP growth rate was 1.6 for Poland in 2009, while the average for 27 EU countries was −4.3). Poland came through the subprime crisis without a negative GDP in the economy, but with problems for exporters due to the growth of the exchange rate risk of the Polish zloty against the dominant world currencies.

In order for Poland to join the eurozone and introduce the common European currency euro, it should meet economic convergence criteria, that is, 1) price stability, 2) sound and sustainable public finances, 3) exchange-rate stability and 4) long-term interest rates. The convergence criteria help to ensure that a country is ready for integration into the monetary regime of the euro area. The reasons for not adopting the euro in Poland are the failure to meet the convergence criteria of budgetary deficits and also the fear that the Polish economy would suffer from the inability of the Polish zloty exchange rate to depreciate in the event of an economic crisis (the zloty then weakens, which stimulates exports and weakens imports). Such a situation is believed to be what took place in Portugal, which is said to have suffered from an economic slowdown due to adopting the euro at too high an exchange rate. Greece, for example, was not able to defend its economy by means of the domestic currency exchange rate against the euro (Kasimati and Veraros, 2013).

Poland primarily does not meet the euro convergence criteria for the budgetary deficit (Figure 8.1). In the case of the public debt, the situation of Poland is better than the average for the euro area, although the COVID-19 pandemic also poses a threat that Poland may fail to meet the national debt-to-GDP criterion as well (Figure 8.2).

Table 8.1 shows the evolution of the exchange rate system in Poland. As shown in Table 8.1, Poland has slowly followed the entire path of easing the exchange rate starting from the fixed-rate system and has been using the free-floating exchange rate system since 2000. The Central Bank allows for interventions in the zloty exchange rate only if the inflationary target is endangered (this is the main goal of the monetary policy pursued by the Polish Central Bank NBP).

The advantages and disadvantages of Poland having its own currency can be seen in Figure 8.3. The rates significantly fluctuate over time (the figure shows changes in the Polish zloty against the euro and the US dollar). On the one hand, it is a normal mechanism of adjustments to the changes in economic relations between countries, but on the other, the uncertainty of the exchange rate may be difficult to overcome by exporters and importers. An excellent example of these fluctuations can be seen in the year 2008 when the United States economy was already under the impact of the subprime crisis. Poland felt the effects of the crisis with a delay, therefore the exchange rate of the zloty in 2007, until mid-2008, was strengthening against the dollar and the euro, and only in the second half of 2008 did it begin to weaken quite rapidly (from 2 PLN/USD to 4 PLN/USD).

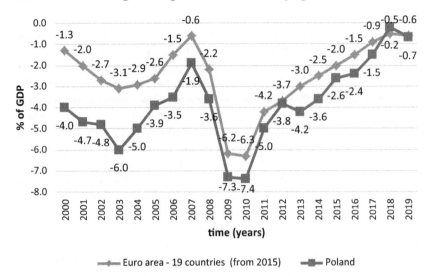

Source: Eurostat.

*Figure 8.1   Budgetary deficits in Poland compared to the average for the
euro area countries, 2000–2019, percentage*

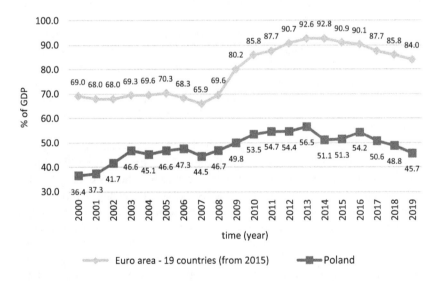

Source: Eurostat.

*Figure 8.2   Government debt in relation to GDP for Poland compared to the
average for the euro area countries, 2000–2019, percentage*

Table 8.1   Exchange system evolution in Poland

Period	Exchange rate system
Jan 1990–Apr 1991	Fixed rate against US dollar.
May 1991–Oct 1991	Fixed rate against a basket of five currencies. Devaluation in May 1991, by 16.8%.
Oct 1991–Feb 1992	Crawling peg with a monthly rate of devaluation declining steadily from 1.8% to 1.2%. Two devaluations, by 12% in Feb 1992 and 8% in Aug 1993.
May 1995–Apr 2000	Crawling band system, with fluctuation band increasing from ± 7% to ± 15%. Steady decrease in monthly devaluation rate from 1.2% to 0.3%. Revaluation of the central parity by 6% in Dec 1995.
Apr 2000–	Free-floating exchange rate system.

Source: Polish Central Bank, after Banbula et al. (2010).

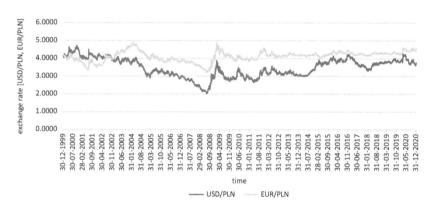

Source: Polish Central Bank.

Figure 8.3   Exchange rate of the Polish zloty against US dollar and euro, 2000–2020

The variance of the Polish złoty foreign exchange rate for USD and euro increased sharply in 2008, 2009 and 2010, that is, during the subprime crisis in Poland and immediately after it. The Polish economy came out relatively unscathed from the subprime crisis, but the fluctuations in the exchange rate show that the economy experienced disruptions that were translated into sudden changes in the exchange rate. From the macroeconomic point of view, the weakening of the Polish zloty that occurred in mid-2008 was beneficial for the economy; the unfavourable part was that it happened through the sudden collapse of the zloty exchange rate, which enterprises completely did not expect (many companies speculated at that time on further strengthening of the zloty).

What happened to imports and exports during the crisis can be seen in the years 2008 and 2009, when both imports and exports fell sharply in response to the economic crisis and the weakening of the Polish zloty. However, imports fell stronger than exports and they almost levelled off then, while in 2006 and 2007, when the zloty was very strong against the dollar and the euro, imports were clearly higher than exports. In the following years, the Polish zloty has never been so strong in relation to foreign currencies as before 2008, and as one can see, since 2012, exports have exceeded imports (Figure 8.4). This shows a strong dependence of the trade balance on the zloty exchange rate.

The analysis of the data for 2007–2009 showed that it is not easy to clearly determine whether the exchange rate fluctuations hurt or helped the economy. In the first phase of the subprime crisis, the Polish zloty strongly appreciated, and then weakened sharply. The weakening of the zloty helped export sales, which fell much less than imports, and the imports became equal to exports. This behaviour strengthened the domestic economy. However, the drop in the exchange rate was sharp and unexpected by the majority of companies (it took place after a very long period of the zloty appreciation) and negatively impacted the financial costs of entrepreneurs and enterprises.

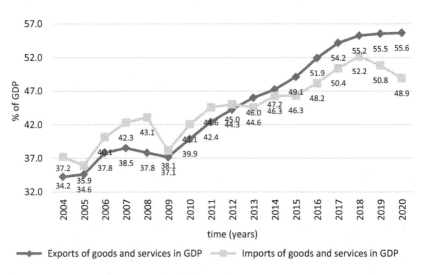

Source: Central Statistical Office of Poland.

Figure 8.4   Exports and imports of goods and services as a percentage of GDP, Poland, 2003–2020

The appreciation of the Polish zloty since Poland's accession to the European Union in 2004 was the reason exporters had less and less revenue in domestic currency each year. After a few years, exporters began hedging in the OTC derivatives markets, but their business experience motivated them to hedge against further appreciation of the Polish zloty. The macroeconomic environment in the forex market is very important to understand the behaviour of exporters, who ultimately, instead of hedging, exposed themselves to huge risks in case of trend changes, as will be described in the next section.

8.3   CURRENCY OPTIONS STRATEGIES

Firms can hedge their exposition on currency risk by means of different types of financial instruments, including currency derivatives (Bailly et al., 2003; Benatti and Napolitano, 2019). Besides natural hedge, both exporters and importers may reduce the risk of their future cash flow by matching derivatives, like future contacts or options, to their risk exposure. Firms with extensive foreign-exchange-rate exposure and economies of scale in hedging activities are more likely to use currency derivatives (Géczy et al., 1997). Polish entrepreneurs used option strategies in 2007–2008 in Poland, creating big volume. Most of the foreign-exchange option strategies were offered on the OTC market, and these instruments turned out to cause the largest losses during the subprime crisis in Poland (Liberadzki, 2015). Table 8.2 shows the average daily turnover on OTC and regular market at the Warsaw Stock

Table 8.2   Average daily turnover in the domestic foreign-exchange market by instrument in millions of USD, transactions in foreign currencies into/from PLN

	2004	2005	2006	2007	2008	2009
OTC derivatives	5987.7	8677.6	9244.9	13159.4	14817.0	6325.3
• price derivatives	4597.6	7047.8	7397.4	10227.4	11373.4	4316.0
• currency derivatives	1390.1	1629.8	1847.5	2932.0	3443.6	2009.3
Stock exchange derivatives	251.5	498.9	797.6	1411.0	1255.2	1003.7
• interest rate derivatives	0.0	15.0	5.3	0.8	0.0	0.0
• currency derivatives	0.5	0.8	0.4	0.7	14.4	26.9
• related to the stock market	251.0	483.1	791.9	1409.5	1240.8	976.8
including WIG20 futures	239.6	448.8	742.8	1343.2	1198.7	939.4

Source: Polish Central Bank.

Exchange. The highest turnover took place in 2007 at the bottom of the trend for the exchange rate of the Polish zloty against USD and EUR, just before the trend reversal (Figure 8.3). The highest turnover was just before the subprime crisis in Poland; it returned to the level from 2007 in 2019.

Exporters being non-financial companies should consider classic instruments like selling futures contracts (short futures) or purchasing a put option (long put). The payout functions of these financial instruments are illustrated in Figure 8.5, both of which provide positive settlement in the event of further appreciation of the Polish zloty (falling exchange rate). A futures contract is a zero-cost symmetrical derivative, but it can only offer an exchange rate that is the forward rate. Exporters did not open positions in futures contracts because they considered the exchange rate unattractive. With a put option, they could choose any exchange rate, but they had to pay an option premium. The more attractive the exchange rate, the more expensive the option was, so there was not much interest from exporters in this derivative. Negative and positive characteristics of derivatives hedging exporters' foreign-exchange risk are summarized in Table 8.3. Banks in the OTC market offered option strategies that had a good exchange rate and were costless. Option strategies were very popular in the Polish market. An example of this strategy is highlighted in the black line in Figure 8.5; it is a payoff function of a combination of a long put and a short call, where the call option had a double nominal value (volume) compared to the put option. A strategy built in this way offered

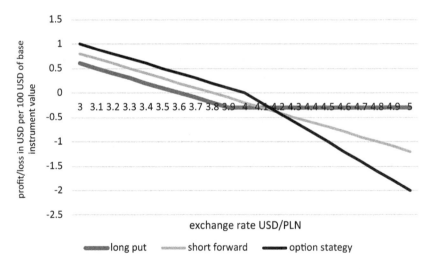

Figure 8.5   Payoff functions of derivatives hedging exporters' foreign-exchange risk

Table 8.3 Positive and negative aspects of the derivatives hedging export-ers' foreign-exchange risk

	Positive aspects of the transaction	Negative aspects of the transaction
Long put	The possibility of getting a more favourable exchange rate than the forward rate	Premium paid
Short forward	Zero cost	Lack of the possibility of getting a more favourable exchange rate than the forward rate
Zero-cost options strategies	Zero cost Favourable exchange rate	Double amount of currency sold by the company in the case of negative settlement Limits for positive settlements (barriers, expiration in the case of positive settlement)

a more favourable exchange rate than the forward contract and it was zero-cost (short-call contract premium covered the cost of the long-put contract premium), but in the case of an exchange rate trend reversal, the settlement of the transaction was negative based on the double volume of short call options.

After many years of stable and slow appreciation of the Polish zloty, as a result of joining the EU, a rapid reversal of the Polish zloty exchange rate took place in 2008. It resulted in enormous losses for exporters. Most of the option strategies were structures that expired throughout the whole year, which resulted in losses in subsequent periods. Polish financial supervision authority reported that losses of exporters were 9 billion PLN (that is 2 billion EUR) in March 2009. In fact, the option strategies were hazardous instruments and resulted in large losses due to negative settlement under trend reversal conditions.

A puzzling question is why Polish exporters took so much risk in the forex market, even though they should just do only hedging. There is a large literature on hedging against exchange-rate movements by non-financial firms. For example, Géczy et al. (1997) showed that firms with greater growth opportunities and tighter financial constraints are more likely to use currency derivatives. Bartram et al. (2009) proved that derivative usage is determined by other financial and operating decisions in ways that are intuitive but not related to specific economic theories. For example, they point out that derivative usage helps determine the level and maturity of debt, dividend policy, holdings of liquid assets and international operating hedging. In our opinion, referring to the Polish case, the long-term trend over several years, which was also not in favour of exporters, contributed to their risk-taking in currency options. This is related to the reaction to losses, which is the subject of behavioural finance research (Shiller, 2003). We believe that apart from economic factors, motivational factors play an important role in explaining the popularity of option strategies in Poland in 2007, and it is described in the next section.

8.4   BEHAVIOURAL ASPECTS OF DECISIONS ON INVOLVEMENT IN CURRENCY OPTION STRATEGIES

Substantial evidence indicates that entrepreneurial, financial risk-taking is strongly influenced by behavioural factors that affect risk perception. Such inclinations may lead to underestimation of risk, overestimation of expected profit or improper information analyses. Consequently, as documented by the research in the field of behavioural finance, investment decision-making processes of investors and entrepreneurs can be significantly impaired (Gilovich et al., 2002). In our opinion, the factors that may influence the decision to open a precarious position in toxic options are related to the intuitive processing of information and not analysing all available factors by succumbing to heuristics, such as availability or conservatism. Besides, the propensity to take risks and overconfidence can also motivate to take positions in toxic options.

Two of the essential heuristics that influence economic decisions on involvement in currency option strategies are conservatism (Edwards, 1982) and availability heuristic (Tversky and Kahneman, 1973). Conservatism can be defined as the individual's tendency to revise their beliefs slowly and insufficiently when presented with new evidence. The result is that people tend to over-weight older experiences and under-weight new evidence (Kariofyllas et al., 2017). Availability is yet another cognitive heuristic bias, and it can be defined as the human tendency to believe that things that come first to mind (recent events, key events, things easy to remember) are more reliable and deserve more weight in the decision-making process than less memorable events (Cossette, 2014). Another important factor that can explain entrepreneurial decisions is related to information processing. The cognitive reflection test (CRT) measures the propensity for an intuitive way of processing information (Frederick, 2005). Intuitive thinking is unfocused, nonlinear, views the big picture, is heart-centred and ignores details. It used to be beneficial in difficult situations with time pressure, especially when the observer had experience in similar situations. It helped to find a workable solution to the problem, in contrast to the best solution usually looked for with analytical thinking.

Risk attitudes can be considered as another bias in human reasoning that influences decisions on involvement in currency option strategies. People tend to have different perceptions of risk – some are risk-averse, and others are risk seekers. Risk-aversion involves low tolerance for the risks, and the person sees the risks as more significant than they are. Risk-seekers have high (often too high) tolerance for the risks and may underestimate their severity. According to the classical theories of finance, investors are characterized by risk aversion, which implies the occurrence of a risk premium. On the other hand, the basic theory of behavioural finance, prospect theory, assumes risk aversion in the area of profits and risk preference in the area of losses under the condition of medium and high probabilities (Kahneman and Tversky, 1979). According to the prospect theory, we observe in the behaviour of investors risk avoidance in the area of profits, manifested in the quick closing of profitable positions because its continued holding would be associated with the risk of a price drop and loss of profits. On the other hand, in the area of losses, investors show a tendency to take the risk, which manifests itself in the form of holding losing positions, even though such action carries the risk of a further decline in the price and deepening of losses. One of the measurement methods of risk preferences in the field of economic psychology is based on the lottery approach (Kahneman and Tversky, 1979; Holt and Laury, 2002; Wärneryd, 1996).

People are also very prone to overestimating their skills or knowledge, which represents a very common judgemental error called overconfidence (Glaser et al., 2010). Overconfidence is the bias that makes humans put more confidence in their personal judgements than the objective accuracy of their opinions. Overconfidence can be explained as the lack of calibration of our opinions, an egotistical belief that we are better than we actually are. The literature mentions three forms of overconfidence, and they are as follows: 1) miscalibration, consisting in narrowing down the confidence intervals for the predicted feature in comparison with the interval determined based on the rules of the probability calculus (Lichtenstein et al., 1982), 2) a tendency to consider oneself a better person in some area than an average person (Svenson, 1981) and 3) illusion of control, that is, a tendency to overestimate the probability of success in comparison to the objective probability (Langer, 1975). This bias makes investors too confident about their skills and knowledge and ignores risks inherent in the investments (Ahmad and Shah, 2020).

8.5 SURVEY CARRIED OUT AMONG SMALL AND MEDIUM-SIZED ENTERPRISES

In this subsection we present the results of a questionnaire survey analysing the propensity to take risks in the foreign-exchange derivatives market, taking into account economic and behavioural variables. The research was

a part of the project 'Socio-economic consequences of the fourth industrial revolution' under the Regional Initiative of Excellence programme in
Poland.[2]

The survey was conducted in a group of micro, small and medium enterprises operating in the Podkarpackie voivodship. It was carried out with the
personal participation of the organizer of the survey after prior notification
by e-mail and after setting the date of the meeting in a telephone conversation. The participants took part in the survey without any compensation; the
survey took on average 60 minutes to complete. In the group of economic
questions, we asked about (knowledge of) currency risk-related issues, risk
exposure and whether respondents used any simple or more advanced hedging
strategies. We asked whether the respondent's company accounted for losses
in 2007–2009 due to toxic options. There was also a group of questions about
sources of funds that were used in the company and what sources of funds
the company planned to use in the future. Respondents could choose different
sources of funds out of the proposed list. Behavioural questions were focused
on heuristics and biases representing the economic psychology approach and
risk attitude in the area of profits or losses; the motivational part focused on
overconfidence.

8.5.1   Participants

The questionnaire was addressed to 392 micro, small and medium enterprises operating in the Podkarpackie voivodship in 2018. The survey questions concerned the form of conducted activity, its scale, age of the company,
entrepreneur's knowledge of finance and financing, choices regarding toxic
options and selected behavioural characteristics. As for behavioural traits, we
studied the level of self-confidence in respondents, loss aversion, cognitive
styles (intuitive/analytical), loss aversion, disposition effect and conservatism
heuristics. For behavioural research, we used ready-made psychological tasks
from psychological economic literature.

Most of the surveyed companies were very small: 57.7 per cent employed
up to nine employees, 37.2 per cent employed between ten to 49 employees
and only 5.1 per cent employed more than 50 employees. Around 70.4 per cent
of surveyed companies have been operating for more than five years, only 6.1
per cent existed no longer than one year, and the remaining companies, that
is, 23.5 per cent of surveyed firms, lasted from one to five years. The median
and mode age of respondents turned out to be the bracket of 41–50 years.
Due to the short history of many surveyed companies (companies where our
respondents worked), we limited our research to 271 companies. These businesses were established at least five years prior to the survey.

8.5.2 Comparison of Behavioural and Economic Factors between Entrepreneurs Who Were Involved

In order to identify the behavioural and economic factors that influence risk-taking in the currency derivatives market by entrepreneurs, we have divided them into two groups. We divided the respondents into those who used complex derivatives such as option structures and those who did not, based on the answers to the following question: *'have you ever hedged against currency risk in financial markets with the following financial instruments, complex derivative instruments such as option strategies?'*. It allows us to test behavioural and economic determinants that led entrepreneurs to take a position in complex derivative instruments such as option strategies.

Table 8.4 compare the mean values of behavioural factors between two groups on which we run the t-test of the means. Processing information was verified by three questions from CRT:

- A bat and a ball cost $1.10 in total. The bat costs $1 more than the ball. How much does the ball cost?
- If it takes five machines five minutes to make five widgets, how long would it take 100 machines to make 100 widgets?
- In a lake, there is a patch of lily pads. Every day, the patch doubles in size. If it takes 48 days for the patch to cover the entire lake, how long would it take for the patch to cover half of the lake?

There were two questions measuring the tendency to follow the availability heuristic:

- Do you think more words start with K or end with K?
- Do you think more people die in car accidents or suicide attempts?

Answers that more words start with K and more people die in car accidents are coherent with the availability heuristic; they are immediate examples that come to mind when trying to find the answers, although the objective facts state the opposite.

In the question on conservatism heuristics, we have adopted the classical question of Edwards (1968):

- There are two bookbags, one containing 700 red and 300 blue chips, the other containing 300 red and 700 blue. Take one of the bags. Now, you sample, randomly, with replacement after each chip. In 12 samples, you get eight reds and four blues. What is the probability that this is the predominantly red bag?

Table 8.4 Behavioural variables for two groups that use or do not use hedging with complex derivative instruments such as option strategies

| | Hedging with complex derivative instruments such as option strategies | | | | t-test (no equality of variance was assumed) | | |
| | Yes N = 46 | | No N = 225 | | | | |
	Mean	St. dev.	Mean	St. dev.	t	df	p-value (two-sided)
Number of correct answers in CRT	0.30	0.59	0.17	0.56	1.38	62.59	0.172
Availability heuristics (1 = more words starting with the letter)	0.78	0.42	0.73	0.44	0.72	67.46	0.473
Availability heuristics (1 = more deaths caused by a car)	0.52	0.51	0.54	0.50	−0.25	64.27	0.803
Availability heuristics – number of answers coherent with the bias in two tasks	1.30	0.59	1.28	0.56	0.30	62.76	0.763
Conservatism task – correct answer 3.26	41.09	32.58	48.09	59.83	−1.12	117.27	0.264
The number of risky choices in two decision problems expressed in gains	1.48	0.69	1.30	0.72	1.56	66.41	0.123
The number of risky choices in two decision problems expressed in losses	1.70	0.47	1.34	0.73	4.21	96.45	0.000
Number of answers 'better than the average entrepreneur' out of 5 possible	4.04	0.92	2.89	1.48	6.90	99.59	0.000

The question was transformed into a story about two advising companies on the market that help in obtaining funds for financing enterprises; we stated that one company is 70 per cent efficient and the other company is 30 per cent. The correct answer in both tasks is 3.26 per cent.

Four questions measured risk attitude. In these questions, the respondents had to choose between a safe and a risky option. Two questions concerned losses and two concerned gains.

Questions about risk preference in the gains domain were the following:

- Imagine you are visiting a friend you haven't seen for a long time. You receive 500 PLN as a welcome gift. Being in a good mood, your friend suggests a game. You must choose one answer from the following:
  - You accept PLN 500 as a welcome gift from your friend and do not participate in the game.
  - You take part in a game for 500 zlotys. You toss a coin; if it falls heads you win 1,000 zlotys; if tails you lose 500 zlotys.
- Imagine that Poland is preparing for the arrival of an attack of a certain disease that will result in 600 deaths. Two alternative programmes have been proposed to fight the disease: programme A and programme B. Every effort has been made to evaluate the effectiveness of these programmes. Results were obtained:
  - If programme A is followed, 200 people will be saved.
  - If programme B is applied, with probability 1/3 all will be saved and with probability 2/3 no one will be saved.
  Which programme do you choose?

Questions about risk preference in the losses domain were the following:

- Imagine you are paying a friend another visit. He proposes the same game, but this time you are the payer. Choose one of the following options:
  - You do not play and you pay 500 as a welcome gift to your friend.
  - You play and flip a coin: if it falls heads you pay 1,000 for a welcome gift for the two of you; if it falls tails your friend pays for himself and for you.
- Imagine that Poland is preparing for an attack of a certain disease that will kill 600 people. Two programmes have been proposed to fight the disease: programme C and programme D. Every effort has been made to evaluate the effectiveness of these programmes.
  - If programme C is followed 400 people will die.
  - If programme D is followed, with probability 1/3 no one will die and with probability 2/3 everyone will die.
  Which programme do you choose?

Respondents were also asked to express their opinion about their knowledge, competencies and skills in different areas of everyday life. We put forth the statements:

- I am more financially competent than the average entrepreneur.
- I know politics better than the average entrepreneur.
- I have more knowledge about culture than the average entrepreneur.
- I have a better sense of humour than the average entrepreneur.
- I'm more observant when watching a movie than the average viewer.

The number of Yes answers, where the respondents admit that they are better than the average entrepreneur, is the measure of overconfidence.

As shown in Table 8.4, there are no statistically significant differences in processing information. Both groups have very low CRT results, answering correctly only less than one question out of three on average. The two groups of respondents have similar levels of propensity for heuristic processing of information, and they have similar results in the tasks of availability and conservatism heuristics. They have similar results by giving immediate examples that come to our mind when asked about words starting with the letter K or deaths caused by a car. Both groups did not revise prior beliefs sufficiently when presented with new evidence. The correct answer in both tasks is 3.26 per cent, but in both groups, the average answers are more than 40 per cent and the difference is not statistically significant. There were no statistically significant differences in the domain of gains, but we observed statistically significant differences in the domain of losses. The entrepreneurs who decided to use hedging with complex derivative instruments (such as option strategies) were more risk-seeking in the domain of losses. Comparing the level of overconfidence in the form of a better-than-average effect, those entrepreneurs who decided to use hedging with complex derivative instruments gave around four yes answers, while the other group provided less than three positive answers. The entrepreneurs who decided to use hedging with complex derivative instruments (such as option strategies) revealed higher overconfidence than those who have never been involved in complex derivative instruments.

Table 8.5 compares the mean values of economic factors between those two groups on which we run the t-test of the means. In the group of economic questions, we asked whether or not (1 = yes, 0 = no) they:

- were exposed to currency risk,
- used simple derivatives such as currency options, futures, swaps,
- hedge against currency risk in their company,
- suffered losses in 2007–2009 due to toxic options.

Table 8.5 Economic variables for two groups that use or do not use hedging with complex derivative instruments such as option strategies

| | Hedging with complex derivative instruments such as option strategies | | | | t-test (no equality of variance was assumed) | | |
| | Yes N = 46 | | No N = 225 | | | | |
	Mean	St. dev.	Mean	St. dev.	t	df	p-value (two-sided)
Exposure to currency risk (1 = yes, 0 = no)	1.00	0.00	0.40	0.49	18.33	224.00	0.000
Use of simple derivatives such as currency options, futures, swaps (1 = yes, 0 = no)	0.07	0.25	0.04	0.20	0.65	56.93	0.521
Company does not hedge against currency risk (1 = yes, 0 = no)	0.02	0.15	0.96	0.20	−36.97	81.42	0.000
No. of sources of funds already used in the company	8.24	4.31	4.26	2.89	6.00	53.60	0.000
No. of sources of funds, that are going to be used in the company	10.04	5.11	14.04	5.01	−4.85	63.91	0.000
Losses in 2007–2009 due to toxic options (1 = yes, 0 = no)	0.98	0.15	0.03	0.16	39.23	68.94	0.000

In the group of economic factors, there were questions about sources of funds that respondents

- already used in the company,
- had been planning to use in the future.

They could choose different sources of funds out of the proposed list of 22 items. The list comprised 22 items: 1) self-financing, 2) retained profit, 3) sale of redundant assets, 4) depreciation write-offs, 5) owners' surcharges, 6) share issue, 7) bond issue, 8) long-term loan, 9) short-term loan, 10) loan, 11) operating lease, 12) financial leasing, 13) subsidies, 14) state subsidies, 15) EU grants, 16) factoring, 17) issue of securities other than bonds, 18) venture capital, 19) business angels, 20) supply chain financing, 21) overdraft and 22) trade credit. The variables were determined as the sum of the indications of funding sources.

If one looks at Table 8.5, all entrepreneurs who decided to use hedging with complex derivative instruments confirmed that they had exposure to currency risk. These results demonstrate that they had an actual position in a foreign currency, and hedging was not carried out from purely speculative motives. There are no statistically significant differences in the reported use of simple derivatives such as currency options, futures and swaps. Both groups used classical simple currency derivatives to the same extent. The group that used hedging with complex derivative instruments did not differ from the other group in terms of using classical simple currency derivatives. It is worth noting that the use of complex derivative instruments was not preceded by more extensive experience with simple instruments. Entrepreneurs who used complex derivative instruments reported a similar level of the use of classical simple currency derivatives as those who had not used complex derivative instruments. Another difference between toxic-option takers and non-takers was the selection of the sources of funds. Those entrepreneurs who decided to use hedging with complex derivative instruments used more sources of funds already in the company, but the group that has not used hedging with complex derivative instruments declared to use more sources of funds in the future. Entrepreneurs who refused complex options were significantly more open to trying new sources in the future. Entrepreneurs who decided to use hedging with complex derivative instruments confirmed that they had experienced losses in 2007–2009 due to toxic options. Complex currency derivatives were present in the Polish OTC forex market mainly in the period of 2007–2009.

The results presented here show that taking a position in FX options and exposing oneself to a huge risk of loss was linked to other economic factors such as risk exposure but also a much greater activity of companies. In addition, the purchase of relatively complex derivatives was also influenced by behavioural factors such as overconfidence and risk-seeking in the area of losses. Variables examining information processing did not influence the decision to take a position in currency options. The factors analysed show that not only economic factors are taken into account in hedging decisions, but also behavioural factors related to risk propensity and overconfidence. The study shows that the currency option settlement crisis in Poland, observed at an aggregate level, is also due to behavioural aspects of individual decision-makers. Behavioural factors significantly influence the propensity of traders to take excessive risks, and any actions aimed at prevention should also take these factors into account.

8.6   CONCLUSION

The analysis of the reaction of the Polish economy to the subprime crisis and the resulting currency crisis showed that at the macroeconomic level, despite the high exposure to currency risk, the country managed the crisis relatively well. Unfortunately, at the microeconomic level, that is, individual entrepreneurs, the situation was completely different. Exporters' open currency positions in the over-the-counter market have caused enormous financial losses across the corporate sector, due to negative settlement of currency options in the conditions of a trend reversal.

When one looks at the aggregated data it strikes an observer how big the volume of risky contracts acquired at the time was, despite the considerable currency risk. Entrepreneurs who should have concentrated on making profits in their core businesses made risky investments in currency markets. Such behaviour is puzzling, and it spurred the questionnaire research conducted to find the relationship between behavioural inclinations and economic activities with the decisions of involvement in toxic currency options.

The survey results suggest that the way of information processing and susceptibility to heuristics did not underlie the acquisition of risky option strategies. This is in line with research showing individual differences; for example, Bailly et al. (2003) were analysing the derivative practices of UK non-financial firms after large losses on derivatives transactions. In our research, we were focused also on behavioural motivation supporting decisions about the use of currency derivatives. Information-processing methods are not crucial, while risk attitudes and overconfidence played an essential role in differentiating the groups which sustained and did not sustain losses from foreign-exchange contracts.

NOTES

1.   The analysis of the crisis in 2008 was carried out without analysing the costs of the Polish Central Bank intervention in the currency market, as such data was not available.

2.   The research has been carried out as part of a research initiative entitled 'Socio-economic consequences of the fourth industrial revolution' financed by the Ministry of Science and Higher Education within the 'Regional Initiative of Excellence' Programme for 2019–2022. Project no.: 021/RID/2018/19. Total financing: 11,897,131.40 PLN.

REFERENCES

Ahmad, M., and Shah, S. Z. A. 2020. 'Overconfidence heuristic-driven bias in investment decision-making and performance: Mediating effects of risk perception and moderating effects of financial literacy.' *Journal of Economic and Administrative Sciences*, 39: 1–31. DOI: 10.1108/JEAS-07-2020-0116.

Bailly, N., Browne, D., Hicks, E., and Skerrat, L. 2003. 'UK corporate use of derivatives.' *The European Journal of Finance*, 9(2): 169–193. DOI: 10.1080/135 18470110071218a.

Banbula, P., Kozinski, W., and Rubaszek, M. 2010. 'The role of the exchange rate in monetary policy in Poland.' *The Bank for International Settlements*, 57: 285–295.

Bartram, S. M., Brown, G. W., and Fehle, F. R. 2009. 'International evidence on financial derivatives usage.' *Financial Management*, 38: 185–206. DOI: 10.1111/j.1755-053X.2009.01033.x.

Benatti, Nicola, and Napolitano, Francesco. 2019. 'An insight into the derivatives trading of firms in the euro area,' IFC Bulletins chapters, [In:] Bank for International Settlements (ed.), Are post-crisis statistical initiatives completed?, vol 49, Bank for International Settlements. https://EconPapers.repec.org/RePEc:bis:bisifc: 49–20.

Carlson, M., Carroll, C., Chan, I., Cooper, G., Lehner, V., Montgomery, K., Tran, D., Mody, Ashok, and James, Marzenna. 2016. 'Should Poland join the Euro?: An economic and political analysis.' Woodrow Wilson School of Public & International Affairs, Princeton University. http://arks.princeton.edu/ark:/88435/dsp01df65vb64m.

Cossette, P. 2014. 'Heuristics and cognitive biases in entrepreneurs: A review of the research.' *Journal of Small Business and Entrepreneurship*, 27(5): 471–496.

Edwards, W. 1968. 'Conservatism in Human Information Processing'. [In:] Kleinmuntz B. [Ed.], Formal Representation of Human Judgment, Wiley, New York, 17–52.

Edwards, W. 1982. Conservatism in human information processing (excerpted). In Kahneman, Slovic, Paul, and Tversky, Amos (eds.). *Judgment Under Uncertainty: Heuristics and Biases*. New York: Cambridge University Press.

Frederick, S. 2005. 'Cognitive reflection and decision making.' *Journal of Economic Perspectives*, 19(4). DOI: 10.1257/089533005775196732.

Géczy, C., Minton, B. A., and Schrand, C. 1997. 'Why firms use currency derivatives.' *The Journal of Finance*, 52: 1323–1354. DOI: 10.1111/j.1540-6261.1997.tb01112.x.

Gilovich, T. D., Griffin, D., and Kahneman, D. 2002. *Heuristics and Biases: The Psychology of Intuitive Judgment*. New York, NY: Cambridge University Press.

Glaser, M., and Weber, M. 2010. 'Overconfidence' [in:] Baker, H.K., Nofsiner, J. [eds.], 'Behavioral finance: investors, corporations, and markets', John Wiley & Sons, Inc., New York, 241–258.

Holt, C. A., and Laury, S. K. 2002. 'Risk Aversion and Incentive Effects', *The American Economic Review*, 92(5): 1644–1655.

Kahneman, D., and Tversky, A. 1979. 'Prospect theory: An analysis of decision under risk.' *Econometrica*, 47(2): 263–291.

Kariofyllas, S., Philippas, D., and Siriopoulos, C. 2017. 'Cognitive biases in investors' behaviour under stress: Evidence from the London stock exchange.' *International Review of Financial Analysis*, 54: 54–62.

Kasimati, E., and Veraros, N. 2013. 'Should Greece adopt a dual-currency regime to resolve its economic crisis?' *Journal of Policy Modeling*, 35(4): 588–600.

Langer, E. J. 1975. 'The illusion of control'. *Journal of Personality and Social Psychology*, 32(2): 311–328.

Liberadzki, K. 2015. 'The issue of 'toxic' foreign exchange options in Poland.' *Jordan Journal of Economic Sciences*, 2(1): 87–95.

Lichtenstein, S., Fischhoff, B., and Phillips, L. D. 1982. 'Calibration of Probabilities: The State of the Art to 1980,' [In:] Kahneman, D., Solvic, P., Tversky, A. [eds.], 'Judgment under Uncertainty: Heuristics and Biases', Cambridge University Press, Cambridge, New York, 306–224.

Shiller, Robert J. 2003. 'From efficient markets theory to behavioral finance.' *Journal of Economic Perspectives*, 17(1): 83–104.

Svenson, O. 1981. 'Are we all less risky and more skillful than our fellow drivers?' *Acta Psychologica*, 47(2): 143–148.

Tversky, Amos, and Kahneman, Daniel. 1973. 'Availability: A heuristic for judging frequency and probability.' *Cognitive Psychology*, 5(2): 207–232.

Wärneryd, K. E. 1996. 'Risk attitudes and risky behavior', *Journal of Economic Psychology*, 17(6): 749–770.

9. Real exchange rate, demand growth and labour productivity: a growth model of cumulative and circular causation

Hugo C. Iasco-Pereira, Fabrício J. Missio, Frederico G. Jayme Jr and Douglas Alencar

9.1 INTRODUCTION

There is extensive literature related to the influence of real exchange rate (RER) on long-run growth. Many articles have confirmed the positive impact of a competitive RER on long-run performance. Rodrik's (2008) article is a widespread study in the literature on this topic. Rodrik's findings suggest that a competitive RER spurs long-run growth, especially for developing countries. His argument is that pursuing a competitive RER acts as a second-best policy, or a substitute for industrial policy, to foster economic growth. The competitive RER counterbalances the negative consequences of bad institutions over the profitability of investments and acts as a substitute for industrial policy. Moreover, Rodrik suggests additional effects of the competitive RER via its enlarging effects in tradable sectors and in the diversification of the mix of produced goods in the productive structure.

This chapter provides a growth model of cumulative and circular causation, in the Kaldorian tradition, to explain the association between a competitive RER and long-run economic growth. For that, we follow the articles of Cornwell and Setterfield (2002) and Naastepad (2005) to build up a theoretical approach. Our model is constructed under the Kaldorian demand-led tradition, in which economic growth comes from the interaction between demand growth and labour productivity growth.

Regarding the canonical growth model of Dixon and Thirlwall (1975), we extend the demand regime to consider the domestic demand in addition to exports as sources of demand growth in a manner in which a competitive RER can increase, or damage, the demand growth, depending on the regime of demand (wage- or profit-led). We model labour productivity behaviour as a function of demand growth. Hence, the growth rate of labour productivity is determined by the Kaldor-Verdoorn mechanism via the increasing returns of scale.

The chapter's contribution to the existing literature is to introduce the RER directly as a determinant of labour productivity. The argument is that a competitive RER, by influencing the capital accumulation (which embodies technological progress) via its effects on the profit rate, determines, in part, the labour productivity. However, such influence is associated with the regime of capital accumulation of the economy. In economies under a profit- (wage-) led regime of capital accumulation, a competitive RER increases (damages) the labour productivity, given the pace of demand growth. The results indicate that a competitive RER, in an economy under a profit- (wage-)led regime of demand and capital accumulation, increases (damages) the long-run growth due to the expansionary (contractionary) effect over the demand growth, which is reinforced by the expansionary (contractionary) effect over the labour productivity growth.

The chapter provides a simple econometric exercise to test the effect of a competitive RER on the labour productivity of OECD countries over the period 1974–2019. The empirical findings suggest that a competitive RER increases the growth rate of labour productivity, on average. Moreover, the results indicate heterogeneous effects of a competitive RER over the countries.

The chapter is composed of five sections, besides this introduction. Section 9.2 exposes a brief literature review. Section 9.3 presents the fundamentals of our model. Section 9.4 discusses the influence of RER on economic growth. Section 9.5 provides some econometric exercises to test the association between the RER and the growth rate of labour productivity. Section 9.6 completes the study with the main conclusions.

9.2   A BRIEF LITERATURE REVIEW

There exists a vast literature documenting the empirical association between RER and growth: Cottani et al. (1990), Dollar (1992), Razin and Collins (1997), Bahlla (2012), Gala (2007), Rodrik (2008), Rapetti et al. (2011), Vieira and MacDonald (2012), Missio et al. (2015), among others, are some examples. The results of these studies indicate that pursuing a competitive (non-competitive) RER spurs (damages) growth. Rapetti (2020) delivers an extensive survey of the empirical studies, confirming the previous association. Rapetti (2020) points out that the volatility of RER has a negative effect on growth. In other words, the empirical literature suggests that a stable and competitive RER has a positive impact on economic growth.

In the theoretical field, multiple transmission channels account for the positive influence of a devalued RER over the growth. Rapetti (2020) also offers a survey about this topic. On the one hand, an undervalued RER favours capital accumulation and economic growth by reducing macroeconomic volatility and, on the other, stimulates a structural change towards the cutting-edge tradable sectors (Rapetti, 2020). Such an effect is stronger in developing countries, as devaluations of RER act as a second-best policy, which counterbalances the influence of its bad institutions over growth (Rodrik, 2008). In addition, pursuing a non-competitive RER is a symptom of bad institutions because it obstructs the emergence of new productive activities, favouring the elite in power (Acemoglu et al., 2003).

A competitive RER acts by means of favouring the investments' profitability. A competitive RER expands the investment/saving; it transfers income from workers (with lower propensity to save) to entrepreneurs (with greater propensity to save). Consequently, the investment capacity of the economy is enlarged (Bahmani-Oskooe and Hajilee, 2010; Glüzmann et al., 2012). Provided that the capital accumulation, induced by a devalued RER, materializes in fact, the labour productivity is boosted, as well as the long-run economic performance.

The Kaldorian literature, in turn, explains the association between RER and economic growth in the terms of the balance-of-payments-constrained growth models, or simply by means of Thirlwall's law. The parameter of income-elasticities of exports is endogenized with respect to the structural change induced by the RER's policy. Pursuing a competitive RER promotes a structural change in the productive structure towards the manufacturing/ modern sectors. On the condition that the income-elasticities of exports of these sectors are greater, the growth rate of output consistent with the equilibrium in the balance of payment becomes greater. The studies of Missio and Jayme (2012) and Missio et al. (2017) are examples from this literature. The theoretical model is developed in the next section.

9.3   A CUMULATIVE AND CIRCULAR CAUSATION GROWTH MODEL

Considering the Kaldorian tradition, our model assumes that economic growth is a cumulative and circular process, following Myrdal (1957) and Kaldor (1970). The growth cumulativeness comes from the interaction between the demand regime (DR) and productivity regime (PR) (Setterfield and Cornwall, 2002). The DR states how the demand growth is determined. The canonical version of Dixon and Thirlwall's (1975) model assumes that demand growth is uniquely represented by exports. The PR points out the determinants of productivity growth, which is represented by the Kaldor-Verdoorn mechanism:

productivity cohesively increases with demand growth (Setterfield and Cornwall, 2002).

It is argued that there is a feedback interaction between demand growth and productivity growth. The greater the demand growth, the greater the productivity growth and the gains in international competitiveness of domestic goods. This leads to a better performance of exports that reinforces the process. Then, the DR and the PR constitute a system of equations, in which both equations influence each other, providing the cumulative and circular logic of economic growth. The theoretical model developed hereafter is built up upon this tradition. However, we extend some aspects of this cluster of growth models by assuming that:

(1) The DR is not compounded exclusively by the exports. We have extended the model by introducing consumption and investment as additional sources of demand growth.
(2) The RER is an exogenous variable, determined by the monetary authority: positive (negative) values of RER mean that the national currency is cheaper (more expansive) in relation to the foreign currency. It is assumed that the monetary authority pursues a competitive RER.
(3) The RER influences demand growth indirectly by changing the functional income distribution between workers and entrepreneurs and by its effects on the growth rate of labour productivity – in other words, by influencing consumption (wage share), investment (profit rate) and exports (international competitiveness of domestic goods).
(4) The RER is directly introduced in the PR together with the demand growth as a determinant of productivity growth. The argument is that the RER influences the profit rate of firms, influencing the firm's decision of making new investments (that embodies technological progress). We have modelled the DR and the PR and their interaction in what follows. Given that, firstly, we have modelled the link between productivity, price and income distribution. Next, we model the association between RER and DR, and, ending the section, we have modelled the PR.

9.3.1 RER, Prices and Income Distribution

The domestic price of the economy is modelled as a function of labour costs in the following way, assuming the existence of one sector:[1]

$$P_{d,t} = (1 + M_t) b_t W_t \qquad (9.1)$$

where the variables P_t, M_t, b_t and W_t represent the price, the markup rate under the nominal wages W_t, while b_t is the labour coefficient (labour hours per unit of output). Rearranging the equation (9.1) as a function of the labour productivity and taking the log-difference:[2]

$$r_t = m_t + (w_t - p_{d,t}) \qquad (9.1.1)$$

The growth rate of labour productivity is represented by r_t. Equation (9.1.1) shows how the gains in labour productivity are distributed between entrepreneurs (markup) and workers (real wage).

Blecker (1989) claims that the markup rate is endogenous regarding the RER. A competitive RER expands the markup rate because the domestic firms increase their prices to benefit from the elevated competitiveness in relation to the foreign goods, and vice versa (Blecker, 1989). Then, changes in the markup rate can be described as:

$$m_t = b_1 r_t + b_2 \text{rer}_t \qquad (9.2)$$

Increases in labour productivity, as well as RER devaluations, spur the markup rate. Equation (9.2) indicates that:

(1) The first term of the right side of equation (9.2) suggests the possibility of changes in the markup rate (and, then, in the functional income distribution) without, necessarily, occurring changes in the domestic prices. In other words, if changes in labour productivity are absorbed by the markup rate, the profit margin expands without inflationary pressures. This is the case in developing economies. The gains from labour productivity are not shared between workers and entrepreneurs due to the numerous unemployed people. The social conflict regarding the gains from labour productivity is feeble/low. Workers do not have the bargaining power to claim gains in the real wage. Workers obtain a real wage barely adequate for the means of subsistence.
(2) The second term, in turn, is associated with changes in domestic prices. In this case, the parameter b_2 captures the effect of changes in the RER over the markup rate and, consequently, over the prices. Such an expanded markup rate represents the lower real wages induced by the RER devaluations (especially in developing countries due to the reasons set out earlier).

Moreover, it should be emphasized that, when dealing with an open economy, the RER influences the prices of domestic goods in the international market. Considering that the international price $P_{i,t}$ is $P_{d,t} * RER_t$, then:

$$p_{i,t} = m_t + w_t - r_t - \text{rer}_t \qquad (9.3)$$

Equation (9.3) represents the changes in the domestic goods' prices, in the international market. RER devaluations make domestic goods cheaper. Introducing (9.2) into (9.3) and rearranging:

$$p_{i,t} = (b_1 - 1) r_t + (b_2 - 1) \text{rer}_t \tag{9.3.1}$$

On the other hand, within the Kaleckian tradition, the functional income distribution between workers and capitalists results from the firm's markup. The total profits and the profit as a share of GDP π_t (in growth rate) depend positively on the markup rate (Kalecki, 1956). Equation (9.2), then, becomes:

$$\pi_t = b_1 r_t + b_2 \text{rer}_t \tag{9.4}$$

Increases in labour productivity, or RER devaluations, expand the profits as a share of GDP.

Taking the equations (9.3.1) and (9.4) together, the parameter b_1 captures how much of the labour productivity is absorbed by an expanded profit as a share of GDP (equation 9.4), while $(b_1 - 1)$ captures how much of the labour productivity is passed onto the prices in the international market (equation 9.3.1). The parameter b_2, in turn, captures how much of the devaluations in RER are passed onto the markup rate (equation 9.4), while $(b_2 - 1)$ captures how much of the devaluations in RER are passed onto the prices.[3]

9.3.2 Demand Regime, Productivity Growth and RER

The DR is compounded by consumption c_t, investment i_t, exports x_t and imports m_t:

$$y_t = c_t + i_t + x_t - m_t \tag{9.5}$$

The growth rate of consumption is represented as:

$$c_t = (1 - \sigma_\omega) \omega_t + (1 - \sigma_\pi) \pi_t \tag{9.6}$$

where ω_t, σ_ω and σ_π stand for the growth rate of wage share in GDP and the marginal propensity to save of workers and entrepreneurs, respectively. As ω_t can be represented as $-\pi_t$, the equation (9.6) can be rearranged as:

$$c_t = (\sigma_\omega - \sigma_\pi) \pi_t \tag{9.7}$$

Equation (9.7) reveals that the effects of changes in the functional income distribution on the growth rate of consumption depend on the difference between the parameters σ_ω and σ_π. The behaviour of investment is modelled in accordance with Bahduri and Marglin (1990):

$$i_t = i_0 + i_1 y_t + i_2 \pi_t \tag{9.8}$$

where i_0 is the '*animal spirits*' (or simply the expectations) of the entrepreneurs, following Lavoie (2015). The parameter i_1 is the response of investment to changes in demand (accelerator effect), while i_2 is the response of investment to the profit share (markup rate) (Bahduri and Marglin, 1990).

The growth rate of exports is modelled as a positive function of foreign demand growth $y_{f,t}$ and as a negative function of the changes in domestic prices p_t (we assume that the foreign price is constant over time):

$$x_t = x_1 y_{f,t} - x_2 p_t \tag{9.9}$$

The growth rate of imports is modelled as a positive function of domestic demand growth y_t:

$$m_t = m_1 y_t \tag{9.10}$$

Introducing (9.3), (9.4.1), (9.7), (9.8), (9.9) and (9.10) into equation (9.5) we get the DR:

$$y_t =$$
$$\frac{\left(\sigma_\omega - \sigma_\pi\right)\left(b_1 r_t + b_2\, \mathrm{rer}_t\right) + i_0 + i_2\left(b_1 r_t + b_2 \mathrm{rer}_t\right) + x_1 y_{f,t} - x_2\left(\left(b_1 - 1\right)r_t + \left(b_2 - 1\right)\mathrm{rer}_t\right)}{\left(1 - i_1 + m_1\right)} \tag{9.11}$$

Taking the first difference of (9.11) in relation to r_t and rer_t:

$$\frac{dy_t}{dr_t} = \frac{\left(\sigma_\omega - \sigma_\pi\right)b_1 + i_2 b_1 - x_2\left(b_1 - 1\right)}{\left(1 - i_1 + m_1\right)} \tag{9.12}$$

$$\frac{dy_t}{drer_t} = \frac{\left(\sigma_\omega - \sigma_\pi\right)b_2 + i_2 b_2 - x_2\left(b_2 - 1\right)}{\left(1 - i_1 + m_1\right)} \tag{9.13}$$

Assuming that $(1 - i_1 + m_1)$ is positive, the derivatives signal is ambiguous and is associated with the parameter setting. In economies under a regime of demand profit- (wage-)led reduction of wage share of GDP spurs (harms) the demand growth. The lower consumption is (is not) compensated by higher investment and exports. The scenario of a profit-led regime occurs when the signal of (9.12) or (9.13) is positive. Otherwise, the regime of demand is wage-led.

Before all else, it should be noticed that the parameters b_1 and b_2 are essential in this analysis. In the case in which $b_1 = b_2 = 1$, the growth rate of labour productivity and the changes in RER do not influence the international competitiveness because firms absorb them by increasing their markup (profit share): the determination of the demand regime depends on the parameters of consumption and investment. In the case in which $b_1 = b_2 = 0$, the growth rate of labour productivity and the changes in RER do not influence the profit share because firms entirely pass them on into the prices: the demand regime is profit-led. Let us assume that the parameters b_1 and b_2 are lower than the unity.

The wage-led regime of demand occurs when $|b_1\sigma_\pi| > (|b_1\sigma_w| + |b_1 i_2| + |x_2(b_1 - 1)|)$ in (9.12), or $|b_2\sigma_\pi| > (|b_2\sigma_w| + |b_2 i_2| + |x_2(b_2 - 1)|)$ in (9.13): increases in productivity growth and devaluations of RER, by reducing increasing the profit share, reduce the demand growth. Figure 9.1 illustrates the wage-led regime of demand.

In turn, the profit-led regime of demand occurs when $|b_1\sigma_\pi| < (|b_1\sigma_w| + |b_1 i_2| + |x_2(b_1 - 1)|)$ in (9.12), or $|b_2\sigma_\pi| < (|b_2\sigma_w| + |b_2 i_2| + |x_2(b_2 - 1)|)$ in (9.13): increases in productivity growth and devaluations of RER, by reducing increasing the profit share, increase the demand growth. Figure 9.2 illustrates the profit-led regime of demand.

9.3.3 Productivity Regime, Demand Growth and RER

In our model, the growth rate of labour productivity is determined by the demand growth and by technological progress:

$$r_t = r_0 + \lambda y_t + \theta i_t \tag{9.14}$$

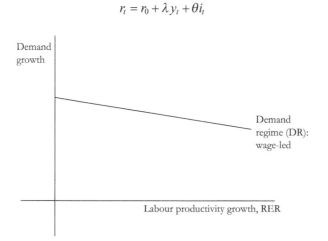

Figure 9.1 Demand regime: the wage-led case

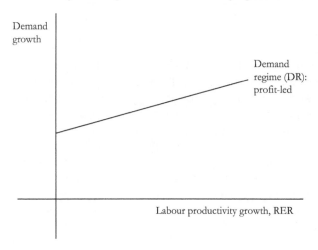

Figure 9.2   Demand regime: the profit-led case

r_0 is the autonomous growth of labour productivity. The parameter λ, positive and around 0.5, captures the Kaldor-Verdoorn mechanism: the faster the pace of demand growth, the greater the labour productivity growth. The parameter θ captures the effects of investment on the growth rate of labour productivity. The argument pursued in this chapter is that the RER influences capital accumulation (that embodies technological progress) by its effects on the profit rate, which affects the growth rate of labour productivity: the higher the technological progress induced by RER, the greater the labour productivity growth. The PR is described graphically in Figure 9.3.

The ambiguous effects of RER on investment should be highlighted. In a profit-led regime of capital accumulation, increases in productivity growth and devaluations of RER increase the demand growth and the profit share, elevating the capital accumulation. As a result, the line of productivity regime dislocates to the right. In a wage-led capital accumulation regime, increases in productivity growth and RER devaluations reduce the demand growth and increase the profit share. It turns out that the smaller demand growth is not compensated by the greater profit share. As a result, capital accumulation reduces, and the productivity regime line dislocates to the left.

Therefore, devaluations of RER have different effects on the growth rate of labour productivity in economies under distinct regimes of capital accumulation. A competitive RER, *ceteris paribus*, increases (reduces) the growth rate of labour productivity within an economy under a profit- (wage-)led regime of capital accumulation: the PR dislocates towards the right (left).

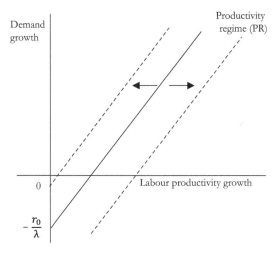

Figure 9.3 Productivity regime: demand growth and capital accumulation

The next section discusses the impact of pursuing a competitive RER in our theoretical model.

9.4 INTERACTION BETWEEN THE DEMAND AND PRODUCTIVITY REGIMES

Following Naastepad (2005), we express our model as:

$$y_{t,dr} = \alpha_{1,t} + \alpha_2 \text{rer}_t + \alpha_3 r_t \tag{9.15}$$

$$y_{t,pr} = 1/\lambda \left(r_t - r_0 - \theta i_t \right) \tag{9.16}$$

where $\alpha_{1,t}$ is $[(i_0 + x_1 y_{ft})/(1 - i_1 + m_1)]$, α_2 is $[((\sigma_\omega - \sigma_\pi)b_2 + i_2 b_2 - x_2(b_2 - 1))/(1 - i_1 + m_1)]$ and α_3 is $[(\sigma_\omega - \sigma_\pi)b_1 + i_2 b_1 - x_2(b_1 - 1)/(1 - i_1 + m_1)]$. The variable $y_{t,dr}$ represents the growth rate of demand permitted by productivity growth and the devaluation of RER. In turn, the variable $y_{t,dr}$ represents the growth rate of demand required to sustain the productivity growth.

The equilibrium requires that $y_{t,dr}$ equals $y_{t,pr}$:

$$r_t^* = \left(-r_0 - \theta i_t - \alpha_{1,t} - \alpha_2 \text{ rer}_t\right)(\alpha_3 - 1/\lambda)^{-1} \tag{9.17}$$

Introducing (9.17) into (9.15):

$$y_t^* = \alpha_{1,t} + \left(\alpha_2 - \alpha_3\alpha_2\left(\alpha_3 - 1/\lambda\right)^{-1}\right)\mathrm{rer}_t$$

$$+ \alpha_3\left(\left(-r_0 - \theta i_t - \alpha_{1,t}\right)\left(\alpha_3 - 1/\lambda\right)^{-1}\right)$$

(9.18)

Equations (9.17) and (9.18) provide the equilibrium value of r_t and y_t, respectively.

9.4.1   The Effects of RER Devaluations

The equilibrium expressions (9.17) and (9.18) allow comprehending how the RER influences the model's equilibrium. The first difference between (9.17) and (9.18) is presented below:

$$\frac{dr_t^*}{d\mathrm{rer}_t} = -\left(\theta i_t' + \alpha_2\right)\left(\alpha_3 - \frac{1}{\lambda}\right)^{-1}$$

(9.19)

$$\frac{dy_t^*}{d\mathrm{rer}_t} = \left(\alpha_2 - \left(\alpha_3\left(\theta i_t' + \alpha_2\right)\right)\right)\left(\alpha_3 - \frac{1}{\lambda}\right)^{-1}$$

(9.20)

The effects of RER devaluations on economic growth are associated with the regimes of demand and capital accumulation (i.e. with the parameters α_2, α_3, and with i_t'). Before examining the consequences of devaluations in RER, it is important to stress some aspects of equations (9.19) and (9.20). The parameters α_2 and α_3 represent the regime of demand of the economy: negative (positive) values indicate a wage- (profit-)led demand regime. In turn, the expression $(\alpha_3 - 1/\lambda)^{-1}$ is crucial in determining the signal of the expressions (9.19) and (9.20). It should be noticed that Verdoorn's coefficient is around 0.5, which produces a value around 2 for the expression $1/\lambda$. As it is very unlikely that the parameter α_3 (the sensibility of demand growth to changes in labour productivity) may be greater than 2, we assume that the expression $(\alpha_3 - 1/\lambda)^{-1}$ is negative:

(1) When the regimes of demand and capital accumulation are wage-led (α_2, α_3, i_t are negative): devaluations of RER reduce the equilibrium productivity growth. The PR dislocates from PR_0 to PR_1 due to its contractionary effects on demand growth and technological progress. The effects on demand growth are not straightforward. Although the devaluations in RER reduce the wage share (contractionary effect), a lower labour

productivity growth induced by the devaluations in RER increases the wage share (expansionary effect). Therefore, its effects depend on if the lower wage share induced by the devaluations in RER offset the greater wage share induced by the lower labour productivity growth. In this sense, in the expression (9.20), α_2 is negative and $-\left(\alpha_3\left(\theta i_t + \alpha_2\right)\right)\left(\alpha_3 - \dfrac{1}{\lambda}\right)^{-1}$ is positive: if $|\alpha_2| > |\left(\alpha_3\left(\theta i_t + \alpha_2\right)\right)\left(\alpha_3 - \dfrac{1}{\lambda}\right)^{-1}|$, the demand regime is wage-led (otherwise, it is profit-led).

We assume that $|\alpha_2| > |\left(\alpha_3\left(\theta i_t + \alpha_2\right)\right)\left(\alpha_3 - \dfrac{1}{\lambda}\right)^{-1}|$. As a result, devaluations of RER dislocate the DR from DR_0 to DR_1, towards a slower pace of demand growth. Figure 9.4 displays this dynamic graphically. Devaluations of RER harm the equilibrium value of r_t, y_t and, then, the long-run growth of economies under wage-led regimes of demand and capital accumulation.

(2) When the regimes of demand and capital accumulation are profit-led (α_2, α_3, i_t' are positive): devaluations of RER boost the equilibrium productivity growth. The PR dislocates from PR_0 to PR_1 due to its expansionary effects on demand growth and technological progress.

In turn, devaluations of RER dislocate the DR from DR_0 to DR_1, towards a faster pace of demand growth. Both the lower wage share and the greater labour

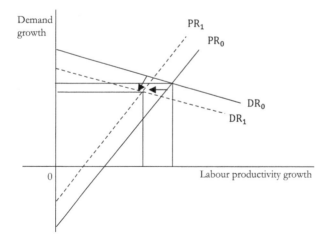

Figure 9.4   The effects of devaluations in RER: the wage-led case

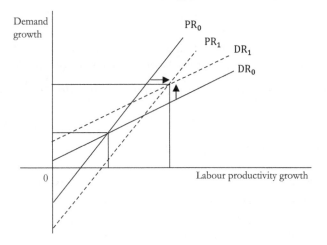

Figure 9.5   The effects of devaluations in RER: the profit-led case

productivity induced by the devalued RER boost the demand growth. Therefore, devaluations of RER enhance the equilibrium value of r_t, y_t and, consequently, the long-run growth of economies under profit-led regimes of demand and capital accumulation. Figure 9.5 illustrates graphically this dynamic.

The following section provides a set of simple econometric regressions to test whether the RER has an impact on the labour productivity of OECD countries.

9.5   RER AND LABOUR PRODUCTIVITY: EMPIRICAL EVIDENCE FOR OECD COUNTRIES (1974–2019)

We have performed a simple econometric exercise to test the effect of RER devaluations on the labour productivity growth of OECD countries over the period 1974–2019. The complete sample is compounded by 24 countries, presented in Table A.9.1 (in appendix). Not all OECD countries are presented in our sample due to the absence of data for multiple years. The first econometric specification performed is:

$$y_{t,i} = b_0 + b_1 mis_{t,i} + u_{t,i} \tag{9.21}$$

the subscript t and i represent the year and the country, respectively. The dependent variable is the growth rate of labour productivity, represented by the GDP per hour worked (constant prices and adjusted by the 2015's Purchasing Power Parity). This variable comes from the OECD productivity database.[4]

The dependent variable, $mis_{t,i}$, represents the measure of RER misalignment calculated by Couharde et al. (2017).[5] Negative values of $mis_{t,i}$ indicate that the RER is devalued in relation to its fundamentals (Balassa-Samuelson effect, terms of trade and net asset position). A negative parameter estimated of b_1 indicates that a devalued (valued) RER increases (harms) the growth rate of labour productivity.

The second model estimated is:

$$y_{t,i} = b_0 + b_1 mis_{t,i} + b_2 \left(mis_{t,i} * \text{country dummy} \right) + u_{t,i} \qquad (9.22)$$

The estimation of equation (9.22) aims to capture the heterogeneous effects of a competitive RER on the labour productivity for distinct countries. For that, we introduce the variable ($mis_{t,i}$*country dummy) that represents the variable $mis_{t,i}$ multiplied by 23 dummies for countries. Therefore, we estimate the individual effect of a competitive RER.

As our database variables have a more extensive number of years than individuals ($T > N$), we chose to run the estimates using the methodology of panel-corrected standard errors (PCSE).[6] Estimates are performed by controlling countries' fixed-effect and time fixed-effect. This procedure is useful to capture, to some extent, unobserved characteristics across the sectors and over time. Moreover, it should be noticed that this econometric methodology does not address the likely issue of endogeneity in our regressions. We argue that this potential weakness of our estimates is mitigated by the fact that the variable $mis_{t,i}$ is calculated discounting the influence of the Balassa-Samuelson effect, terms of trade and net asset position on the real exchange rate. Table 9.1 reports the estimates.

The estimates of equation (9.21) (columns 1 and 2) suggest that a devaluation of 10 per cent in RER increases the growth rate of labour productivity by 0.2 per cent. This is the 'common' effect, on average, in all countries of our sample. Columns 3 and 4, in turn, report the results of estimates of equation (9.22). The 'particular' effect of a competitive RER has proven statistically significant in few countries. The results of column 3 indicate that a devaluation of 10 per cent in RER increases the growth rate of labour productivity by 0.1 per cent (Canada), 0.3 per cent (Denmark), 0.3 per cent (Finland), 0.9 per cent (France), 0.4 per cent (Greece), 0.7 per cent (Israel), 0.5 per cent (Italy), 0.2 per cent (Japan), 0.4 per cent (Portugal), 0.3 per cent (Spain) and 0.4 per cent (Sweden). The results of column 4 confirm these results, except for Finland and Greece.

9.6   FINAL DISCUSSION

This chapter provides a Kaldorian model to study the RER influence on long-run growth. The contribution to the existing literature is to consider the influence of RER on labour productivity growth, in addition to the Kaldor-Verdoorn

Table 9.1   RER and labour productivity growth

	(1)	(2)	(3)	(4)
y_{t-1}		0.07* (0.04)		0.05 (0.04)
$mis_{t,i}$	−0.02** (0.01)	−0.02* (0.01)	0.03***(0.01)	0.009 (0.02)
Australia			−0.01 (0.03)	0.005 (0.03)
Belgium			−0.02 (0.03)	−0.02 (0.03)
Canada			−0.05* (0.02)	−0.04* (0.20)
Chile			0.02 (0.06)	0.04 (0.06)
Denmark			−0.06* (0.03)	−0.04 (0.03)
Finland			−0.06* (0.03)	−0.03 (0.03)
France			−0.12*** (0.03)	−0.11*** (0.03)
Germany			−0.05 (0.03)	−0.04 (0.03)
Greece			−0.07* (0.03)	−0.05 (0.03)
Iceland			−0.08 (0.06)	−0.02 (0.04)
Ireland			−0.08 (0.06)	−0.06 (0.05)
Israel			−0.10* (0.05)	−0.10* (0.05)
Italy			−0.08*** (0.02)	−0.07*** (0.02)
Japan			−0.05** (0.02)	−0.04* (0.02)
Korea			0.01 (0.03)	0.01 (0.03)
Netherlands			−0.07** (0.03)	−0.05* (0.03)
Norway			−0.01 (0.02)	−0.007 (0.02)
Portugal			−0.07*** (0.02)	−0.05** (0.02)
Spain			−0.06** (0.02)	−0.05** (0.02)
Sweden			−0.07** (0.03)	−0.06** (0.02)
Switzerland			−0.01 (0.03)	−0.02 (0.03)
United States			−0.005 (0.02)	0.01 (0.02)
United Kingdom			−0.007 (0.03)	−0.01 (0.02)
constant	0.01*** (0.003)	0.03*** (0.003)	0.01*** (0.003)	0.03*** (0.003)
R^2	0.28	0.33	0.32	0.36

Notes:
1) All variables are in logarithm form.
2) The dependent variable is the log-diff of labour productivity.
3) All regressions are estimated controlling both country fixed-effect as time fixed-effect.
4) The panels are performed using the option correlation of AR(1) in the error term.
5) The panel is unbalanced (the number of observations per group [24] is: min 32, avg 42.7 and max 44; the number of observations is 1,025).
6) We introduce the variable mis in lagged values (not reported, but available upon request).
7) The standard error is between the parentheses.
8) *, ** and *** represent statistically significant at 10, 5 and 1 per cent, respectively.

mechanism, via its effects on capital accumulation. We argue that the RER influences the firms' profit rate and, consequently, their decision to invest.

Our theoretical model indicates that a competitive RER may spur long-run growth, under certain conditions. In economies under a profit-led regime of demand and capital accumulation, a competitive RER increases the growth rate of demand and labour productivity. As a result of the circular and cumulative process, the long-run growth spurs. Moreover, the faster pace of capital accumulation, induced by the competitive RER, increases the labour productivity growth, reinforcing the greater long-run growth. Yet, in economies under a wage-led regime of demand and capital accumulation, a competitive RER damages the long-run growth.

The chapter also provided a simple econometric exercise to estimate the effects of RER on the growth rate of labour productivity of OECD countries over the period 1974 to 2019. The results indicate a positive influence of a competitive RER on labour productivity growth, on average, and especially for Canada, Denmark, Finland, France, Greece, Israel, Italy, Japan, Portugal, Spain and Sweden.

Future research should identify the RER influence on labour productivity via other channels than capital accumulation and demand growth. Furthermore, in the empirical field, it is up to future studies to perform additional regressions (controlling other variables, using various econometric methods, providing robustness checks, etc.) in order to deliver new and more robust evidence about how the RER may influence the growth rate of labour productivity.

NOTES

1. This is a simple model. The intermediary inputs are not considered in order to simplify the analysis.
2. Lowercase letters mean the growth rate of the variables.
3. See Krugman (1986) for a similar argument.
4. For more details, access the link https://stats.oecd.org/Index.aspx?DataSetCode=PDBI_I4 (accessed by the authors: 11/30/2020).
5. For more details, access the link www.cepii.fr/CEPII/en/bdd_modele/download.asp?id =34 (accessed by the authors: 11/30/2020).
6. The unit root tests Fisher and Im-Pesaran-Shin indicate the variables are stationary (available upon request).

REFERENCES

Acemoglu, D., Johnson, S., Robinson, J., and Thaicharoen, Y. 2003. 'Institutional causes, macroeconomic symptoms: Volatility, crises and growth.' *Journal of Monetary Economics*, 50: 49–123.
Bahmani-Oskooee, M., and Hajilee, M. 2010. 'On the relation between currency depreciation and domestic investment.' *Journal of Post Keynesian Economics*, 32(4): 645–660.

Bhaduri, A., and Marglin, S. 1990. 'Unemployment and the real wage: The economic basis for contesting political ideologies.' *Cambridge Journal of Economics*, 14: 375–393.

Bhalla, S. 2012. *Devaluing to Prosperity Misaligned Currencies and Their Growth Consequences*. Washington, DC: Peterson Institute for International Economics.

Blecker, R. 1989. 'International competition, income distribution and economic growth.' *Cambridge Journal of Economics*, 13(3): 395–412.

Cornwall, J., and Setterfield, M. 2002. "A neo-Kaldorian perspective on the rise and decline of the Golden Age," in M. A. Setterfield (ed.). The Economics of Demand-Led Growth: Challenging the Supply Side Vision of the Long Run (Cheltenham: Edward Elgar), pp. 67–82.

Cottani, J., Cavallo, D., and Khan, M. 1990. 'Real exchange rate behavior and economic performance in LDCs.' *Economic Development and Cultural Change*, 39(1): 61–76.

Couharde, C., Delatte, A., Grekou, C., Mignon, M., and Morvillier, F. 2017. *EQCHANGE: A World Database on Actual and Equilibrium Effective Exchange Rates*. Working Paper CEPII 2017-14.

Dixon, R., and Thirlwall, A. P. 1975. 'A model of regional growth-rate differences on Kaldorian lines.' *Oxford Economic Papers, New Series*, 27(2): 201–214.

Dollar, D. 1992. 'Outward-oriented developing economies really do grow more rapidly: Evidence from 95 LDCs, 1976–1985.' *Economic Development and Cultural Change*, 40(3): 523–534.

Gala, P. 2007. 'Real exchange rate levels and economic development: Theoretical analysis and empirical evidence.' *Cambridge Journal of Economics*, 32: 273–288.

Glüzmann, P., Levy-Yeyati, E., and Sturzenegger, F. 2012. 'Exchange rate undervaluation and economic growth: Díaz Alejandro (1965) revisited.' *Economic Letters*, 117: 666–672.

Kaldor, N. 1970. 'The case for regional policies.' *Scottish Journal of Political Economy*, 17(3): 337–443.

Kalecki, M. 1956. *Theory of economic dynamics*. George Allen and Unwin.

Krugman, P. 1986. Pricing to Market When the Exchange Rate Changes. *NBER Working Paper No. 1926*.

Lavoie, M. 2015. *Post-Keynesian Economics New Foundations*. Cheltenham: Edward Elgar.

Missio, F., Araujo, R., and Jayme, F., Jr. 2017. 'Endogenous elasticities and the impact of the real exchange rate on structural economic dynamics.' *Structural Change and Economic Dynamics*, 42: 67–75.

Missio, F., and Jayme, F., Jr. 2012. 'Structural heterogeneity and endogeneity of elasticities on the balance of payments constrained growth model.' In: Soukiazis, E., and Cerqueira, A. P. (eds.). *Models of Balance of Payments Constrained Growth History, Theory and Empirical Evidence*. Basingstoke: Palgrave Macmillan.

Missio, F., Jayme, F., Britto, G., and Oreiro, J. 2015. 'Real exchange rate and economic growth: New empirical evidence.' *Metroeconomica*, 66(4): 686–714.

Myrdal, G. 1957. *Economic Theory and Under-Developed Regions*. London: G. Duckworth.

Naastepad, C. 2005. 'Technology, demand and distribution: A cumulative growth model with and application to the Dutch productivity growth slowdown.' *Cambridge Journal of Economics*, 30(3): 403–434.

Rapetti, M. 2020. 'The real exchange rate and economic growth: A survey.' *Journal of Globalization and Development*, 11(1): 1–54.

Rapetti, M., Skott, P., and Razmi, A. 2011. 'The real exchange rate and economic growth: Are developing countries different?' *International Review of Applied Economics*, 26(6): 735–753.

Razin, O., and Collins, S. 1997. Real exchange rate misalignments and growth. *NBER Working Paper Series, Working Paper 6174.*

Rodrik, D. 2008. *The Real Exchange Rate and Economic Growth: Theory and Evidence.* John F. Kennedy School of Government, Harvard University.

Setterfield, M., and Cornwall, J. 2002. A neo-Kaldorian perspective on the rise and decline of the golden age. In: Setterfield, M. (ed.). *The Economics of Demand-Led Growth Challenging the Supply-Side Vision of the Long Run.* Cheltenham: Edward Elgar.

Vieira, F., and MacDonald, R. 2012. 'A panel data investigation of real exchange rate misalignment and growth.' *Estudos Econômicos*, 42(3): 433–456.

APPENDIX

Table A9.1   Complete list of countries

Country	Available sample
Australia	1974–2019: 46 years
Belgium	1974–2019: 46 years
Canada	1974–2019: 46 years
Chile	1986–2019: 33 years
Denmark	1974–2019: 46 years
Finland	1974–2019: 46 years
France	1974–2019: 46 years
Germany	1974–2019: 46 years
Greece	1983–2019: 36 years
Iceland	1976–2019: 44 years
Ireland	1974–2019: 46 years
Israel	1984–2019: 35 years
Italy	1974–2019: 46 years
Japan	1974–2019: 46 years
Korea	1974–2019: 46 years
Netherlands	1974–2019: 46 years
New Zealand	1974–2019: 46 years
Norway	1974–2019: 46 years
Portugal	1974–2019: 46 years
Spain	1974–2019: 46 years
Sweden	1974–2019: 46 years
Switzerland	1974–2019: 46 years
United Kingdom	1974–2019: 46 years
United States	1974–2019: 46 years

PART III

COVID-19 and open economy

10. Capital flows and emerging market economies since the global financial crisis

Otaviano Canuto

10.1 INTRODUCTION

The decade after the global financial crisis (GFC) of 2007–2009 saw significant changes in the volume and composition of capital flows in the global economy. Portfolio investments and other non-bank financial intermediaries (NBFIs) are behind an increasing share of foreign capital flows, while banking flows have shrunk in relative terms. This chapter approaches the implications of such a metamorphosis of finance for capital flows to emerging market economies (EMEs).

Changes in capital flows accompanied structural shifts in financial intermediation in capital-source countries, with NBFIs increasingly shaping the demand for and supply of liquidity in financial markets. The channels of systemic risk propagation have changed with the higher profile acquired by NBFIs, with leverage fluctuations through changes in margins rising in weight.

Risks associated with capital flows to EMEs have changed accordingly. Foreign capital potentially brings benefits to EMEs. However, wide swings in capital flows carry high risks to macroeconomic and financial stability, including the adverse effects of sudden stops to capital inflows and challenges faced by economies with weaker institutions and less-developed financial markets.

Capital inflows in emerging market economies are driven by both global and country-specific drivers. The abundance of global liquidity since the GFC has pushed investors to search for yield, with shifts in risk appetite becoming a source of fluctuations. On the other hand, changes in the macroeconomic fundamentals and institutional frameworks of EMEs have made investors more selective.

The weight of global factors came to the fore in the first half of 2020, when the financial shock in advanced economies caused by coronavirus outbreaks led to a substantive wave of capital outflows from emerging markets, with unprecedented speed and magnitude. The shock was mitigated subsequently by central banks' counter-shock policy moves in source countries, as well as by EME policy tools in managing the risks associated with extreme shifts in capital flows.

The chapter first examines the metamorphosis of finance and of capital flows after the GFC, up to the shock to capital flows to EMEs during the 2020–2021 coronavirus crisis. Then we analyse the extent to which normalization of monetary policies in advanced economies may lead to shocks in those flows, as well as why exchange-rate fluctuations between the US dollar and other major currencies can affect capital flows to EMEs. Finally, we assess the range of policy instruments that EME policymakers tend to resort to when managing risks derived from capital-flow volatility.

10.2   THE METAMORPHOSIS OF FINANCE

10.2.1   Global Capital Flows after the GFC

After a strong rising tide starting in the 1990s, gross capital flows reached a peak with the GFC. Inflows rose rapidly between 2002 and 2007, reaching US$12 trillion (close to 22 per cent of global GDP). After falling steeply during the GFC, flows have trended sideways, never recovering their pre-GFC upward momentum (BIS, 2021).

As detailed in Canuto (2017) and BIS (2021), the decade after the GFC (2007–2009) brought substantial changes both in the volume and composition of global capital flows. When one excludes the significant flows to China, the volume declined globally.

The overall stabilization at lower flow levels has taken place alongside a deep reshaping of cross-border financial flows, featuring de-banking and an increasing weight of non-banking cross-border financial transactions. Sources of potential instability and long-term funding challenges have morphed accordingly.

The post-GFC descent in flows was pronounced for bank loans. Portfolio debt and equity flows were also lower in the post-GFC period, while foreign direct investment (FDI) maintained its strength. Market-based sources of funding replaced banks, while foreign participation in the local markets of EMEs grew. On the borrowers' side, banks were also substituted by corporates and public-sector entities. The US dollar has remained the dominant currency for cross-border operations and investments, but the currency composition of flows has become more diversified. As we will discuss later, that has consequences for EMEs.

Another change in composition accompanied the decline in global flows after the GFC, namely, a substantial decline in flows between advanced economies, while EMEs became more prominent as destinations. Financial globalization had mainly happened among advanced economies (AEs). Rising cross-border movements of financial assets from the mid-1990s were remarkable among AEs. Levels of financial openness (the sum of foreign assets and liabilities as a proportion of GDP) relative to trade openness (the sum of exports and imports as a proportion of GDP) were similar for both AEs and EMEs until the mid-1980s, when they shifted upward in the case of AEs, rising rapidly particularly after the mid-1990s (Canuto, 2017). Cross-border financial assets and liabilities went from 135 per cent to above 570 per cent of GDP after the mid-1990s for AEs, whereas they moved from approximately 100 per cent to 180 per cent of GDP for EMEs.

The post-GFC global trend mainly reflects changes in flows to AEs, which corresponded to 18 per cent of world GDP in 2007, and then moved down to below 7 per cent after the GFC (BIS, 2021). Flows to financial centres comprised part of the trend increase before 2007 but became more volatile between 2009 and 2019. Although the share of world GDP of assets located in financial centres declined, they have remained ascendant over the past decade. Such flows to financial centres have reflected the financial and tax strategies of multinational enterprises, aimed at minimizing costs and the tax burden. BIS (2021) called it the 'financialization of foreign direct investment (FDI)'.

Also worthy of mention is the deeper regional integration among EMEs. That is the case particularly for EMEs as FDI and portfolio investors in other EMEs, even though AEs remain the most important funding sources in EMEs across all types of investment. Some features of 'the new dynamics of financial globalization' may bring greater stability (McKinsey, 2017). Higher capital buffers and minimum amounts of liquid assets have reduced the weight of bank lending and the intrinsic features of mismatch and volatility of banks' balance sheets. The larger share of equity and FDI, in turn, may carry longer-term return horizons and closer alignment of risks between asset purchasers and originators. The unwinding of huge debt-financed current-account imbalances characteristic of the global economy in the run-up to the GFC has also contributed to such a view of global finance entering a more stable phase (Canuto, 2021b, ch. 7).

On the other hand, as previously noted, flows of FDI partially correspond to disguised debt flows and/or transfers motivated by tax arbitrage or regulatory evasion. Cross-border debt flows – including securities – in turn, are also sensitive to global factors, besides being highly sensitive and procyclical with respect to monetary-financial conditions in either source and/or destination countries. There are also 'blind spots' left by de-banking, hitherto not preempted by non-banking financial transactions. For instance, cross-border de-risking by global banks has entailed the closure of correspondent banking relations in many countries, in which the paucity of alternatives has led to negative consequences for local financial dynamics (Canuto and Ramcharan, 2015).

Furthermore, the arms-length distance between asset holders and liability issuers intrinsic to debt securities and portfolio equity, in the absence of the project-finance role played in the past by international investment banks, often constrains the cross-border financing of greenfield investment projects. Additionally, as we will see in the following, the rise of NBFIs and market-based intermediation has brought a greater likelihood of, at times of stress, liquidity/maturity transformation and leverage procyclicality, leading NBFIs to a heightened 'dash for cash' and sudden increases in demand for liquidity.

10.2.2 European Banks at the Core of Both Surge and Pause of the Wave of Financial Globalization since the 1990s

European banks have been at the core of both the surge and pause of the wave of financial globalization since the 1990s. The substantial piling up of European banks' foreign claims in the run-up to the GFC was followed by an equally substantial retrenchment (McKinsey, 2017). From 2007 to 2016, Eurozone banks reduced their foreign claims by US$7.3 trillion, and other Western European banks reduced their foreign claims by US$2.1 trillion.

Lending by European banks was behind two of the major contributing factors to the rising wave of financial globalization. First, the inauguration of the euro, which was followed by markets initially converging their assessments of risk premiums across the zone downward towards German levels, boosted cross-border transactions. According to BIS (2017):

> Between 2001 and 2007, 23 percentage points of the increase of the ratio of advanced economies' external liabilities to GDP was due to intra-euro area financial transactions and another 14 percentage points to non-euro area countries' financial claims on the area.
>
> (p. 102)

European banks also played an active role in the asset bubble-blowing process in the US financial system that preceded the GFC. European banks used US wholesale funding markets to sustain exposures to US borrowers through the shadow banking system. Despite their small presence in the domestic US commercial banking sector, their weight in overall credit conditions was magnified through the shadow banking system in the United States that relies on capital market-based financial intermediaries, which intermediate funds through securitization of claims (Shin, 2012).

From the standpoint of the balance of payments between the US and Europe, those transactions netted out. Nonetheless, in an accounting sense, they represented short-term borrowing combined with long-term lending by European banks, with a corresponding double counting as cross-border financial transactions. The retrenchment of European banks' foreign claims followed both the US asset-bubble burst starting in 2007 and the Eurozone crisis from 2009 onward. Alongside business-driven reasons – losses, decisions to deleverage balance sheets – tighter banking regulation and the orientation towards domestic assets assumed by post-crisis unconventional monetary policies also weighed. These factors have also led to deleveraging, balance-sheet shrinking and domestic reorientation by banks in the other crisis-affected AEs. Although some banks from outside the latter have expanded their foreign lending, levels of global financial openness have been maintained, thanks to growing flows of non-lending instruments (debt securities, portfolio equity and FDI).

10.2.3   Morphing Financial Intermediation in Advanced Economies behind the Metamorphosis of Capital Flows

The metamorphosis of global capital flows accompanied the evolution of market-based intermediation in advanced economies, after the global financial crisis of 2008, when the weight of NBFIs in the financial system has risen. Banks – and their affiliated broker-dealers – remain an important component of the mosaic, but they are now part of a broader set of institutions that route the flow of funds and facilitate trading. NBFIs have become more important in debt intermediation, with implications for risk sharing in the financial system.

According to the Financial Stability Board, NBFIs accounted in 2020 for about 50 per cent of global financing activities, with the rise of NBFIs in financing US corporate debt (FSB, 2020). While, in the 1980s, banks funded about 30 per cent of non-mortgage debt through loans, their share has fallen to 10 per cent; market-based finance (bonds and commercial paper) now comprises 65 per cent of corporate debt. Mutual funds, insurance companies and pension funds held almost 80 per cent of corporate and foreign bonds as of 2020, with a substantial increase for mutual funds (Aramonte et al., 2021). Similar trends have also appeared internationally, with a rising role played by NBFIs in Europe, particularly by asset managers.

The bond holdings of broker-dealers – which are often part of banking groups – diminished after the GFC, even as the overall market expanded. This is quite different from the dynamics pre-GFC, when broker-dealers played a major role in driving the shift from a bank-centric financial system towards a market-based one, and their balance sheets saw a tenfold expansion between 1990 and 2008, with a corresponding increase in leverage. The role played by European banks that we previously highlighted illustrates that. Since the GFC, regulatory tightening over the activities of banks and their affiliated broker-dealers, demographic changes and a greater weight of capital markets in providing for retirement, as well as technological change and the pursuit of operational efficiencies, have led to a rising role of market intermediation and NBFIs (Aramonte et al., 2021). How do stability properties tend to change with such a metamorphosis? NBFIs bring a range of attributes to the financial system and the economy, such as greater diversity in the ecosystem, and the advantage of less correlated trading motives among intermediaries. NBFIs may fill the gap when banks retreat from certain intermediation activities.

On the other hand, like banks, NBFIs can also feed systemic risk, that is, disruptions to the activity of a financial intermediary generating substantial costs – particularly as externalities – for other financial institutions or non-financial firms. At times of stress, liquidity/maturity transformation and leverage procyclicality may lead NBFIs to a heightened 'dash for cash', suddenly increasing demand for liquidity. The roles of market prices and of balance sheet management by NBFIs raise new issues. The debt capacity of an investor is increasingly dependent on the debt capacity of other investors in the system, so that leverage enables greater leverage, and spikes in margins can lead to system-wide deleveraging. Deleveraging and 'dash for cash' scenarios become two sides of the same coin, rather than being two distinct channels of stress propagation (Aramonte et al., 2021).

The greater weight of NBFIs means that risk exposures are increasingly intermediated and held outside the banking system. Instead of banks warehousing liquidity and credit risks on their balance sheets, such risks are increasingly outsourced to NBFIs. Such structural changes have mitigated counterparty credit risk but have led to a financial system more sensitive to large swings in liquidity imbalances. After all, the business models of NBFIs are typically built around exploiting liquidity mismatches, and tend to, on net terms, provide liquidity in good times. During periods of financial turmoil, however, NBFIs often retrench, and their liquidity supply can suddenly turn into substantial liquidity demand.

We saw such an intense 'dash for cash' turmoil in March 2020, at the apex of the pandemic financial shock, when investors shifted away abruptly and massively from risky assets to cash-like assets, thereby making explicit such structural NBFI vulnerabilities with spillovers that impacted other participants in the financial system. Ultimately, it was the central banks' flexible use of their balance sheets, including the crossing into areas previously considered outside their territory, that stopped the adverse feedback loops and helped to restore market functioning. Such features of NBFI-based, market-based financial intermediation have been carried over to global capital flows, as the latter have accompanied the former.

10.3   CAPITAL FLOWS TO EMEs

10.3.1   Capital Flows to EMEs from the
GFC to the Pandemic Shock

Capital inflows to EMEs held up well after the GFC, even if occasionally passing through high turbulence (BIS, 2021). They slowed sharply in some years (Canuto, 2013a, 2016, 2018, 2021a). In June 2013, then-Fed Chair Ben Bernanke suggested that the Federal Open Market Committee (FOMC) might soon start to slow down its bond purchases. With that one statement, made in passing, Bernanke unwittingly triggered a wave of interest-rate hikes and capital flight from emerging markets.

At the time, the 'fragile five' – South Africa, Brazil, India, Indonesia and Turkey – had high current-account deficits and were strongly dependent on inflows of foreign capital. For years, they experienced the spillover effects of ultra-loose US monetary policies, which sent investors seeking higher yields towards emerging markets. When Bernanke raised the possibility of gradual monetary-policy tightening, investors briefly panicked. Market jitters also happened in 2015 when commodity prices fell and the economic outlook for China deteriorated.

Another bout of capital outflows from emerging markets occurred in May 2018, when the Fed really did start to reduce its asset holdings. But this tapering – followed by a sell-off in US bond markets and dollar appreciation – was halted in 2019. This time, the 'fragile five' had been reduced to the fragile two of Turkey and Argentina, both with high current-account deficits and acute vulnerability to exchange-rate fluctuations, owing to their large volumes of foreign-currency debt. Emerging Asia stands out as the one region that saw a sustained increase in capital flows after the GFC. Boosted by China, inflows to emerging Asia doubled between the 2000–2007 period and the 2009–2019 period, from around 0.4 per cent of global GDP to an average of 0.8 per cent.

10.3.2   The Pandemic Shock to Capital Flows to EMEs

During periods of heightened uncertainty, the typical response of markets is a flight to safety because of risk aversion. Capital flows to EMEs faced such a deep shock at the beginning of the COVID-19 crisis. Although short-lived, capital outflows were larger than at any point during the GFC (Canuto, 2021b, ch. 23). While banks' broker-dealers were in the epicentre of the GFC shock, this time the new features of global capital flows led to a dramatic shock to capital flows to EMEs.

The extraordinary monetary and financial support in major economies stabilized flows to EMEs in the months after May 2021. Overall, the net capital flows have diverged significantly between China and EMEs excluding China (IMF, 2021). That reflects the simultaneous presence of both common-to-EMEs and country-specific capital-flow drivers, including some substitution effects of capital flows between China and other EMEs. International bond issuance has partially compensated for the outflows from local equities and bonds. In fact, the diversity in the composition of the non-resident flows to EMEs excluding China in 2021 illustrates the diversity of country-specific determinants of capital flows (IMF, 2021).

Overall flows to EMEs have performed better than initially expected, particularly considering the severity of the shock, even if the recovery was uneven and incomplete in some market segments. The loss by the governments of several countries of foreign funding in local currency did not reverse. Capital flows to EMEs in 2021 have not maintained the strong pace of the second half of 2020 (IIF, 2021). As attention has shifted to possible implications of reorientation of monetary policies of major AEs to capital flows to EMEs, we consider next what the likelihood is of new capital outflows once it happens.

10.3.3 Will Another Taper Tantrum Hit Emerging Markets?

Market movements in mid-2021 led to renewed fears that changes in US financial and monetary conditions would trigger a painful wave of capital flight from emerging markets, as happened in 2013. But times have changed, and the greatest risks to emerging markets are now elsewhere (Canuto, 2021a). In early July 2021, the yield on US ten-year Treasury bonds fell to its lowest level in four months, and stock markets dipped because of fears that the year's rosy projections for economic growth would not be borne out. Still, as we write, the prevailing view is that the 2021 spike in inflation will be temporary, allowing the US Federal Reserve to pursue a smooth unwinding of its balance sheet at some point in the future.

The July 2021 market episode could be partly traced back to February and March 2021, when US long-term rates rose in anticipation that the Fed might soon start tightening its monetary policy. With US President Joe Biden's large fiscal packages came new fears about inflation and economic overheating. Ten-year Treasury yields duly increased from below 1.2 per cent to close to 1.8 per cent, before stabilizing and falling back to previous levels. And ten-year Treasury yields started to rise substantially in September and October as it became clear that the US Fed would start tapering its QE before the end of the year and basic interest-rate hikes would probably come in 2022.

Though there were some jitters following the June meeting of the policy-setting Federal Open Market Committee, when some FOMC members assumed a more hawkish attitude, the Fed nonetheless managed to keep markets cool by promising to give plenty of advance notice before beginning to taper its monthly bond purchases. Since then, interest rates have declined at a notable pace. But uncertainties remain for emerging markets, most of which suffered capital flight as a result of the February–March tantrum and the attendant hike in US market interest rates. Although these outflows have since reversed, there is always a possibility that the Fed will feel obliged to change tack, leaving open the question of whether we are heading for another 'taper tantrum' of the kind that shook global markets in 2013 (see section 10.2.1).

The February–March market tantrum was enough to generate a significant reduction in non-resident portfolio flows to emerging markets. Although these losses were partly recovered over the following three months, worries of a 'taper tantrum 2.0' will remain over the next two years, especially if it starts to look like the Fed will tighten faster than it is currently projecting. But it is important to remember that we are no longer in 2013. Back then, the fragile five's (South Africa, Brazil, India, Indonesia and Turkey) current-account deficits averaged around 4.4 per cent of GDP, compared to just 0.4 per cent in 2021 (Canuto, 2021a). Moreover, the flow of external resources into emerging markets in recent years has been nowhere close to as large as in the years before the 2013 tantrum. Nor are real exchange rates as overvalued as they were then. Except for Turkey, the fragile five's gross external financing needs as a proportion of foreign reserves have fallen substantially.

Two additional mitigating factors are also worth considering. First, if stronger economic growth drives up US interest rates, positive trade linkages for some emerging markets might help to offset any negative financial spillover. Second, it is reasonable to assume that the Fed will offer more appropriate 'signalling' this time around, thereby minimizing the risk of another panic episode.

What about the problem of 'twin deficits' in many emerging economies? One cannot dismiss the fact that emerging markets suffered large capital outflows last year just as their fiscal deficits were rising in response to the pandemic. But despite the COVID-19 crisis, emerging markets generally have been able to finance their larger fiscal deficits by relying on domestic investors and, in some cases, their central banks (Canuto, 2020). And starting in the second half of 2020, purchases of government securities by non-residents in some emerging markets started to pick up again.

True, because some issuance of foreign-currency-denominated securities may still be necessary, the risks associated with changing foreign-exchange flows have not been eliminated entirely. Countries such as Colombia and Chile still have relatively high levels of dollar-denominated debt, and in some emerging markets, portfolio inflows will remain crucial to financing fiscal deficits. But, ultimately, the bigger risks facing emerging markets lie elsewhere. Rather than worrying about another taper tantrum, we should be more concerned with the slow pace of COVID-19 immunizations leading to an anaemic post-pandemic recovery, commodity price hikes generating inflation and economic strategies that merely restore the low growth rates of the pre-pandemic era.

10.3.4   Why a Weakening Dollar Tends to be Good for EMEs

After peaking against other currencies in March 2020, the dollar fell by almost 15 per cent by the end of that year. Asset portfolio managers have been taking 'short' positions against the dollar, that is, betting on its future fall. The dollar is expected to end 2021 much more devalued against the euro, the yen and the Chinese RMB.

The peak during the coronavirus financial shock reflected the search for a safe haven in short-term US bonds or cash that happens in times of heightened global aversion to risk. The dollar rose almost 10 per cent in the first quarter of the year. The mood improvement in the subsequent months reduced the search for safety. There is currently a convergence of views that, gradually or not, US current-account deficits and insufficient domestic savings tend to slide down the relative value of the dollar (see, for example, Roach, 2020; Rogoff, 2020). This is good news for emerging economies in 2021, judging from an essay by Hofmann and Park (2020), included in the Bank for International Settlements (BIS) *Quarterly Report* of December 2020. Loose financial conditions and sustained expansion of global credit favour growth on the real side of emerging economies, with the presence of the dollar as an influential factor in this transmission. According to the authors' estimates, a shock of 1 per cent appreciation of the dollar against a wide basket of other currencies reduces by 0.3 percentage points the economic growth of a group of 21 emerging countries that they consider. One may expect an impact in the opposite direction in the event of a devaluation of the dollar.

The authors highlight four 'channels of dollar transmission' to explain the negative correlation between the dollar's strength and the growth of the global economy. First, the demand for the currency reflects, as a barometer, the global appetite for risk by investors. When the latter collapses, the search for refuge raises the price of the dollar, at the same time as capital outflows and worsening financial conditions at the origins are witnessed, in addition to retraction with respect to higher-risk assets and clients. The dollar rises, while the level of economic activity tends to fall.

Second, there is a mismatch between currencies on the sides of liabilities and assets in global credit in dollars outside the United States, the magnitude of which is considerable. When the dollar falls, balance sheets in which liabilities decline relative to assets in other currencies get stronger. The supply of credit, in turn, increases due to the improvement in risk assessment. This tends to happen even with short-term trade finance.

Third, something in the same direction occurs in the markets for government bonds in local currencies, not least because global investors who carry securities from various countries adjust their portfolios according to the risk conditions of the group as a whole. It is interesting to note that Hofmann and Park (2020) mention a study showing that changes in the dollar against a broad set of currencies weigh more for securities markets in local currency individually than changes in the value of the country's own currency against the dollar. The fourth channel of dollar transmission is foreign trade. A devaluation of the dollar tends, of course, to negatively affect competitiveness in relation to dollarized economies on the part of those whose currencies appreciate. However, particularly in cases in which invoices are in dollars, there is price rigidity in the short term.

Now, these four channels are particularly relevant in the case of emerging economies. Despite the 'deepening' and development of the financial systems of these countries in recent decades, including the expansion of local-currency securities markets, their financial systems still do not have the density of those in advanced economies and are dependent on external financing. It is not by chance that they have relatively high dollar-denominated debt and a significant presence of foreign investors as holders of local currency sovereign bonds. When the availability of sources of foreign-exchange hedge is not adequate, local borrowers of dollar funds and external buyers of local currency securities tend to be exposed in relation to exchange-rate variations. Finally, dollar trade invoicing is more widespread in emerging market economies than in advanced economies (Hofmann and Park, 2020).

As long as a future downward shift in the dollar is not abrupt, while low interest rates in advanced economies and an abundance of global liquidity continue, its transmission via financial channels to emerging economies in general tends to be favourable in the near future. The weights of the four channels differ by country. For instance, while the trade relationship with the United States and the fourth channel matters a lot to Mexico, the financial transmission channels are more powerful in the case of Brazil. Overall, the estimates of Hofmann and Park (2020) point to a gain.

This is consistent with a previous paper by Samer Shousha, from the Federal Reserve Board, showing that the transmission of dollar movements to emerging economies takes place mainly through financial conditions rather than net exports and that (Shousha, 2019):

> the central role of the U.S. dollar in global trade invoicing and financing – the dominant currency paradigm – and the increased integration of EMEs into international

supply chains weaken the traditional trade channel. Finally, as expected if financial vulnerabilities are prominent, EMEs with higher exposure to credit denominated in dollars and lower monetary policy credibility experience greater contractions during dollar appreciations.

It is worth keeping in sight the weight of domestic, country-specific factors. In the experience of the negative financial effect of the appreciation of the dollar in May 2018, it was not by chance that Argentina and Turkey were captured by the storm, because of their particular vulnerability to dollar fluctuations. In Brazil, the possibly favourable tide from abroad will only be taken advantage of if the domestic fiscal mooring is firm. In any case, most EMEs tend to welcome dollar depreciation against a wide basket of currencies.

10.4   A POLICY TOOLKIT TO DEAL WITH CAPITAL FLOW VOLATILITY IN EMEs

Major risks accompany the benefits of financial development and international financial integration for EMEs (Canuto and Ghosh, 2013). There is the inherent procyclicality of the financial system, amplifying business cycles. Positive shocks tend to lead financial institutions and markets to move in the same direction, feeding asset price and credit booms, and boosting a generalized expansion of economic activity. When the cyclical tide changes, asset prices decline, credit shrinks and the economic slowdown tends to be deeper because of the enthusiasm during the upside phase. At the extreme, financial crises with major real sector dislocations and large fiscal costs can happen.

Such procyclicality and the accompanying risks of financial crises are also present in international financial integration, and capital flows often have volatile features. But the evolution of financial intermediation in the last few decades, as we have discussed, has accentuated such features as a 'downside' accompanying its 'upside' consequences. In AEs, the buildup of banking systems' vulnerabilities prior to the GFC occurred through complex chains of credit intermediation and related to large gross capital flows, as we have noted. After the GFC, countries undertook measures to strengthen the resilience of their financial systems, including against risks originating abroad. A key component has been to attempt to curb the propensity of financial systems to behave procyclically. Cross-border spillovers have also been tentatively dealt with in the financial architecture.

However, EMEs face greater challenges in dealing with international financial integration and cross-border flows (Claessens and Ghosh, 2013; Canuto, 2013b). First, capital flows to EMEs, even in net terms, are often large relative to their domestic economies and overall absorptive capacity – especially relative to the size and depth of their financial systems. Financial flows correspond to much larger shares of the domestic capital markets of EMEs than of AEs.

A second challenge comes from the fact that EMEs are more likely to undergo larger shocks. Their economies are smaller and less diversified, and negative shocks – domestic or from abroad – tend to be exacerbated and propagated more easily in EMEs because of structural and institutional features (such as weaker enforcement of property rights and deficient information infrastructures). Large capital inflows tend to interact with and amplify the domestic financial and real business cycles in EMEs to a greater extent than in AEs.

The challenges to economic and financial sector stability in EMEs brought by international financial integration are significant. Business cycles and financial cycles are more volatile in EMEs than in AEs (Canuto and Ghosh, 2013). Adverse financial cycles combined with recessions, although not necessarily more frequent or longer, tend to lead to worse and deeper losses in EMEs than in AEs. Conversely, recoveries combined with favourable financial cycles tend to be stronger (and faster) in EMEs than in AEs. Capital flow surges and sudden capital outflows are associated with the greatest amplification in business cycles in EMEs.

To manage these risks, as argued by Canuto and Cavallari (2013), EMEs must use a different and broad set of policies, including macroprudential tools, in addition to monetary, fiscal and microprudential policies. EMEs are also subject to tighter constraints than AEs on fiscal and monetary policies, and relatedly, more limited headroom. EMEs are likely to have to use a more heterodox mix of policy tools, notably including macroprudential policies, but also capital-flow management (CFM) tools. Global financial integration has challenged the belief that floating exchange rates would suffice as a response to the 'Mundell trilemma', that is, that free capital mobility, pegged exchange rates and independent monetary policies are incompatible (Obstfeld and Taylor, 2004). As argued by Rey (2013):

> The most appropriate policies are those aiming directly at the main source of concern (excessive leverage and credit growth). This requires a convex combination of macroprudential policies guided by aggressive stress-testing and tougher leverage ratios. Depending on the source of financial instability and institutional settings, the use of capital controls as a partial substitute for macroprudential measures should not be discarded.

The IMF's integrated policy framework designed to help policymakers to face frequent difficult tradeoffs in pursuing domestic and external stabilization objectives recognizes that, under some circumstances, independent monetary policies are possible if and only if the capital account is managed, directly or indirectly.

A strong macroprudential structure was erected after the GFC but dealing with the pandemic emergency led to the relaxation of regulations in

2020–2021. As discussed by Edwards (2021), in every country regulatory for-bearance was given a key role in the response to COVID-19. Rebuilding the macroprudential fabric – including CFM controls as macroprudential instru-ments – will be key to reducing the costs of future systemic shocks.

10.5   CONCLUSION

The transformation of global finance has not suppressed the need for policies to monitor and cope with risks. The greater weight of NBFIs and market-based intermediation has brought changes to the risk landscape.

On the side of recipients of net capital inflows, domestic strategies of insti-tutional strengthening to reinforce the alignment of risks between investors and countries, together with regulatory vigilance against excess financial euphoria or depression, remain necessary. The bar in terms of domestic insti-tutional quality – corporate governance standards, business environment – has been raised in the new phase of global finance.

To finalize, it is also worth referring to the potentially transformative impact – and corresponding need for regulatory adaptation – of digital tech-nologies on cross-border finance. We may well be on the brink of an addi-tional metamorphosis of global finance and the instability that could bring.

REFERENCES

Aramonte, S., Schrimpf, A., and Shin, H. Y. 2021. *Non-Bank Financial Intermediaries and Financial Stability*. BIS Working Papers No. 972, October.

BIS – Bank for International Settlements. 2017. *Annual Report*, July.

BIS – Bank for International Settlements. 2021. *CGFS Papers No. 66: Changing Patterns of Capital Flows*.

Canuto, O. 2013a. "QE tapering as a wake-up call for emerging markets." *Capital Finance International*, Fall Issue.

Canuto, O. 2013b. *Currency War and Peace*. Project Syndicate, March 12.

Canuto, O. 2016. "China's spill-overs on Latin America and the Caribbean." *Capital Finance International*, Summer Issue.

Canuto, O. 2017. *The Metamorphosis of Financial Globalization*. Policy Center for the New South, September 15.

Canuto, O. 2018. *Argentina, Turkey and the May Storm in Emerging Markets*. Policy Center for the New South, June 6.

Canuto, O. 2020. *Quantitative Easing in Emerging Market Economies*. Policy Center for the New South, November 19.

Canuto, O. 2021a. *Will Another Taper Tantrum Hit Emerging Markets?* Project Syndicate, July 14.

Canuto, O. 2021b. *Climbing a High Ladder: Development in the Global Economy*. Policy Center for the New South, June 6.

Canuto, O., and Cavallari, M. 2013. "Monetary policy and macro prudential regulation: Whither emerging markets." In Canuto, O., and Ghosh, S. R. (eds.).

2013. Dealing With the Challenges of Macro Financial Linkages in Emerging Markets. Washington, DC: World Bank, pp. 119–154.

Canuto, O., and Ghosh, S. R. (eds.). 2013. *Dealing With the Challenges of Macro Financial Linkages in Emerging Markets*. Washington, DC: World Bank.

Canuto, O., and Ramcharan, V. 2015. *De-Risking Is De-Linking Small States From Global Finance*. Nasdaq.com, October 23.

Claessens, S., and Ghosh, S. R. 2013. "Capital flow volatility and systemic risk in emerging markets: The policy toolkit." In Canuto, O., and Ghosh, S. R. (eds.). 2013. Dealing With the Challenges of Macro Financial Linkages in Emerging Markets. Washington, DC: World Bank, pp. 91–118.

Edwards, S. 2021. *Macroprudential Policies and the Covid-19 Pandemic: Risks and Challenges for Emerging Markets*. NBER Working Paper No. 2944, October.

FSB – Financial Stability Board. 2020. *Global Monitoring Report on Non-Bank Financial Intermediation*. Financial Stability Board Report, December 16.

Hofmann, B., and Park, T. 2020. "The broad dollar exchange rate as an EME risk factor." *BIS Quarterly Review*, December.

IIF – Institute of International Finance. 2021. *Capital Flows Tracker – September 2021 Bond Issuance Saves the Day*, October.

IMF – International Monetary Fund. 2021. *EM Capital Flows Monitor*, September 13.

McKinsey Global Institute. 2017. *The New Dynamics of Financial Globalization*, August.

Obstfeld, M., and Taylor, A. M. 2004. *Global Capital Markets: Integration, Crisis and Growth*. Cambridge: Cambridge University Press.

Rey, H. 2013. *Dilemma Not Trilemma: The Global Financial Cycle and Monetary Policy Independence*. VoxEU, August 13.

Roach, S. 2020. "The end of the dollar's exorbitant privilege." *Financial Times*, October 5.

Rogoff, K. 2020. *The Calm Before the Exchange-Rate Storm?* Project Syndicate, November 10.

Shin, H. S. 2012. "Global banking glut and loan risk premium. 2011 Mundell-Fleming lecture." *IMF Economic Review*, 60: 155–192.

Shousha, S. 2019. *The Dollar and Emerging Market Economies: Financial Vulnerabilities Meet the International Trade System*. Federal Reserve System, October.

11. The Lebanese banking crisis: an exploration of the impaired banking system

Samar Issa

11.1 INTRODUCTION

Conventional banks highly rely on leveraging, which is considered one of the main causes of the 2008 global financial crisis. Banks continued to leverage after 2008, and Lebanese banks specifically conducted a Ponzi scheme wherein they borrowed fresh money to lend the government to pay their existing debt obligations. This led to a collapse of the banking system, which will be discussed later on in detail. Some economists state that this could mean the end of Lebanon.

Now the questions are: Can Lebanese conventional banks withstand the current financial crisis as well as the impact of COVID-19? Are there any capital and liquidity buffers left that could be sufficient to overcome their borrowing costs and survive the most dramatic economic disaster in history? Would there be a rise in non-Western conventional banking or specifically Islamic banking? It is generally argued that Islamic banks are safer than conventional banks and the prime reason is that their product structure is essentially asset-backed financing.

Islamic banks (IBs) currently possess less than 1 per cent of deposits and assets. Because the Lebanese Muslim population is more than 60 per cent, some believe that Islamic banking has great potential to grow its market share. Nonetheless, IBs should address the lack of diversification and attempt to offer products that satisfy customers' varied needs. Moreover, IBs in Lebanon should consider the possibility of expanding into capital markets, such as through the issuance of Sukuk.

This chapter presents a model of bank capital structure that lends itself to capturing the mechanism between the optimal or sustainable leverage of a bank and the actual debt level as measured by the Stein model (2012). This research addresses if and how the excess debt defined by Stein (2012) can be considered an early warning signal for banks and takes an additional dimension by comparing the excess leverage between IBs and conventional banks before, during and after the 2008 global financial crisis as well as the 2019 Lebanese crisis.

Overleveraging is derived and estimated for a sample of eight Lebanese banks, both Islamic and conventional, for the period 2000–2018. The model, similar to the Stein model, in essence postulates that the optimal debt/net worth ratio depends significantly on the stochastic process concerning the capital gains variable and that the expected growth of net worth is maximal when the debt ratio is at the optimal level. However, this analysis is double-sided. On one hand, this chapter shows that excess debt, rather than the mere holding of debt, is the reason behind the vulnerability of the financial sector; on the other hand, the chapter finds that IBs in Lebanon exhibit a lower level of excess leverage, which posits them as better survivors after the current economic crisis as well as the crisis of COVID-19. One should be careful, however, when comparing the COVID-19 shock to the current Lebanese financial crisis or the 2008 crisis. The former is a purely exogenous shock, whereas the latter two are the result of a vulnerable financial system.

This chapter is organized as follows. Following the introduction and rationale of the study in section 11.1, section 11.2 provides the chronological events leading to the Lebanese debt crisis. Section 11.3 reviews the literature on Islamic banks in Lebanon. Section 11.4 provides the theoretical model and the empirical/graphical analysis of the results. Section 11.5 presents the policy implications and section 11.6 concludes. The appendix provides the calculations of the optimal and excess debt for all eight banks.

11.2   LEBANESE BANKING CRISIS

2020 was a unique year for everyone. The global economy suffered from what are continuing concerns about COVID-19 effects. However, for Lebanon, 2020 was at a whole other level as the country experienced the worst financial and economic crisis in its modern history. It is not simply a financial crisis; the whole institutional framework of society and the economy has crumbled and half the country's population is now expected to enter poverty as a result. Did this happen overnight? Well, the answer is 'No'. Lebanon's financial meltdown is a consequence of many years of corruption and mismanagement. This section will provide the chronological events that led to the current economic situation.

Tremendous government debt was accumulated following the 1975–1990 civil war and borrowing occurred with little to no restraints, and at interest rates reaching 21 per cent. Currently, Lebanon's debt equals 170 per cent of its national output, which marks one of the largest debt burdens faced by any country in the world. How did the country borrow so much? The truth is that Lebanon is the first country where a Ponzi scheme was conducted at the whole financial system level, including the central bank. According to economists, Lebanese officials essentially steered a Ponzi scheme where they borrowed new money to pay existing debt obligations at higher and higher rates (Blair, 2020). What must be realized is that Lebanon was called 'the Switzerland of the East' in the 1970s. It was one of the most advanced and prosperous countries in the Middle East. Even after the multi-decade civil war, Lebanon benefited financially in a number of ways, including tourism, foreign aid, its own financial sector and largesse from other Arab countries.

However, the most effective means for the country to raise funds was through its diaspora. Many Lebanese citizens went internationally for employment and many would send funds back to their home country and stimulate the economy. For instance, the World Bank estimates the inflows of expatriates' remittances to Lebanon at $7.2bn in 2018, equivalent to 12.7 per cent of GDP during that year. Lebanon was the 24th largest recipient of remittances in the world and the 18th largest among 123 developing economies in 2018.

Things changed in 2011 as a result of some political controversy. The budget deficit surged to new heights and the balance of payments hit new lows. In 2016, banks offered very high interest rates for dollar deposits and higher rates for Lebanese pound deposits. This resulted in an influx of dollars and Lebanese pounds back into the economy. The central bank of Lebanon introduced this approach, which may be the reason for Lebanon's current state. This approach possibly led to tremendous amounts of liabilities being assumed by the central bank. It is believed by some that as a result, the central bank's liabilities are significantly more than its assets. This is all while servicing the country's debt became so expensive that it became a third of the country's budget spending (Blair, 2020). In 2018, the country sought to lower spending but ended up spending large amounts on a pay raise for the public sector, which exacerbated the situation. Because the resigned government was not able to form a new one that could achieve any reforms regarding its financial system, many foreign countries withdrew the pledges of foreign aid they had made. This meant that Lebanon lost out on receiving billions of dollars in foreign aid.

In October 2019, Lebanon looked to tax WhatsApp calls, which led to civil unrest. For one, the cost of communication in Lebanon is extremely expensive: more than 20 times the cost of calls in the US. Second, there are around five million Lebanese living in Lebanon and 15 million outside of it. Thus, Lebanese utilize WhatsApp heavily to communicate with friends and family. Additionally, the country's tax system at the time was favourable for wealthier citizens. This meant that the country was looking to target the not-as-well-off citizens trying to communicate with loved ones rather than wealthier citizens.

This led to mass protests across the nation. As a result, foreign exchange rate inflows declined as many dollars left the country's economy. Many banks did not have an adequate amount of dollars to pay those who deposited in their banks, which led to many banks having to close their doors. The Lebanese pound also collapsed, dropping from 1,500 to as much as 13,000 today (Mroue, 2020). In March of 2020, the country defaulted for the first time on a debt payment. Then, the country's debt reached $90 billion, which equates to 170 per cent of its GDP. Other factors also exacerbated the economic issues. A historically powerful explosion, ranked fourth in strength after Hiroshima, occurred on August 4 in Beirut port, killing 190 people and causing billions of dollars in property damage. Additionally, the ongoing global COVID-19 epidemic contributed to this already worsening situation.

Despite all of this, there is still no enactment of necessary reformative measures for the country's recovery taking place. According to the World Bank, the real GDP is expected to drop by 19.2 just this year. Moreover, the country is currently experiencing triple-digit inflation (365 per cent) due to the almost 80 per cent crash of the Lebanese pound. Also, Lebanon's consumer price index ranked first among 26 Arabic countries and 57 among 598 countries according to numbeo.com.

The inflation rate for Lebanon (368 per cent) surpassed Zimbabwe (343 per cent)[1] for the second most hyperinflation in the world after Venezuela (2,436 per cent). According to the International Monetary Fund (IMF), the economy is expected to contract by 25 per cent this year. The IMF estimates that per capita GDP decreased from $14,500 in 2019 to $10,900 in 2020. Moreover, imports have declined by over 50 per cent as spending power has declined due to the fall of the Lebanese pound (Coles and Osseiran, 2020). Inflation here has been the normal consequence; as Milton Friedman says: 'Inflation is always and everywhere a monetary phenomenon in the sense that it is and can be produced only by a more rapid increase in the quantity of money than in output'. This is partially what we see in Lebanon, where money creation continues while the GDP has been contracting by almost 10 per cent annually since 2019.

As of mid-2021, the economic situation in Lebanon is not hopeful. Hundreds of thousands of people lost their jobs over the past year, causing many to look for work in foreign markets. This outflow of skilled labour is detrimental to the long-term success of the country's economy as it only has five million citizens in the country.

Financial engineering and restructuring still seem to be far out of reach. Last year, the country contracted Alvarez & Marsal, a New York–based firm, to conduct a forensic audit of the country's central bank. Alvarez & Marsal actually backed out of the deal because they were unable to obtain any of the documentary evidence or information requested for the audit. This is all driven by the highest level of corruption found within the ranks of Lebanese officials. Lebanon ranked 149 out of 180 in a corruption index published by transparency.org, where it ranked 138 the year before (Transparency International, 2021). Due to the country's lack of effort to seek a serious solution, foreign countries have announced that they will not provide aid until necessary reforms are implemented. These reforms need to address the country's ongoing issues of corruption and mismanagement. Capital inflow will continue to suffer as exchange market pressures continue to suffocate trade finance and corporate finance in the highly dollarized economy. The struggle of entering international markets for foreign currencies with the impaired domestic banking system will result in continuous capital controls, and probably haircuts, especially since Lebanon is a primary commodity-importing emerging market. As mentioned by Gevorkyan (2019), the foreign exchange market, interest rates and domestic credit cycles altogether generate volatility for structurally weaker economies. The paper presents interesting results on the short-term sensitivity between exchange market pressure and domestic and external factors in primary commodity-exporting emerging markets.

11.3 LEBANON-SPECIFIC ISLAMIC BANKING LITERATURE REVIEW

Islamic banks prohibit any sort of interest and money is considered capital and not an asset. There are no pure monetary flows and all transactions should be asset-backed (i.e. no derivatives, short selling or debt selling). Suppliers of funds become investors and not creditors, and the provider of financial capital and the entrepreneur share business risks in return for a share of the profits. Islamic banks focus on investment, with an emphasis on the soundness of the project. Bankers coordinate with partners in resource mobilization and apply moral criteria in investment. All of this is believed to boost the economic system. On the other hand, conventional banks focus on lending, with an emphasis on the ability of the borrower to repay. Banks' lending depends on resource mobilization and applies only financial criteria.

Over the last decade, the annual growth rate of IBs reached 15 per cent and these banks are currently present in over 51 countries (Juan Solé, 2007). This constant growth has been due to the fact that competition among banks has pushed toward innovation accompanied by the stability that IBs offer in a way. Many banks opened an Islamic banking window where they adopted some Islamic banking operations or established full-fledged Islamic banking (Turk-Ariss, 2009). This expansion of Islamic banking has attracted many researchers to conduct comparison studies between Islamic and conventional banks. Prior studies of Islamic banks focused primarily on their conceptual issues and issues of liquidity, capital adequacy, operations and customer satisfaction.

However, research studies that address Lebanese Islamic banking and finance in Lebanon are very limited and are presented in the following.

Bizri (2014) examines the status of Islamic banking in Lebanon by looking into existing and potential clients. The author uses interviews with ten key informants and industry experts using a qualitative approach. She finds that banks' clients do want to be assured that IBs are truly compliant with Shariah. Moreover, they want to consider the cost of financing and other transactions, the accessibility of IBs and the quality of service offered by those banks.

Chammas (2006) questions the reasons behind the limited growth of IBs in Lebanon. He conducts a qualitative market analysis of Islamic finance in Lebanon through a series of interviews with key players in the industry and backs his research with secondary data and analysis. The author suggests the application of Islamic financial instruments to most financial areas to increase the volume of operations of Islamic financial institutions in Lebanon.

Saleh and Zeitun (2005) use ratio analysis to examine the growth and performance of IBs in Lebanon and conclude that competition with conventional banks is the main factor. Moreover, they find that lack of public awareness and acceptance is one of the challenges limiting the growth of the industry. They conclude that the industry has potential in Lebanon due to its profit-sharing nature, which is a popular notion that can attract capital into the country, especially because the projects that IBs support are related to popular industries such as telecommunications, agriculture and other industry sectors in the Lebanese economy.

Hammoud (2006) analyses the challenges and opportunities of IBs in Lebanon. The author conducts interviews and reports the results of a two-phase research project. The author identifies the percentage of Muslim population in Lebanon as a key opportunity along with the possibility of expansion into capital markets. He also states that all interviewees agreed that the present legal and regulatory framework is a serious challenge.

11.4   EMPIRICAL APPROACH AND DEFINITION OF VARIABLES

11.4.1   Background

According to Stein (2012b), the US financial crisis in 2008 was caused by excessive financial obligations/mortgages of private households, that is, bubbles in the mortgage market defined as unsustainable debt/income ratios. Essentially, Stein argues that although debt problems may have originated in either the public or private sectors in different nations, the result was still declining asset values and the mechanisms at work resulted in a contagion effect either from the US to Europe and/or from one European nation to another depending on the debtor-to-debtee relationship under examination. Of course, in each scenario, Stein makes it clear that the primary source of the problem is not the presence of debt but excess debt within the country under analysis.

Stein derives an optimal debt ratio and builds on it to identify an early warning signal (EWS) of a debt crisis, which is defined as the excess debt of households (actual debt ratio less than the optimal debt ratio). As the excess debt level rises, the probability of a debt crisis increases. It has been shown that rising house prices since the late 1990s have led to above-average capital gains for households, thereby increasing owner equity. The supply of mortgages increased and, consequently, financial obligations as a percentage of disposable income increased for private households. At the same time, the quality of loans declined (subprime mortgages). Of course, this process was not sustainable. As capital gains[2] dropped below the interest rate, debtors could no longer service their debts and foreclosures led to a collapse in the value of financial derivatives.

Before delving into the theoretical model and empirical analysis presented in this chapter, it is important to briefly provide background information regarding IBs' mortgage-loan operations. As mentioned earlier, their operations do not involve interest rates; rather, they have a proprietary programme called the LARIBA (interest-free) model that uses an equity-participation or profit/loss sharing system. First, profit sharing (Murabaha) is where the bank does not lend money to the buyer to purchase the home or other property; rather, the bank buys the home itself and then resells it to the buyer at a profit. The buyer typically pays a fairly large down payment and the price at which the bank buys the property is disclosed to the end buyer. The second method is decreasing rent (Ijara). The bank purchases the home and resells it to the buyer; however, unlike the first method, in this case, the home remains in the bank's name until the total price is paid. The buyer takes up residence immediately and makes payments to the bank on the purchase price and pays a fair market rent. This method is preferred in countries such as the United Kingdom to avoid double payments of taxes (Khan, 2010).

This research uses a model of optimal leverage that helps define overleveraging as per Issa (2020). The model sketched here is a low-dimensional stochastic variant of a model of bank leveraging and follows Issa (2020), Stein (2010, 2012a) and Sannikov and Brunnermeier (2012). Overall, the model of Issa (2020) is very similar to those of Sannikov and Brunnermeier (2012) and Stein (2012a). All models are stochastic and have leveraging and payouts as choice variables, and net worth as a state variable. Similar to this study, Sannikov and Brunnermeier (2012) specifically focus on the banking sector; however, their setting is more general compared to the one used in this chapter. There are households that save and financial experts representing financial intermediaries that invest in capital assets owned by households and financial intermediaries. Both have different discount rates. Here the focus is solely on the behaviour of financial intermediaries.

In this model, preferences are used in the objective function and Brownian motions as state variables similar to both studies. The Stein (2012a) model, assuming certain restrictions, uses log utility and allows us to exactly compute excess leveraging. Capital return is also stochastic due to capital gains and the interest rate is stochastic as well, similar to the model in this chapter and in contrast with that of Sannikov and Brunnermeier (2012) where only the capital return is stochastic and the interest rate is taken as constant. Both Sannikov and Brunnermeier (2012) and Stein (2012a) employ a continuous time version, but the problem in this chapter is formulated as a discrete time variant with a discounted instantaneous payout and an optimal leveraging function.

Moreover, Sannikov and Brunnermeier (2012) and Stein (2012a) both state that a shock to asset prices creates a vicious cycle through the balance sheets of banks. In other words, risk-taking and excessive borrowing occur when asset prices are volatile. They define what they refer to as the 'volatility paradox' as the shock to asset prices that negatively affects the banks' balance sheets and subsequently disrupts the real sector. Thus, when the prices of banks' assets decrease – and, thus, their equity value and net worth decrease – margin-loan requirements increase. For financial intermediaries to remain liquid, they take haircuts and deleverage. Consequently, a fire sale of assets begins that further decreases the asset price and net worth declines, thus triggering an endogenous jump in volatility and a risk for all of a downward spiral. This is in accordance with the findings of this chapter.

The asset price channel through which the banking system's instability is triggered is also studied by Mittnik and Semmler (2012, 2013). In this model, the unconstrained growth of capital assets through excessive borrowing, facilitated by the lack of regulations imposed on financial intermediaries, is considered the main cause of banking sector instability.[3] On the other hand, large payouts with 'no skin in the game' affect banks' risk-taking behaviours, equity development and leveraging. The higher the payout the more leveraged the bank becomes, which increases the aggregate risk and risk premia for all. In summary, the increased risk spreads and risk premia, especially at a time when defaults begin, expose banks to vulnerabilities and financial stress triggered by security price movements.

To derive an optimal debt ratio, Stein uses stochastic optimal control (SOC). A hypothetical investor selects an optimal debt ratio $f(t)$ to maximize the expectation of a concave function of net worth $X(t)$, where t is the terminal date. The model assumes that the optimal debt/net worth ratio significantly depends on the stochastic process concerning the capital gain variable. The expected growth of net worth is also maximal when the debt ratio is at the optimal level.

Optimal leverage is given by:

$$f^*(t) = \left[(r-i) + \beta - \alpha y(t) - \frac{\left(\frac{1}{2}\right)\left(\sigma_p^2 - \sigma_i \sigma_p \rho\right)}{\sigma^2} \right] \tag{11.1}$$

such that

$$Risk = \sigma^2 = \sigma_i + \sigma_p - \left(2\rho_{ip}\sigma_i\sigma_p\right), \tag{11.2}$$

where r is the bank's capital gain/loss; i is the credit cost of banks; β is the productivity of capital; $y(t)$ is the deviation of capital gain from its trend; σ^2 is the variance; and ρ represents the negative correlation coefficient between interest rate and capital gain. Through the presented model, Stein could determine excess debt as an early warning signal of a potential crisis. As mentioned, it is this mechanism that played a role in decreasing the net worth of individuals, households and institutions in the US, and that was amplified by the increased leverage and pricing volatility of complex securities.

To measure the excess leveraging of banks, the introduced and defined Stein model was followed with a focus on the solution of the dynamic version of the model, which allowed for using time-series data on banks. One difference from Stein is that in this case, each bank's productivity of capital was not assumed to be deterministic or constant as in the Stein model; rather, it was calculated for the years 2000–2018.

The optimal debt level was calculated for the years 2000–2018; thus, excess debt, which is the measure of overleveraging in this chapter, was estimated. To calculate the banks' optimal debt ratios, data on the banks' capital gain/loss, market interest rates and the productivity of capital were collected. Using these variables, the risk and return components of the model were then calculated. Using the aforementioned variables, the optimal and actual debt ratios were calculated for a sample of eight banks (four Islamic and four conventional banks) in Lebanon. The full calculations are presented in eight tables (Tables A11.1 through A11.8) with 18 columns each, presented in the appendix. Data were derived from Bloomberg and Factset, the banks' annual reports, balance sheets and financial statements. The calculations are summarized in the following.

Column 1 consists of capital gain/loss that represents the return in percentage to the investors of the bank from capital appreciation or loss in a particular year. This capital gain/loss is calculated by dividing the change in each bank's stock market cap by the beginning market cap at each period. The market caps were Hodrick–Prescott (HP)-filtered to eliminate the effects of daily stock market swings. HP filtering is a data-smoothing technique frequently applied on time-series data to remove short-term fluctuations associated with the business cycle.

Column 2 represents the market interest rate. The ten-year Treasury yield was used to represent the market interest rate and is, therefore, presented in percentage.[4] In Column 3, beta (β) represents the productivity of capital. The beta is calculated as the bank's annual gross revenue divided by total capital. The total capital here is calculated as shareholder equity plus half of both short-term and total long-term debt.[5] To determine shareholder equity, I obtain the annual value of each bank's shareholder equity from the balance sheet. Short-term debt comprises all the bank's current liabilities that are usually due within 12 months. Long-term debts, on the other hand, are calculated as the combination of long-term and other liabilities in the bank's balance sheets. These are basically all bank liabilities due in more than one year's time. Therefore, each bank's productivity of capital is calculated for the years 2000–2018 and is not constant as in Stein (2012b).

Columns 4–9 are the risk elements in Stein's model (2012a). Column 4 represents beta variance calculated as the difference between each year's beta from the mean beta for the years 2000–2018, representing the deviation of each period's beta from the mean. Column 5 is also a component of the risk element. This is calculated as one-half of the square of the capital gain variable. Column 6 is the statistical correlation between interest rate and capital gain variables over the period 2000–2018. Columns 7 and 8 are the variance for the interest rate and capital gain variables, respectively. Each period's variance is calculated as the deviation of that period's value from the mean. Therefore, interest rate variance is the difference between each year's ten-year Treasury yield and the mean interest rate from 2000 to 2018. Similarly, capital gain variance is the difference between each year's capital gain/loss and the mean capital gain from 2000 to 2018.

Column 9, which is the product of the correlation between the stochastic variables (interest rate and capital gain) and interest-rate and capital-gain variance, represents an additional component of the risk element. It is calculated as the product of the correlation factor of the stochastic variables (Column 6), interest rate variance (Column 7) and capital gain variance (Column 8).[6] Columns 10–12 are used to determine the risk that investors bear when they decide to hold equity in the bank, which is a critical issue for investors' decision-making.

Columns 10 and 11 represent the standard deviations of the interest rate and capital gains, respectively. Therefore, Column 10 is the standard deviation of values in Column 2 while Column 11 is the standard deviation of values in Column 1. Here, standard deviations are constant over the periods as in the Stein model.

Column 12, on the other hand, is calculated as twice the value of variances of the two stochastic variables and their correlation. This is, therefore, calculated as 2 multiplied by Column 9. Column 13 is, hence, the risk of an investor holding the equity of the bank at each time period as in equation (11.2). The risk is calculated using Columns 10–12. The risk is calculated by adding the standard deviations of the interest rate (Column 10) plus the standard deviation of capital gain (Column 11) minus the risk component in Column 12.

In the model, the optimal debt ratio maximizes the difference between net return and risk term. Therefore, only if the net return exceeds the risk premium does the optimal debt ratio become positive. The optimal debt ratio, therefore, is not a constant as Stein also noted (2012a), but rather varies directly with net return and risk.

In Column 14, I then calculated, using all the aforementioned variables, the Stein optimal debt ratio $f^*(t)$. Debt ratios were normalized to remove the effects of seasonality. Therefore, normalized $f^*(t)$ measures the deviation of the optimal debt ratio away from the mean. Negative values in Column 14 represent lower optimal debt ratios away from the mean ratio during the applicable periods. The components of the optimal debt ratio are, therefore, primarily the capital gains for equity holders of the bank's stock, the market interest rate and the risk term. The optimal debt ratio maximizes the difference between mean return and risk term. The formula for calculating optimal debt ratio using the aforementioned column numbers is: ((Column 1 − Column 2) + Column 3 − Column 4 − Column 5 + Column 9)/Column 13 (Ebisike, 2014). This reiterates what was mentioned earlier that the optimal debt ratio is positive only if the net return is greater than the risk premium and this can be seen intuitively.

In Column 15, I calculated normalized optimal debt ratios using Column 14, the mean and standard deviation of the optimal debt values.[7] In addition to calculating the optimal debt ratio, I calculated the banks' actual debt ratio in order to calculate the excess debt ratio. The actual debt ratio of the banks was equal to long-term debt divided by total assets, which are given in the banks' annual reports as well. Actual debt ratios are also normalized in the same way as optimal debt ratios and are presented in Column 16. After optimal and actual debt ratios are calculated as discussed earlier, excess debt is calculated in the last columns as normalized actual minus optimal debt. The graphs of the two ratios, namely, optimal and excess debt ratios, are presented in Figures 1–8 followed by an empirical analysis.

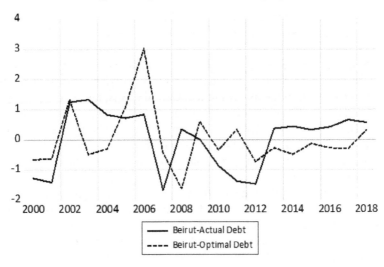

Source: author's calculations.

Figure 11.1   Actual vs optimal debt for Bank of Beirut (conventional)

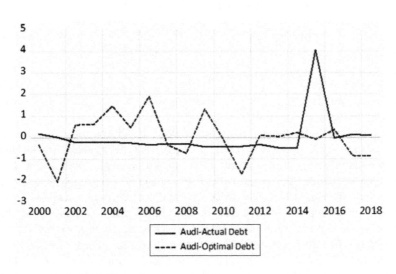

Source: author's calculations.

Figure 11.2   Actual vs optimal debt for Bank Audi (conventional)

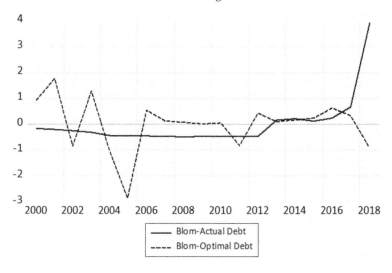

Source: author's calculations.

Figure 11.3 Actual vs optimal debt for Blom Bank (conventional)

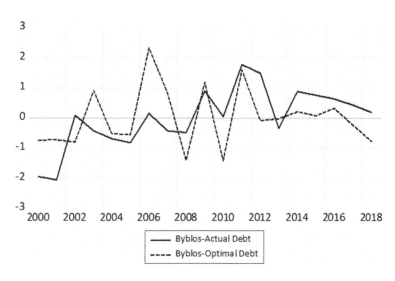

Source: author's calculations.

Figure 11.4 Actual vs optimal debt for Byblos Bank (conventional)

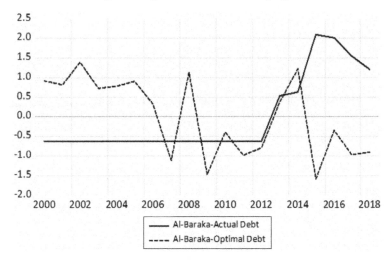

Source: author's calculations.

Figure 11.5   Actual vs optimal debt for Al-Baraka Bank (Islamic)

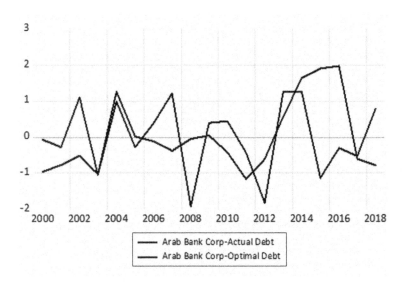

Source: author's calculations.

Figure 11.6   Actual vs optimal debt for Arab Bank (Islamic)

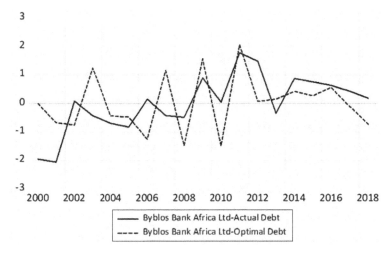

Source: author's calculations.

Figure 11.7 Actual vs optimal debt for Byblos Bank Africa Ltd (Islamic)

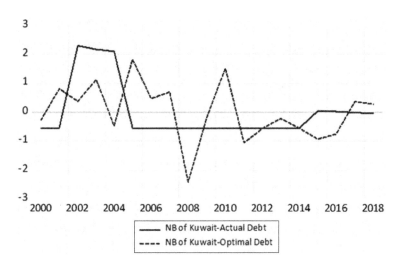

Source: author's calculations.

Figure 11.8 Actual vs optimal debt for National Bank of Kuwait Ltd (Islamic)

11.4.2   Empirical Results

Next, applying the methodology presented in the previous section, optimal and excess leverage were calculated for a sample of eight Lebanese banks: four conventional and four Islamic banks.

For the banks under study, this analysis was performed using the bank's total long-term debts and total assets. As noted, total long-term debt represents a bank's total debt with a maturity date of more than one year from the balance sheet date and total assets represent the value of a bank's total assets.

The vertical axes of the figures represent the debt ratios while the horizontal axes represent the years. Each of the banks' optimal and actual debt ratios was calculated. As shown in Figures 11.1–11.8, most of the banks exhibited an increase in actual debt ratio over the years prior to the 2008 financial crisis as well as prior to the 2019 Lebanese financial crisis, with a smoother and less severe increase in the debt ratio of the IBs.

Figures 11.1–11.8 show the optimal versus actual debt ratio for each bank.

The optimal debt ratios for most of the banks exhibited similar trends, although the trends were more pronounced for conventional than for Islamic banks. For a number of years preceding the 2007–2009 financial crisis these banks had high optimal debt ratios. For most of the banks, about a year or two prior to 2007, optimal debt ratios began to drop and the decrease was severe in most cases. Overall, optimal debt for most Islamic banks was not as high as optimal debt for conventional banks in this context. On the other hand, the drastic drop in optimal debt right before the crisis for both types of banks exhibited the same behaviour. Another interesting observation is that optimal debt for IBs was more stable during the years immediately following the crisis when compared with that of conventional banks. Moreover, the trend of actual debt exceeding optimal debt clearly reversed post-crisis for most banks in the sample, until the year 2013, when banks started to leverage at an even higher level. It should be noted that most of the banks started to excessively leverage in 2016, which is approximately three years before the Lebanese crisis. Therefore, this could have been considered an early warning signal for the crisis along with other indicators.

For further analysis, the deviation of banks' actual debt ratios from the optimal debt over the period 2000–2018 was calculated as a proxy for excess debt ratio. Excess debt ratios were calculated for the eight aforementioned banks. For this calculation, each bank's total assets and long-term debts were used to calculate debt ratios as previously noted. Total assets represent the bank's total balance sheet assets at the end of the period. Long-term debts are the balance of each bank's debts that are more than one year due at the end of each period. On the basis of the presented calculation method, the excess debts of the respective banks were calculated and graphs of the excess debt ratios are exhibited in Figures 11.1–11.8. The vertical axis represents the excess debt ratios while the horizontal axis represents the years. The graphs show that all banks in this study exhibited a similar movement in debt ratio for most of the period, with excess debt rising between 2007 and 2009 (during the financial crisis) as well as between 2013 and 2016, the years preceding the Lebanese crisis. However, we clearly see that overall, IBs were leveraged less than conventional banks. It should be noted that in 2014, Lebanon had no president and suffered from some internal political instability, which allowed the banks to undertake some unregulated excessive levels. However, when it comes to public finance, Lebanon's fiscal balance significantly improved in 2014, with the deficit tightened by 27 per cent according to a Macro report conducted by Blom Bank. In the next paragraphs, each bank is separately discussed. First, the IBs will be discussed, followed by conventional banks.

Al-Baraka Bank exhibited a low actual debt ratio. The bank started to over-leverage after 2012, where we see some high excess debt ratios, especially after 2014. In 2014, the Lebanese economy realized relative improvement in performance and an increase in investment. This movement may have induced loans by Al-Baraka Bank. Arab Bank did not have excess debt throughout the years except between 2014 and 2016, where we see high debt ratios. Byblos Bank Africa Ltd exhibited moderate debt levels even after 2014 and when most banks were overleveraged, but did have some excess leverage after 2014. National Bank of Bahrain had excess debt between 2002 and 2004 but maintained low levels after the financial crisis, with some higher levels between 2014 and 2016.

Bank Audi is one of the largest banks in Lebanon. The debt levels were sustainable until 2014, when the bank leveraged at an excessive level, reaching an excess debt ratio of five, the highest among the banks in context. Beirut Bank seems to have exceeded its optimal debt for most of the years except the period following the financial crisis of 2008, with 2002–2004 and 2014–2018 being the periods of most excess debt. Blom Bank exhibited lower debt levels until 2016, when it skyrocketed and continued to do so until 2018. Byblos Bank managed its debt well even before and during the 2008 financial crisis. However, the bank started to move beyond this threshold in 2010 and onwards, with the highest debt levels being in 2010–2012. The bank benefited from the recovery from the financial crisis when investments, especially real estate investments and mortgages, began to pick up in Lebanon.

In general, the results in this chapter are in accordance with most of the literature, whether in terms of the reasons behind the financial crisis or when it comes to comparing Islamic and conventional bank riskiness and performance. The overall picture is very clear regarding debt. Before 2002, over-leveraging was not a serious problem and leveraging was on a sustainable/optimal level for banks; however, leveraging subsequently increased, leading to instability in the overall banking sector in Lebanon. The same behaviour seen after 2014 also preceded the 2019 Lebanese crisis.

It is now the serious advice of the International Monetary Fund to developing countries that they should avoid debt-creating flows and rely mostly on foreign direct investment. If these countries have to borrow, then they should ensure that their debt obligations are not geared toward short-term maturities and that their economy is producing enough primary surplus to meet their debt obligations, a problem that led Lebanon to its current disastrous situation. Moreover, developing countries in general, and Lebanon specifically, should ensure that their sovereign bonds incorporate better risk-sharing mechanisms to avoid moral hazards. Finally, Lebanon should put in place an efficient debt management structure. In these circumstances, IBs can provide a viable financial system in Lebanon, with growth opportunities on many sides.

11.5   POLICY IMPLICATIONS

With respect to the main endeavour of this chapter, empirical analysis showed that leverage is lower in general at IBs compared with their conventional counterparts. How should policymakers think about IBs? Are these interest-free banks safer than interest-based conventional banks? Are IBs safer than conventional banks and yet profitable enough to survive and be a viable alternative to the impaired Lebanese banking system?

A better understanding of these policy questions requires specific knowledge about the riskiness of banks and the leverage level and profitability of IBs. Indeed, the performance and stability of IBs are especially important today. In view of what is going on in Lebanon and the world, we can probably anticipate a rise in non-conventional banking/leveraging activities. It would seem logical that as conventional funds are leaving some countries, especially in emerging markets, these economies have to rely on their specific advantages to draw additional funds, hence the rise of Islamic banking activity.

Although IBs exhibit a lower level of leverage, their operations are characterized by a high degree of financial risk. The reason is that IBs undertake risky operations in order to generate a return that can attract customers when they cannot be guaranteed a return on deposits. What might make IBs unique and attractive in the coming years is the short-term funding and non-interest-earning assets that might be in high need by Lebanese citizens, and are considered the main aspects of their profits.

This chapter's results draw some implications for policy that helps improve the performance of the Lebanese banking sector as well. The first suggestion is to reduce overall risky debt and develop an optimal debt structure that needs to be followed in order to avoid the risk of financial instability and default. The first challenge in designing an effective policy to make optimal debt a fixed ratio on the basis of the net worth of a financial corporation is a regulatory one. High risk implies high return; therefore, decreasing the risk by providing secured lending such as in IBs is a challenging task.

This chapter tried to distinguish between the optimal and actual leveraging of financial institutions. A further policy challenge is to introduce and strengthen risk-weighted capital buffers and the use of collateral that can be liquidated quickly. Collaterals are a powerful tool of stability despite the repossession cost that they impose on the banks. Policymakers should impose higher collaterals on riskier borrowers and also on financial institutions exposed to shocks such as oil price shocks or the COVID-19 pandemic crisis. When banks see that they are suffering from excess debt, stability instead of high profit should be the driving force. Banks can take a corrective measures by keeping cash flowing, increasing capital requirements and limiting lending to high-risk borrowers. All of what has been mentioned should be made while strengthening the management of public funds through public finance, investment and debt management as well as improving transparency and inclusion to regain trust in all sectors, especially the banking sector.

Finally, with diaspora remittances constituting around 13 per cent of the Lebanese GDP, some diaspora mechanisms would be economically beneficial. Currently, all expatriates' remittances are individually motivated; indeed, as mentioned by Gevorkyan (2021), there is slight evidence that individually motivated remittances have helped to support the 'structural transformation of an industrially weaker economy' (Gevorkyan, 2021). Gevorkyan and Gevorkyan (2012) develop a diaspora regulatory mechanism (DRM) to coordinate temporary labour migration in a mutually effective fashion for both the home and host countries, which can be applicable to the case of Lebanon.

11.6 CONCLUSION

This study presented the Lebanese debt crisis as well as an empirical model that helps identify the early warning signs of banking crises based on the presence of excess debt or what is called 'overleveraging'. Here, I presented a measure of overleveraging defined as the difference between actual and sustainable debt. Furthermore, I conducted an empirical study on overleveraging for eight banks in Lebanon and studied the vulnerabilities of banks and credit and output contractions that could subsequently arise when hit by a crisis.

As results showed, all banks in the sample exhibited high excess debt levels preceding the 2008 crisis as well as the Lebanese crisis of 2019. It is argued that excess debt rather than actual debt can serve as an early indicator of crises because the presence of excess debt is actually the reason why banks collapse. In other words, it is not sufficient to examine current capital gains and interest rates alone. Drift and trend parameters must be considered as well. This chapter presents methodologies that can be used to estimate optimal debt ratios in the banking sector. Excess debt is, hence, determined by the difference between actual and optimal debt. Empirical results presented in this chapter showed that although banks have different debt ratios, a significant rise in excess debt ratios often precedes and/or overlaps a banking crisis.

Moreover, this chapter provides evidence that IBs managed debt better prior to and during the 2008 financial crisis, but were subject to the second-round effect of the crisis beginning in 2011. Islamic banks also managed their debt prior to the Lebanese crisis where we witnessed excessive leverage conducted by conventional banks. However, in theory, the unique feature of Islamic banking – profit-and-loss sharing – is not that different from conventional banking in practice. Therefore, Islamic banks should revisit their strategies to provide higher returns while maintaining banking stability.

This chapter has some limitations. For instance, the size of the sample was relatively small. This issue will be addressed in the future by soliciting additional banks. Moreover, the calculated optimal debt showed some swings; hence, there is a need to smooth the capital gain variable. Some techniques, such as the HP filter, were applied for the banks; however, this did not show any difference and some irregular and random fluctuations in results of optimal debt were still observed.

In conclusion, in the aftermath of all that and given what is currently happening, Lebanon's recession is likely to be difficult and prolonged due to the lack of necessary policymaking and the level of corruption still taking place. The narrative of the Lebanese financial crisis is to blame Lebanon for being the architect of its own financial crisis. This reduces the complexity and global nature of the Lebanese financial crisis to a national focus that justifies a strategy of structural adjustment and austerity targeted to reduce the public debt. However, the story is much bigger, and Lebanon's public debt has grown over the course of treatment. A full crisis management strategy is necessary as opposed to a simple and insufficient financial plan that simply aims to reduce the public debt.

Alongside a neoliberal restructuring of the Lebanese economy, entering international markets for foreign currencies should be supported by the International Monetary Fund, credit rating agencies and private investors to ensure discipline, surveillance and control. Capital inflow is extremely necessary in Lebanon to reduce the total pressure on an exchange rate that has been resisted through foreign exchange intervention. Given the large depreciation of the Lebanese currency and its importance as a spillover channel, understanding the role of domestic and external factors, international capital flows and capital controls in determining the exchange market pressure would be interesting for future research.

NOTES

1. Data computed by Steve H. Hanke, Johns Hopkins University.
2. Meaning increases in housing prices.
3. This source of instability is also discussed by Sannikov and Brunnermeier (2012).
4. Variables in the first two columns, capital gain/loss and interest rate, form the uncertainty of the model. The two variables are stochastic in the model and can move in different directions.
5. The reason that total capital is calculated this way is because capital investments in a company comprise both equity capital and debt financing; hence, a company has two types of stakeholders: equity and debt holders.
6. The optimal debt ratio is positive only if the net return is greater than the risk premium.
7. They were normalized such that each variable had a mean of zero.

REFERENCES

Bizri, R. M. 2014. 'A study of Islamic banks in the non-GCC MENA region: Evidence from Lebanon.' *International Journal of Bank Marketing*, 32(2): 130–149.

Blair, E. 2020, September 17. 'Explainer: Lebanon's financial meltdown and how it happened.' *Reuters*. https://www.reuters.com/article/us-lebanon-crisis-financial -explainer/explainer-lebanons-financial-meltdown-and-how-it-happened -idUSKBN26821L.

Chammas, G. 2006. 'Islamic finance industry in Lebanon: Horizons, enhancements, and projections.' Retrieved January 11, 2016, from https://ribh.files.wordpress.com/ 2007/09/islamic-finance-industry-in-lebanon-ghassan-chammas-esa-beirut.pdf.

Coles, I., and Osseiran, N. 2020, November 2. "'We've lost our country': Lebanese Flee an imploding economy.' *The Wall Street Journal*. https://www.wsj.com/articles/ weve-lost-our-country-lebanese-flee-an-imploding-economy-11604324182.

Ebisike, O. 2014. 'Inquiry into US banks' exposures to mortgage securities.' *The New School*.

Gevorkyan, A. V. 2019. 'Exchange market pressure and primary commodity– exporting emerging markets.' *Applied Economics*, 51(22): 2390–2412.

Gevorkyan, A. V. 2021. 'Diaspora and economic development: A systemic view.' *The European Journal of Development Research*. DOI: 10.1057/s41287-021-00432-x.

Gevorkyan, A. V., and Gevorkyan, A. 2012. 'Factoring turbulence out: Diaspora regulatory mechanism and Migration Development Bank.' *International Migration*, 50(1): 96–112.

Hammoud, J. 2017. 'The challenges and opportunities of Islamic banking in Lebanon.' In *Leadership, Innovation and Entrepreneurship as Driving Forces of the Global Economy* (pp. 809–815). Cham: Springer. DOI: 10.1007/978-3-319-43434-6_72.

Issa, S. 2020. 'Life after debt: The effects of overleveraging on conventional and Islamic banks.' *Journal of Risk and Financial Management*, 13(6): 137.

Khan, F. 2010. How 'Islamic' is Islamic Banking? *Journal of Economic Behavior & Organization* 76: 805–20.

Mittnik, S. and W. Semmler. 2012. Regime Dependence of the Multiplier. *Journal of Economic Behavior and Organization* 83: 502–52.

Mittnik, S. and W. Semmler. 2013. The Real Consequences of Financial Stress. *Journal of Economic Dynamics and Control* 37: 1479–99.

Mroue, B. 2020, December 1. *World Bank Warns of 'Prolonged Depression' in Lebanon*. Associated Press. https://apnews.com/article/middle-east-lebanon-coron

avirus-pandemic-financial-markets-financial-crisis-f2b564de3fd25526979b21d
1c2c11a00.

Saleh, A. S., and Zeitun, R. 2005. 'The development of Islamic banking in Lebanon: Prospects and future challenges.' *Review of Islamic Economics*, 9(2): 77–91.

Sannikov, Y., and Brunnermeier, M. 2012. A macroeconomic model with a financial sector. In *2012 Meeting Papers* (No. 507). Society for Economic Dynamics.

Schleer, F., and Semmler, W. 2016. 'Banking overleveraging and macro instability: A model and vstar estimations.' *Jahrbücher für Nationalökonomie und Statistik*, 236(6): 609–638.

Sole, J. A. 2007. Introducing Islamic banks into conventional banking systems.

Stein, J. L. 2010. 'A tale of two debt crises: A stochastic optimal control analysis.' *Economics*, 4(1). Available online: https://doi.org/10.5018/economics-ejournal. ja.2010-3.

Stein, J. L. 2011. The Diversity of the Debt Crisis in Europe. CESifo Working Paper No. 3348. Munich: CESifo, pp. 1–20.

Stein, J. L. 2012a. 'Stochastic optimal control and the US financial debt crisis.' *Public Economy/Public Economics*, 26–27: 271–279.

Stein, J. L. 2012b. The diversity of debt crises in Europe. In Stochastic Optimal Control and the US Financial Debt Crisis. Boston: Springer, pp. 133–54.

Transparency International. 2021. *Our Work in Lebanon*. Transparency International: The Global Coalition Against Corruption. Retrieved May 19, 2021, from https:// www.transparency.org/en/countries/lebanon.

Turk-Ariss, R. 2009. 'Competitive behavior in Middle East and North Africa banking systems.' *The Quarterly Review of Economics and Finance*, 49(2): 693–710.

APPENDIX

Table A11.1   Optimal, actual and excess debt calculations for Bank of Beirut, in mlns USD

Year	Capital gains/ (losses), (r)	Interest rate (i)	Beta (productivity of capital, β)	Beta variance (αγ(t))	Half square of capital gain variance	Correlation of interest and capital gain variables	Interest rate variance	Capital gain variance	Correlation and variances of interest and capital gain	Std deviation of interest rate	Std deviation of capital gain	2 × (correlation and variances of interest and capital gain)	Risk	Optimal debt ratio, f*(t)	Normalized optimal debt ratio	Actual debt ratio	Normalized actual debt	Excess debt
2000	–	0.11	0.93	0.52	–	0.21	0.04	(0.09)	(0.00)	0.02	0.25	(0.00)	0.27	1.11	(0.66)	0.02	(1.28)	(0.62)
2001	–	0.11	0.85	0.44	–	0.21	0.03	(0.09)	(0.00)	0.02	0.25	(0.00)	0.27	1.13	(0.64)	0.01	(1.41)	(0.77)
2002	0.34	0.11	0.45	0.04	0.06	0.21	0.03	0.25	0.00	0.02	0.25	0.00	0.26	2.22	1.35	0.14	1.24	(0.11)
2003	(0.00)	0.09	0.48	0.07	0.00	0.21	0.01	(0.09)	(0.00)	0.02	0.25	(0.00)	0.27	1.21	(0.49)	0.14	1.33	1.83
2004	0.01	0.07	0.48	0.07	0.00	0.21	(0.00)	(0.08)	0.00	0.02	0.25	0.00	0.27	1.31	(0.30)	0.12	0.83	1.14
2005	0.25	0.08	0.38	(0.03)	0.03	0.21	0.01	0.17	0.00	0.02	0.25	0.00	0.27	2.08	1.09	0.11	0.71	(0.37)
2006	1.00	0.08	0.44	0.03	0.50	0.21	0.00	0.91	0.00	0.02	0.25	0.00	0.26	3.15	3.04	0.12	0.84	(2.19)
2007	–	0.08	0.39	(0.02)	–	0.21	0.00	(0.09)	(0.00)	0.02	0.25	(0.00)	0.27	1.24	(0.43)	0.00	(1.68)	(1.25)
2008	(0.16)	0.08	0.41	(0.00)	0.01	0.21	0.00	(0.25)	(0.00)	0.02	0.25	(0.00)	0.27	0.58	(1.63)	0.10	0.35	1.97
2009	0.16	0.07	0.34	(0.07)	0.01	0.21	(0.00)	0.07	(0.00)	0.02	0.25	(0.00)	0.27	1.81	0.61	0.08	0.01	(0.60)
2010	(0.01)	0.06	0.33	(0.08)	0.00	0.21	(0.01)	(0.10)	(0.00)	0.02	0.25	(0.00)	0.27	1.29	(0.35)	0.04	(0.87)	(0.52)
2011	0.10	0.06	0.39	(0.02)	0.00	0.21	(0.02)	0.01	(0.00)	0.02	0.25	(0.00)	0.27	1.66	0.34	0.02	(1.38)	(1.72)
2012	(0.07)	0.06	0.41	(0.00)	0.00	0.21	(0.02)	(0.16)	0.00	0.02	0.25	0.00	0.26	1.07	(0.74)	0.01	(1.47)	(0.74)
2013	(0.00)	0.06	0.26	(0.15)	0.00	0.21	(0.02)	(0.09)	0.00	0.02	0.25	0.00	0.26	1.33	(0.28)	0.10	0.37	0.64
2014	(0.03)	0.06	0.26	(0.15)	0.00	0.21	(0.02)	(0.12)	0.00	0.02	0.25	0.00	0.26	1.21	(0.50)	0.10	0.44	0.93
2015	0.02	0.06	0.25	(0.16)	0.00	0.21	(0.02)	(0.07)	0.00	0.02	0.25	0.00	0.27	1.40	(0.14)	0.10	0.33	0.47
2016	–	0.06	0.24	(0.17)	–	0.21	(0.02)	(0.09)	0.00	0.02	0.25	0.00	0.26	1.32	(0.28)	0.10	0.42	0.70
2017	0.00	0.06	0.24	(0.17)	0.00	0.21	(0.01)	(0.09)	0.00	0.02	0.25	0.00	0.27	1.31	(0.30)	0.11	0.66	0.96
2018	0.11	0.08	0.25	(0.16)	0.01	0.21	0.00	0.02	0.00	0.02	0.25	0.00	0.27	1.66	0.32	0.11	0.56	0.24

Note: Table with optimal debt calculations. Section 11.4 offers additional details.
Source: authors' calculations based on the data from Bloomberg and Factset.

Table A11.2 Optimal, actual and excess debt calculations for Audi Bank, in mlns USD

Year	Capital gains/ (losses), (r)	Interest rate (i)	Beta (productivity of capital, β)	Beta variance (αxy(t))	Half square of capital gain variance	Correlation of interest and capital gain variables	Interest rate variance	Capital gain variance	Correlation and variances of interest and capital gain	Std deviation of interest rate	Std deviation of capital gain	2 × (correlation and variances of interest and capital gain)	Risk	Optimal debt ratio, f*(t)	Normalized optimal debt ratio	Actual debt ratio	Normalized actual debt	Excess debt
2000	–	0.11	1.08	0.42	—	0.04	0.04	(0.11)	(0.00)	0.02	0.31	(0.00)	0.33	1.64	(0.35)	0.02	0.17	0.52
2001	(0.35)	0.11	1.04	0.38	0.06	0.04	0.03	(0.46)	(0.00)	0.02	0.31	(0.00)	0.33	0.43	(2.05)	0.02	0.01	2.06
2002	0.25	0.11	0.74	0.09	0.03	0.04	0.03	0.14	0.00	0.02	0.31	0.00	0.33	2.31	0.59	0.01	(0.22)	(0.81)
2003	0.23	0.09	0.80	0.15	0.03	0.04	0.01	0.12	0.00	0.02	0.31	0.00	0.33	2.34	0.63	0.01	(0.20)	(0.83)
2004	0.54	0.07	0.63	(0.03)	0.14	0.04	(0.00)	0.43	(0.00)	0.02	0.31	(0.00)	0.33	2.93	1.47	0.01	(0.21)	(1.68)
2005	0.18	0.08	0.67	0.01	0.02	0.04	0.01	0.07	0.00	0.02	0.31	0.00	0.33	2.22	0.46	0.01	(0.25)	(0.71)
2006	1.00	0.08	0.54	(0.12)	0.50	0.04	0.00	0.89	0.00	0.02	0.31	0.00	0.33	3.24	1.90	0.01	(0.34)	(2.24)
2007	(0.03)	0.08	0.54	(0.12)	0.00	0.04	0.00	(0.15)	(0.00)	0.02	0.31	(0.00)	0.33	1.63	(0.36)	0.01	(0.29)	0.07
2008	(0.12)	0.08	0.60	(0.05)	0.01	0.04	0.00	(0.23)	(0.00)	0.02	0.31	(0.00)	0.33	1.36	(0.74)	0.01	(0.29)	0.45
2009	0.46	0.07	0.62	(0.03)	0.11	0.04	(0.00)	0.35	(0.00)	0.02	0.31	(0.00)	0.33	2.82	1.31	0.00	(0.44)	(1.75)
2010	0.01	0.06	0.61	(0.04)	0.00	0.04	(0.01)	(0.10)	0.00	0.02	0.31	0.00	0.33	1.84	(0.07)	0.00	(0.44)	(0.37)
2011	(0.32)	0.06	0.66	0.01	0.05	0.04	(0.02)	(0.43)	0.00	0.02	0.31	0.00	0.33	0.67	(1.70)	0.00	(0.42)	1.29
2012	0.05	0.06	0.59	(0.07)	0.00	0.04	(0.02)	(0.06)	0.00	0.02	0.31	0.00	0.33	1.95	0.09	0.01	(0.33)	(0.42)
2013	0.04	0.06	0.66	0.00	0.00	0.04	(0.02)	(0.07)	0.00	0.02	0.31	0.00	0.33	1.91	0.04	0.00	(0.48)	(0.51)
2014	0.08	0.06	0.68	0.02	0.00	0.04	(0.02)	(0.03)	0.00	0.02	0.31	0.00	0.33	2.04	0.21	0.00	(0.49)	(0.70)
2015	0.01	0.06	0.44	(0.22)	0.00	0.04	(0.02)	(0.10)	0.00	0.02	0.31	0.00	0.33	1.82	(0.09)	0.12	4.04	4.13
2016	0.12	0.06	0.72	0.06	0.01	0.04	(0.02)	0.01	(0.00)	0.02	0.31	(0.00)	0.33	2.15	0.37	0.01	(0.03)	(0.39)
2017	(0.15)	0.06	0.48	(0.17)	0.01	0.04	(0.01)	(0.27)	0.00	0.02	0.31	0.00	0.33	1.29	(0.84)	0.02	0.13	0.97
2018	(0.15)	0.08	0.39	(0.27)	0.01	0.04	0.00	(0.26)	(0.00)	0.02	0.31	(0.00)	0.33	1.27	(0.87)	0.02	0.08	0.95

Note: Table with optimal debt calculations. Section 11.4 offers additional details.
Source: authors' calculations based on the data from Bloomberg and Factset.

Table A11.3   Optimal, actual and excess debt calculations for Byblos Bank, in mlns USD

Year	Capital gains/(losses), (r)	Interest rate (i)	Beta (productivity of capital, β)	Beta variance (αγν(t))	Half square of capital gain variance	Correlation of interest and capital gain variables	Interest rate variance	Capital gain variance	Correlation and variances of interest and capital gain	Std deviation of interest rate	Std deviation of capital gain	2 × (correlation and variances of interest and capital gain)	Risk	Optimal debt ratio, f*(t)	Normalized optimal debt ratio	Actual debt ratio	Normalized actual debt	Excess debt
2000	(0.11)	0.11	0.93	0.39	0.01	0.02	0.04	(0.29)	(0.00)	0.02	0.55	(0.00)	0.57	0.55	(0.75)	0.00	(1.96)	(1.20)
2001	(0.11)	0.11	0.69	0.16	0.01	0.02	0.03	(0.29)	(0.00)	0.02	0.55	(0.00)	0.57	0.55	(0.74)	0.00	(2.06)	(1.32)
2002	(0.12)	0.11	0.70	0.16	0.01	0.02	0.03	(0.30)	(0.00)	0.02	0.55	(0.00)	0.57	0.52	(0.81)	0.02	0.08	0.89
2003	0.24	0.09	0.68	0.14	0.03	0.02	0.01	0.05	0.00	0.02	0.55	0.00	0.57	1.16	0.90	0.02	(0.43)	(1.33)
2004	(0.10)	0.07	0.54	0.01	0.01	0.02	(0.00)	(0.28)	0.00	0.02	0.55	0.00	0.57	0.63	(0.53)	0.01	(0.70)	(0.16)
2005	2.10	0.08	0.49	(0.05)	2.21	0.02	0.01	1.92	0.00	0.02	0.55	0.00	0.57	0.61	(0.57)	0.01	(0.83)	(0.26)
2006	1.00	0.08	0.54	0.01	0.50	0.02	0.00	0.82	0.00	0.02	0.55	0.00	0.57	1.68	2.32	0.02	0.15	(2.18)
2007	0.21	0.08	0.56	0.02	0.02	0.02	0.00	0.02	0.00	0.02	0.55	0.00	0.57	1.13	0.82	0.02	(0.43)	(1.25)
2008	(0.26)	0.08	0.45	(0.09)	0.03	0.02	0.00	(0.44)	(0.00)	0.02	0.55	(0.00)	0.57	0.30	(1.42)	0.02	(0.49)	0.93
2009	0.30	0.07	0.43	(0.10)	0.04	0.02	(0.00)	0.11	(0.00)	0.02	0.55	(0.00)	0.57	1.26	1.17	0.03	0.89	(0.29)
2010	(0.27)	0.06	0.43	(0.10)	0.04	0.02	(0.01)	(0.45)	0.00	0.02	0.55	0.00	0.57	0.30	(1.42)	0.02	0.04	1.46
2011	0.41	0.06	0.41	(0.12)	0.08	0.02	(0.02)	0.23	(0.00)	0.02	0.55	(0.00)	0.57	1.41	1.59	0.04	1.77	0.18
2012	(0.03)	0.06	0.44	(0.09)	0.00	0.02	(0.02)	(0.21)	0.00	0.02	0.55	0.00	0.57	0.79	(0.10)	0.04	1.47	1.57
2013	(0.02)	0.06	0.47	(0.06)	0.00	0.02	(0.02)	(0.20)	0.00	0.02	0.55	0.00	0.57	0.81	(0.03)	0.02	(0.35)	(0.31)
2014	0.03	0.06	0.51	(0.03)	0.00	0.02	(0.02)	(0.15)	0.00	0.02	0.55	0.00	0.57	0.90	0.20	0.03	0.87	0.67
2015	0.01	0.06	0.52	(0.01)	0.00	0.02	(0.02)	(0.18)	0.00	0.02	0.55	0.00	0.57	0.85	0.07	0.03	0.75	0.68
2016	0.06	0.06	0.55	0.02	0.00	0.02	(0.02)	(0.12)	0.00	0.02	0.55	0.00	0.57	0.94	0.32	0.03	0.62	0.31
2017	(0.06)	0.06	0.44	(0.09)	0.00	0.02	(0.01)	(0.24)	0.00	0.02	0.55	0.00	0.57	0.73	(0.25)	0.03	0.42	0.67
2018	(0.14)	0.08	0.38	(0.15)	0.01	0.02	0.00	(0.33)	(0.00)	0.02	0.55	(0.00)	0.57	0.53	(0.78)	0.02	0.18	0.96

Note: Table with optimal debt calculations. Section 11.4 offers additional details.
Source: authors' calculations based on the data from Bloomberg and Factset.

Table A11.4 Optimal, actual and excess debt calculations for Blom Bank, in mlns USD

Year	Capital gains/ (losses), (r)	Interest rate (i)	Beta (productivity of capital, β)	Beta variance (αγ(t))	Half square of capital gain variance	Correlation of interest and capital gain variables	Interest rate variance	Capital gain variance	Correlation and variances of interest and capital gain	Std deviation of interest rate	Std deviation of capital gain	2 × (correlation and variances of interest and capital gain)	Risk	Optimal debt ratio, f*(t)	Normalized optimal debt ratio	Actual debt ratio	Normalized actual debt	Excess debt
2000	0.37	0.11	1.13	0.49	0.07	0.36	0.04	0.28	0.00	0.02	0.37	0.01	0.38	2.23	0.91	0.01	(0.18)	(1.09)
2001	1.15	0.11	1.05	0.40	0.66	0.36	0.03	1.06	0.01	0.02	0.37	0.03	0.36	2.90	1.75	0.01	(0.22)	(1.96)
2002	(0.19)	0.11	0.85	0.20	0.02	0.36	0.03	(0.28)	(0.00)	0.02	0.37	(0.01)	0.39	0.83	(0.85)	0.01	(0.26)	0.59
2003	0.54	0.09	0.76	0.12	0.15	0.36	0.01	0.46	0.00	0.02	0.37	0.00	0.38	2.51	1.26	0.01	(0.33)	(1.59)
2004	(0.27)	0.07	0.52	(0.13)	0.04	0.36	(0.00)	(0.35)	0.00	0.02	0.37	0.00	0.38	0.70	(1.02)	0.01	(0.44)	0.58
2005	(0.65)	0.08	0.57	(0.08)	0.21	0.36	0.01	(0.73)	(0.00)	0.02	0.37	(0.00)	0.39	(0.76)	(2.86)	0.00	(0.45)	2.41
2006	0.19	0.08	0.53	(0.11)	0.02	0.36	0.00	0.11	0.00	0.02	0.37	0.00	0.38	1.93	0.53	0.00	(0.46)	(1.00)
2007	0.05	0.08	0.55	(0.10)	0.00	0.36	0.00	(0.04)	(0.00)	0.02	0.37	(0.00)	0.38	1.60	0.12	0.00	(0.48)	(0.60)
2008	0.03	0.08	0.66	0.01	0.00	0.36	0.00	(0.06)	(0.00)	0.02	0.37	(0.00)	0.38	1.56	0.06	0.00	(0.49)	(0.56)
2009	0.01	0.07	0.66	0.01	0.00	0.36	(0.00)	(0.08)	0.00	0.02	0.37	0.00	0.38	1.51	(0.00)	0.00	(0.48)	(0.48)
2010	0.01	0.06	0.68	0.04	0.00	0.36	(0.01)	(0.08)	0.00	0.02	0.37	0.00	0.38	1.54	0.04	0.00	(0.48)	(0.52)
2011	(0.24)	0.06	0.68	0.03	0.03	0.36	(0.02)	(0.32)	0.00	0.02	0.37	0.00	0.38	0.85	(0.83)	0.00	(0.47)	0.36
2012	0.13	0.06	0.64	(0.01)	0.01	0.36	(0.02)	0.04	(0.00)	0.02	0.37	(0.00)	0.39	1.84	0.42	0.00	(0.48)	(0.90)
2013	0.02	0.06	0.55	(0.09)	0.00	0.36	(0.02)	(0.07)	0.00	0.02	0.37	0.00	0.38	1.58	0.09	0.02	0.15	0.06
2014	0.04	0.06	0.54	(0.11)	0.00	0.36	(0.02)	(0.05)	0.00	0.02	0.37	0.00	0.38	1.63	0.15	0.02	0.20	0.05
2015	0.06	0.06	0.54	(0.11)	0.00	0.36	(0.02)	(0.02)	0.00	0.02	0.37	0.00	0.38	1.69	0.22	0.02	0.11	(0.12)
2016	0.20	0.06	0.62	(0.02)	0.02	0.36	(0.02)	0.12	(0.00)	0.02	0.37	(0.00)	0.39	2.00	0.61	0.03	0.23	(0.39)
2017	0.10	0.06	0.48	(0.17)	0.00	0.36	(0.01)	0.01	(0.00)	0.02	0.37	(0.00)	0.38	1.76	0.32	0.04	0.65	0.34
2018	(0.24)	0.08	0.29	(0.36)	0.03	0.36	0.00	(0.32)	(0.00)	0.02	0.37	(0.00)	0.38	0.79	(0.91)	0.14	3.90	4.81

Note: Table with optimal debt calculations. Section 11.4 offers additional details.
Source: authors' calculations based on the data from Bloomberg and Factset.

Table A11.5 *Optimal, actual and excess debt calculations for Al-Baraka Bank, in mlns USD*

Year	Capital gains/ (losses), (r)	Interest rate (i)	Beta (productivity of capital, f)	Beta variance (αy(t))	Half square of capital gain variance	Correlation of interest and capital gain variables	Interest rate variance	Capital gain variance	Correlation and variances of interest and capital gain	Std deviation of interest rate	Std deviation of capital gain	2 × (correlation and variances of interest and capital gain)	Risk	Optimal debt ratio, $f^*(t)$	Normalized optimal debt ratio	Actual debt ratio	Normalized actual debt	Excess debt
2000	–	–	–	(0.21)	–	(0.36)	(0.05)	0.33	0.01	0.03	0.13	0.01	0.15	1.43	0.92	–	(0.62)	(1.54)
2001	–	–	–	(0.21)	–	(0.36)	(0.05)	0.06	0.00	0.03	0.13	0.00	0.16	1.33	0.81	–	(0.62)	(1.43)
2002	–	–	–	(0.21)	–	(0.36)	(0.05)	1.22	0.02	0.03	0.13	0.04	0.12	1.89	1.39	–	(0.62)	(2.01)
2003	–	–	–	(0.21)	–	(0.36)	(0.05)	(0.18)	(0.00)	0.03	0.13	(0.01)	0.17	1.24	0.72	–	(0.62)	(1.34)
2004	–	–	–	(0.21)	–	(0.36)	(0.05)	(0.03)	(0.00)	0.03	0.13	(0.00)	0.16	1.29	0.78	–	(0.62)	(1.40)
2005	–	–	–	(0.21)	–	(0.36)	(0.05)	0.29	0.00	0.03	0.13	0.01	0.15	1.42	0.90	–	(0.62)	(1.52)
2006	–	0.08	0.05	(0.16)	–	(0.36)	(0.05)	(0.23)	0.00	0.03	0.13	0.01	0.16	0.86	0.33	–	(0.62)	(0.95)
2007	(0.20)	0.08	0.28	0.07	0.02	(0.36)	0.03	(0.61)	0.01	0.03	0.13	0.02	0.15	(0.55)	(1.12)	–	(0.62)	0.50
2008	0.19	0.08	0.37	0.16	0.02	(0.36)	0.03	0.84	(0.01)	0.03	0.13	(0.02)	0.18	1.64	1.13	–	(0.62)	(1.75)
2009	(0.25)	0.07	0.35	0.14	0.03	(0.36)	0.03	0.03	(0.00)	0.03	0.13	(0.00)	0.16	(0.90)	(1.48)	–	(0.62)	0.86
2010	(0.12)	0.06	0.32	0.11	0.01	(0.36)	0.02	(0.56)	0.00	0.03	0.13	0.01	0.16	0.15	(0.40)	–	(0.62)	(0.22)
2011	(0.20)	0.06	0.34	0.13	0.02	(0.36)	0.01	1.14	(0.01)	0.03	0.13	(0.01)	0.17	(0.43)	(0.99)	–	(0.62)	0.37
2012	(0.18)	0.06	0.36	0.15	0.02	(0.36)	0.01	0.32	(0.00)	0.03	0.13	(0.00)	0.16	(0.24)	(0.79)	–	(0.62)	0.17
2013	(0.01)	0.06	0.33	0.12	0.00	(0.36)	0.01	0.14	(0.00)	0.03	0.13	(0.00)	0.16	0.89	0.37	0.03	0.53	0.17
2014	0.14	0.06	0.32	0.11	0.01	(0.36)	0.01	(0.07)	0.00	0.03	0.13	0.00	0.16	1.73	1.22	0.03	0.63	(0.59)
2015	(0.28)	0.06	0.33	0.11	0.04	(0.36)	0.01	0.27	(0.00)	0.03	0.13	(0.00)	0.16	(1.01)	(1.58)	0.06	2.10	3.68
2016	(0.11)	0.06	0.37	0.16	0.01	(0.36)	0.01	(0.16)	0.00	0.03	0.13	0.00	0.16	0.20	(0.35)	0.06	2.02	2.36
2017	(0.20)	0.06	0.29	0.07	0.02	(0.36)	0.02	(0.16)	0.00	0.03	0.13	0.00	0.16	(0.41)	(0.98)	0.05	1.55	2.53
2018	(0.18)	0.08	0.32	0.11	0.02	(0.36)	0.03	(0.16)	0.00	0.03	0.13	0.00	0.16	(0.35)	(0.91)	0.04	1.21	2.12

Note: Table with optimal debt calculations. Section 11.4 offers additional details.
Source: authors' calculations based on the data from Bloomberg and Factset.

Table A11.6 Optimal, actual and excess debt calculations for Arab Banking Corporation, in mlns USD

Year	Capital gains/ (losses), (r)	Interest rate (i)	Beta (productivity of capital, β)	Beta variance (αγ(t))	Half square of capital gain variance	Correlation of interest and capital gain variables	Interest rate variance	Capital gain variance	Correlation and variances of interest and capital gain	Std deviation of interest rate	Std deviation of capital gain	2 × (correlation and variances of interest and capital gain)	Risk	Optimal debt ratio, $f^*(t)$	Normalized optimal debt ratio	Actual debt ratio	Normalized actual debt	Excess debt
2000	0.01	0.11	0.24	0.05	0.00	0.07	0.04	0.33	0.00	0.02	0.53	0.00	0.55	0.16	(0.07)	0.06	(0.96)	(0.89)
2001	(0.07)	0.11	0.24	0.05	0.00	0.07	0.03	0.06	0.00	0.02	0.53	0.00	0.55	0.01	(0.27)	0.07	(0.77)	(0.50)
2002	0.78	0.11	0.19	(0.00)	0.30	0.07	0.03	1.22	0.00	0.02	0.53	0.01	0.54	1.03	1.11	0.08	(0.52)	(1.62)
2003	(0.35)	0.09	0.10	(0.09)	0.06	0.07	0.01	(0.18)	(0.00)	0.02	0.53	(0.00)	0.55	(0.56)	(1.04)	0.06	(1.03)	0.01
2004	0.55	0.07	0.12	(0.07)	0.15	0.07	(0.00)	(0.03)	0.00	0.02	0.53	0.00	0.55	0.94	0.99	0.12	1.26	0.27
2005	(0.10)	0.08	0.13	(0.06)	0.00	0.07	0.01	0.29	0.00	0.02	0.53	0.00	0.55	0.01	(0.28)	0.09	0.02	0.30
2006	0.17	0.08	0.18	(0.01)	0.02	0.07	0.00	(0.23)	(0.00)	0.02	0.53	(0.00)	0.55	0.49	0.38	0.09	(0.11)	(0.49)
2007	1.10	0.08	0.18	(0.01)	0.60	0.07	0.00	(0.61)	(0.00)	0.02	0.53	(0.00)	0.55	1.10	1.21	0.08	(0.38)	(1.59)
2008	(0.60)	0.08	0.31	0.12	0.18	0.07	0.00	0.84	0.00	0.02	0.53	0.00	0.55	(1.21)	(1.93)	0.09	(0.05)	1.88
2009	0.17	0.07	0.20	0.01	0.02	0.07	(0.00)	0.03	(0.00)	0.02	0.53	(0.00)	0.55	0.50	0.39	0.09	0.05	(0.35)
2010	0.18	0.06	0.15	(0.04)	0.02	0.07	(0.01)	(0.56)	0.00	0.02	0.53	0.00	0.55	0.54	0.44	0.08	(0.42)	(0.87)
2011	(0.18)	0.06	0.21	0.02	0.02	0.07	(0.02)	1.14	(0.00)	0.02	0.53	(0.00)	0.55	(0.11)	(0.44)	0.06	(1.17)	(0.72)
2012	(0.58)	0.06	0.18	(0.01)	0.17	0.07	(0.02)	0.32	(0.00)	0.02	0.53	(0.00)	0.55	(1.13)	(1.82)	0.07	(0.61)	1.21
2013	1.14	0.06	0.17	(0.02)	0.64	0.07	(0.02)	0.14	(0.00)	0.02	0.53	(0.00)	0.55	1.13	1.25	0.10	0.57	(0.68)
2014	0.87	0.06	0.16	(0.03)	0.38	0.07	(0.02)	(0.07)	0.00	0.02	0.53	0.00	0.55	1.13	1.25	0.13	1.63	0.38
2015	(0.39)	0.06	0.19	(0.00)	0.08	0.07	(0.02)	0.27	(0.00)	0.02	0.53	(0.00)	0.55	(0.62)	(1.13)	0.14	1.91	3.04
2016	(0.13)	0.06	0.17	(0.02)	0.01	0.07	(0.02)	(0.16)	0.00	0.02	0.53	0.00	0.55	(0.01)	(0.30)	0.14	1.97	2.28
2017	(0.20)	0.06	0.25	0.06	0.02	0.07	(0.01)	(0.16)	0.00	0.02	0.53	0.00	0.55	(0.17)	(0.52)	0.07	(0.61)	(0.08)
2018	0.40	0.08	0.23	0.04	0.08	0.07	0.00	(0.16)	(0.00)	0.02	0.53	(0.00)	0.55	0.79	0.78	0.07	(0.78)	(1.57)

Note: Table with optimal debt calculations. Section 11.4 offers additional details.
Source: authors' calculations based on the data from Bloomberg and Factset.

Table A11.7   Optimal, actual and excess debt calculations for Byblos Bank Africa Limited, in mlns USD

Year	Capital gains/ (losses), (r)	Interest rate (i)	Beta (productivity of capital, β)	Beta variance (αγ(t))	Half square of capital gain variance	Correlation of interest and capital gain variables	Interest rate variance	Capital gain variance	Correlation and variances of interest and capital gain	Std deviation of interest rate	Std deviation of capital gain	2 × (correlation and variances of interest and capital gain)	Risk	Optimal debt ratio, f*(t)	Normalized optimal debt ratio	Actual debt ratio	Normalized actual debt	Excess debt
2000	0.01	0.11	0.93	0.39	0.00	0.02	0.04	0.33	0.00	0.02	0.52	0.00	0.53	0.81	(0.01)	0.00	(1.96)	(1.94)
2001	(0.11)	0.11	0.69	0.16	0.01	0.02	0.03	0.06	0.00	0.02	0.52	0.00	0.53	0.59	(0.68)	0.00	(2.06)	(1.38)
2002	(0.12)	0.11	0.70	0.16	0.01	0.02	0.03	1.22	0.00	0.02	0.52	0.00	0.53	0.56	(0.76)	0.02	0.08	0.84
2003	0.24	0.09	0.68	0.14	0.03	0.02	0.01	(0.18)	(0.00)	0.02	0.52	(0.00)	0.53	1.23	1.24	0.02	(0.43)	(1.67)
2004	(0.10)	0.07	0.54	0.01	0.01	0.02	0.00	(0.03)	0.00	0.02	0.52	0.00	0.53	0.67	(0.44)	0.01	(0.70)	(0.26)
2005	2.10	0.08	0.49	(0.05)	2.21	0.02	0.01	0.29	0.00	0.02	0.52	0.00	0.53	0.65	(0.48)	0.01	(0.83)	(0.35)
2006	(0.22)	0.08	0.54	0.01	0.02	0.02	0.00	(0.23)	(0.00)	0.02	0.52	(0.00)	0.53	0.40	(1.25)	0.02	0.15	1.40
2007	0.21	0.08	0.56	0.02	0.02	0.02	0.00	(0.61)	(0.00)	0.02	0.52	(0.00)	0.53	1.20	1.15	0.02	(0.43)	(1.58)
2008	(0.26)	0.08	0.45	(0.09)	0.03	0.02	0.00	0.84	0.00	0.02	0.52	0.00	0.53	0.32	(1.48)	0.02	(0.49)	0.99
2009	0.30	0.07	0.43	(0.10)	0.04	0.02	(0.00)	0.03	(0.00)	0.02	0.52	(0.00)	0.53	1.34	1.56	0.03	0.89	(0.67)
2010	(0.27)	0.06	0.43	(0.10)	0.04	0.02	(0.01)	(0.56)	0.00	0.02	0.52	0.00	0.53	0.32	(1.48)	0.02	0.04	1.52
2011	0.41	0.06	0.41	(0.12)	0.08	0.02	(0.02)	1.14	(0.00)	0.02	0.52	(0.00)	0.53	1.50	2.05	0.04	1.77	(0.28)
2012	(0.03)	0.06	0.44	(0.09)	0.00	0.02	(0.02)	0.32	(0.00)	0.02	0.52	(0.00)	0.53	0.84	0.07	0.04	1.47	1.41
2013	(0.02)	0.06	0.47	(0.06)	0.00	0.02	(0.02)	0.14	(0.00)	0.02	0.52	(0.00)	0.53	0.86	0.14	0.02	(0.35)	(0.49)
2014	0.03	0.06	0.51	(0.03)	0.00	0.02	(0.02)	(0.07)	0.00	0.02	0.52	0.00	0.53	0.95	0.42	0.03	0.87	0.45
2015	0.01	0.06	0.52	(0.01)	0.00	0.02	(0.02)	0.27	(0.00)	0.02	0.52	(0.00)	0.53	0.90	0.26	0.03	0.75	0.49
2016	0.06	0.06	0.55	0.02	0.00	0.02	(0.02)	(0.16)	0.00	0.02	0.52	0.00	0.53	1.00	0.55	0.03	0.62	0.07
2017	(0.06)	0.06	0.44	(0.09)	0.00	0.02	(0.01)	(0.16)	0.00	0.02	0.52	0.00	0.53	0.78	(0.11)	0.03	0.42	0.53
2018	(0.14)	0.08	0.38	(0.15)	0.01	0.02	0.00	(0.16)	(0.00)	0.02	0.52	(0.00)	0.53	0.57	(0.74)	0.02	0.18	0.92

Note: Table with optimal debt calculations. Section 11.4 offers additional details.
Source: authors' calculations based on the data from Bloomberg and Factset.

Table A11.8 *Optimal, actual and excess debt calculations for National Bank of Kuwait, in mlns USD*

Year	Capital gains/ (losse), (r)	Interest rate (i)	Beta (productivity of capital, β)	Beta variance (αy(t))	Half square of capital gain variance	Correlation of interest and capital gain variables	Interest rate variance	Capital gain variance	Correlation and variances of interest and capital gain	Std deviation of interest rate	Std deviation of capital gain	2 × (correlation and variances of interest and capital gain)	Risk	Optimal debt ratio, f*(t)	Normalized optimal debt ratio	Actual debt ratio	Normalized actual debt	Excess debt
2000	–	0.03	0.65	0.44	–	(0.35)	(0.01)	0.33	0.00	0.01	0.27	0.00	0.28	0.66	(0.28)	–	(0.55)	(0.27)
2001	0.29	0.02	0.27	0.06	0.04	(0.35)	(0.01)	0.06	0.00	0.01	0.27	0.00	0.28	1.53	0.81	–	(0.55)	(1.35)
2002	0.13	0.02	0.19	(0.02)	0.01	(0.35)	(0.01)	1.22	0.01	0.01	0.27	0.01	0.27	1.18	0.37	0.03	2.30	1.93
2003	0.40	0.02	0.21	(0.01)	0.08	(0.35)	(0.02)	(0.18)	(0.00)	0.01	0.27	(0.00)	0.29	1.78	1.12	0.02	2.17	1.05
2004	(0.04)	0.03	0.23	0.02	0.00	(0.35)	(0.01)	(0.03)	(0.00)	0.01	0.27	(0.00)	0.28	0.49	(0.48)	0.02	2.10	2.58
2005	0.75	0.02	0.29	0.08	0.28	(0.35)	(0.02)	0.29	0.00	0.01	0.27	0.00	0.28	2.35	1.83	–	(0.55)	(2.38)
2006	0.19	0.02	0.27	0.06	0.02	(0.35)	(0.02)	(0.23)	(0.00)	0.01	0.27	(0.00)	0.29	1.26	0.47	–	(0.55)	(1.02)
2007	0.27	0.03	0.20	(0.01)	0.04	(0.35)	(0.00)	(0.61)	(0.00)	0.01	0.27	(0.00)	0.29	1.44	0.70	–	(0.55)	(1.24)
2008	(0.40)	0.04	0.21	0.00	0.08	(0.35)	0.00	0.84	(0.00)	0.01	0.27	(0.00)	0.29	(1.07)	(2.42)	–	(0.55)	1.87
2009	0.02	0.03	0.17	(0.04)	0.00	(0.35)	(0.01)	0.03	0.00	0.01	0.27	0.00	0.28	0.74	(0.18)	–	(0.55)	(0.37)
2010	0.61	0.04	0.14	(0.07)	0.18	(0.35)	0.00	(0.56)	0.00	0.01	0.27	0.00	0.28	2.10	1.52	–	(0.55)	(2.06)
2011	(0.14)	0.05	0.14	(0.07)	0.01	(0.35)	0.01	1.14	(0.00)	0.01	0.27	(0.01)	0.29	0.03	(1.06)	–	(0.55)	0.51
2012	(0.04)	0.04	0.16	(0.05)	0.00	(0.35)	0.01	0.32	(0.00)	0.01	0.27	(0.00)	0.29	0.43	(0.56)	–	(0.55)	0.02
2013	0.03	0.04	0.14	(0.07)	0.00	(0.35)	0.01	0.14	(0.00)	0.01	0.27	(0.00)	0.29	0.70	(0.22)	–	(0.55)	(0.33)
2014	(0.05)	0.04	0.13	(0.08)	0.00	(0.35)	0.01	(0.07)	0.00	0.01	0.27	0.00	0.28	0.43	(0.56)	–	(0.55)	0.01
2015	(0.12)	0.04	0.13	(0.08)	0.01	(0.35)	0.00	0.27	(0.00)	0.01	0.27	(0.00)	0.29	0.13	(0.93)	0.01	0.04	0.97
2016	(0.08)	0.05	0.14	(0.07)	0.00	(0.35)	0.01	(0.16)	0.00	0.01	0.27	0.00	0.28	0.27	(0.76)	0.01	0.02	0.78
2017	0.19	0.05	0.15	(0.06)	0.02	(0.35)	0.02	(0.16)	0.00	0.01	0.27	0.00	0.28	1.17	0.36	0.00	(0.02)	(0.38)
2018	0.18	0.07	0.17	(0.04)	0.02	(0.35)	0.03	(0.16)	0.00	0.01	0.27	0.00	0.28	1.10	0.27	0.00	(0.04)	(0.32)

Note: Table with optimal debt calculations. Section 11.4 offers additional details.
Source: authors' calculations based on the data from Bloomberg and Factset.

Index